THE LURE OF
PERFECTION

THE LURE OF PERFECTION

Fashion and Ballet, 1780-1830

Judith Chazin-Bennahum

ROUTLEDGE
NEW YORK AND LONDON

Published in 2005 by
Routledge
270 Madison Avenue
New York, NY 10016
www.routledge-ny.com

Published in Great Britain by
Routledge
2 Park Square
Milton Park, Abingdon
Oxon OX14 4RN U.K.
www.routledge.co.uk

Library of Congress Cataloging-in-Publication Data

Chazin-Bennahum, Judith.
    The lure of perfection : fashion and ballet, 1780–1830 / by Judith Chazin-Bennahum.
        p. cm.
    Includes bibliographical references and index.
    ISBN 0-415-97037-7 (hb : alk. paper) — ISBN 0-415-97038-5 (pb : alk. paper)
    1. Ballet—Costume—France—History—19th century. 2. Ballet—Costume—
France—History—18th century. 3. Fashion—Social aspects—France—History—
19th century. 4. Fashion—Social aspects—France—History—18th century. I. Title.
GV1789.2.C59 2004
792.8'4—dc22

                                                                        2004019194

I dedicate this book to all my family:
my dearest husband David,
Nina and Steven, Rachel and Neil, Aaron and Elizabeth,
and especially to Hannah and Maximilian

Contents

Captions   ix

Acknowledgments   xvii

Preface   xix
VIOLETTE VERDY

Introduction   1

Chapter 1   Setting the Stage   9
*Aristocratic Fashion and Baroque Body
Politics before the French Revolution*

Chapter 2   Reformers and *Philosophes* as Forerunners   35
of the Revolution in Fashion

Chapter 3   The Moderate and the Outrageous   65

Chapter 4   Neoclassicism   93
1780–1820

Chapter 5   The Consulate (1799–1804) and   117
the Empire (1804–1815) of Napoléon
Imperial Designs Pervade Street and Stage Fashion

Chapter 6   Restoration—One Bourbon Returns!   147
Louis XVIII and the Restoration (1815–1824)

Chapter 7   Pale Goddesses on the Street   165
during the Romantic Movement
Charles X Ruled France from 1824–1830

Chapter 8   The Kingdom of the Opera   179
             Pale Goddesses on the Stage (1824–1830)

Chapter 9   The Turning Point   207
             "The Ballet of the Nuns," and La Sylphide

Chapter 10   The Dark Side of White   221

Conclusion   239

Endnotes   247

Chronology   259

Bibliography   263

Index   273

Captions

1. Comtesse d'Artois, 1780s. This extravagant court costume began to lose favor toward the time of the Revolution. The Countess was a walking advertisement for outrageously conspicuous consumption. Courtesy of the Cabinet des Estampes, Bibliothèque Nationale.
2. Chapeau à l'Anglaise. Spencer à l'Anglaise, 1810. English influences pervaded French society despite political conflicts. From Horace Vernet's collection of fashion illustrations, in his *Incroyables et Merveilleuses Costumes et Modes d'Autrefois Paris 1810–1818.* Courtesy of the Irene Lewisohn Costume Reference Library, the Costume Institute at the Metropolitan Museum of Art.
3. Painting of Marie Antoinette in lustrous court attire by Elisabeth Vigée-Lebrun found in the Chateau de Versailles et de Trianon. Courtesy of Alinari/Art Resource, New York.
4. Self-portrait of Elizabeth Vigée-Lebrun. Her luminous paintings portrayed courtly figures such as Marie Antoinette with an idealized and tender beauty. Courtesy of the Cabinet des Estampes, Bibliothèque Nationale.
5. "A Modern Venus," fashion and nature collide, 1786. A strange way to create the S-curve on the fashionable body. Courtesy of the British Museum Print Collection.
6. Pattern of stays or corset from Diderot's *L'Encyclopédie* (1776). The corset was the primary means of encouraging an erect and elegant posture. Courtesy of *Dictionnaire Raisonné des Sciences, des Arts et des Métiers,* 1966. Stuttgart-BAD, Cannstatt, Fromann.
7. Madame Favart, actress from the Opéra Comique, was known for her refreshing and radical ideas on stage costuming. Courtesy of the Bibliothèque de l'Opéra.

8. La Clairon, a celebrated tragic actress, brought reform to costuming as well as the status of actresses in society. Courtesy of the Bibliothèque de l'Opéra.

9. François Talma in a Roman costume for his role in *Cinna*. He was among the early French advocates for realism in both scenery and costume.

10. La Camargo (1761), famous for her brilliant "batterie," or jumping beats. They were more easily seen and applauded when she cleverly shortened her skirts. Courtesy of the Theatre Museum, London.

11. Mademoiselle Allard as Hébé. Boquet's elaborately delicate designs characterized the mid- to late-eighteenth century costume designs at the Opéra. Courtesy of the Bibliothèque de l'Opéra.

12. La Guimard's flowing, soft skirts and bodice gave the impression of a fairy-like heroine, whose "grace was more exquisite than beauty itself." Courtesy of the Bibliothèque de l'Arsenal.

13. Madamoiselle Guimard as Nicette in *La Chercheuse d'Esprit* (1787), wearing a charming costume with a lifted skirt for which she became known. Courtesy of the Bibliothèque de l'Opéra.

14. Portrait of Jean-Jacques Rousseau (1761) by Sir Allen Ramsay. He is wearing his famous fur hat. Rousseau's powerful voice reflected a plea for returning to nature and the simpler outdoor life. Courtesy of the Chateau de Coppet, Geneva.

15. Portrait of Jean-Georges Noverre by Jean-Baptiste Perroneau (1764). Noverre's *Letters on Dance and Dancing* became one of the most important texts on eighteenth-century ballet. He was considered the dance encyclopedist though he did not have any articles in the famous publication. Courtesy of the Bibliothèque de l'Opéra.

16. The tragic death of Louis XVI on January 21, 1793. His last words were, "I die innocent of the crimes for which I've been accused. I never wished but for the happiness of my people and in these last vows I hope that God will pardon my death." Courtesy of the Cabinet des Estampes.

17. Figure of a working woman dancing to one of the most important revolutionary songs, "Ah we'll win, we'll win" (1791). The song was sung during the Terror in all the theaters. In addition, people would report lists of the soldiers who fell during the campaigns. Courtesy of the Cabinet des Estampes.

18. Incroyable et Merveilleuse. A characteristic article of clothing was a broad cravat that virtually covered the mouth. The frockcoat of unusual cut was worn with a flowered waistcoat with wide lapels and knee stockings with tassels. The girl, a Merveilleuse, wears a hat with a soaring brim. Courtesy of the Cabinet des Estampes.

19. Théroigne de Méricourt, famed woman revolutionary who fought in the third corps of the Faubourg army in Paris, wore virtually male attire. The title of this illustration is "Frenchwomen have become free." Courtesy of the Cabinet des Estampes.

20. Homage to Liberty. Revolutionary festivals were common during the Revolution. They stirred deep nationalistic feelings meant to replace old attachments to the *ancien regime*. Courtesy of the Cabinet des Estampes.

21. *La Raison,* or Reason, is presented as a new god with a *bonnet rouge* suspended above her head. No longer were people to worship in a mystical and unknowing way; they were free to choose their destinies. Courtesy of the Cabinet des Estampes.

22. In the ballet *Le Déserteur,* uniforms were the starring attraction and meant to instill patriotic sentiments for the armies fighting abroad. These are costume illustrations of a restaging in 1824. Courtesy of the Bibliothèque Nationale.

23. "Liberated as you are, the French Republic has deemed it necessary. Am I not your sister?" The French freed the slaves in Santo Domingo (Haiti) in 1791, but soon Napoléon reassumed hegemony and tyranny when Haiti's hero Toussaint L'Ouverture was imprisoned and died. Courtesy of the Cabinet des Estampes.

24. Mademoiselle Hilligsberg enhanced her reputation as a fascinating dancer by wearing a man's costume in *le Jaloux Puni* in 1793. Stipple engraving by Jean Condé after H. de Janvry. Courtesy of the Theatre Museum, London.

25. Social dancing and popular fashions went hand in hand. In the ballroom, couple dancing and complicated partnering made dancing lessons more necessary than ever to those wishing to climb the social ladder (1791). Courtesy of the Cabinet des Estampes.

26. Statues of Elgin Marbles at The British Museum. Photo by author.

27. Statues of Elgin Marbles at The British Museum. Photo by author.

28. "Too Much and Too Little, or Summer Clothing for 1556 and 1796." Satire by Isaac Cruikshank on the contemporary fashion for antique draperies. Courtesy of the British Museum Print Collection.

29. "Two Sisters," by Adam Buck (1796). Dancing *à la Grecque.* The lyricism of the flowing costumes inspires the sisters to dance. Courtesy of the Theatre Museum, London.

30. The Graces of 1794. Isaac Cruikshank. "It's the watch fob that grabs the eye. Feminine dress of the present fashion is perhaps the most indecent ever worn within this country. The breast is altogether displayed, and the whole drapery is made to cling to the figure. Well may it be necessary to veil the face." Courtesy of the British Museum Print Collection.

31. "No Flower that Blows is Like this Rose." Picture of the ballerina Rose Didelot, wife of the choreographer Charles Didelot, in a costume of "transparent simplicity." Courtesy of the Theatre Museum, London.

32. Early nineteenth-century dress shoe. Light, flexible, and narrow, the evening slipper had no heel and a sole that was slightly too small for the foot, thereby pressing the bones together and creating a slender, elegant appearance. Courtesy of the Victoria and Albert Dress Collection.

33. "Smart Shoes Made to Fit—Without a Last." Isaac Cruikshank satirizes the pain women will endure in order to be fashionably shod (1794). Courtesy of the British Museum Print Collection.

34. Madame Récamier. As one of the lioness *Merveilleuses,* Madame Récamier sought inspiration in Greek attire in order to reconstitute the glory of ancient Greece in Paris. Courtesy of the Chateau de Coppet, Geneva.

35. Jean-Simon Berthélémy, costume sketch, *Proserpine* (1803). Costume designer and painter, Berthélémy was a distinguished artist. His designs have a lively and dramatic action. Courtesy of the Bibliothèque de l'Opéra.

36. Jean-Simon Berthélémy, costume sketch, *Achille à Scyros* (1804). Courtesy of the Bibliothèque de l'Opéra.

37. Pierre Gardel (1809), member of the philotechnical society (or follower of enlightened ideas of philosophy), ran the Paris Opéra from 1787 to 1820, one of the longest-reigning ballet masters in the history of the Paris Opéra. Courtesy of the Bibliothèque de l'Opéra.

38. Mademoiselle Clothide as Calypso in the ballet *Télémaque dans l'Isle de Calypso* (1790). Her beauty is enhanced by the short Grecian dress and sandals. Courtesy of the Bibliothèque de l'Opéra.

39. The *Robe à la Psyché* became one of the most touted fashions of the time. Courtesy of the Cabinet des Estampes.

40. The dancer says, "Wat, you see enof?" to the Bishop of Durham, who, in 1798, made an example of Parisot's immoral dancing and denounced her to the House of Lords. Courtesy of the Theatre Museum, London.

41. Robe de Cour (1809). Napoleon's court dress which, in spite of the relatively long and simple lines, displays rich materials of satin, velvet, and jewels. Courtesy of the Cabinet des Estampes.

42. La Walse (1801). Illustration from *Le Bon Genre.* "La Valse is a German dance adored by the French as the arms are interlaced in the middle of the body, while 15, 20 sometimes 30 groups of dancers turn following a circular direction. The cavalier is like the pivot of the group that's moving." Courtesy of the Irene Lewisohn Costume Reference Library, the Costume Institute at the Metropolitan Museum of Art.

43. Le Trénis (1805). Illustration from *Le Bon Genre*. "The title of a contra dance named after the inventor, a sad celebrity whose mania for pirouettes drove him to distraction, dying at Charenton." Courtesy of the Irene Lewisohn Costume Reference Library, the Costume Institute at the Metropolitan Museum of Art.

44. La Poule (1810). Illustration from *Le Bon Genre*. "The Hen or Lady Bird is a gay and animated dance in which one amuses oneself with decency and sparkles without pretentions." Courtesy of the Irene Lewisohn Costume Reference Library, the Costume Institute at the Metropolitan Museum of Art.

45. Marie-Louise of Austria marries Napoléon after he divorces Joséphine. Marie-Louise holds the future King of Rome in 1813. Courtesy of the Cabinet des Estampes.

46. Madame Queriau in the ballet *Sauvages de la Floride,* which was the site for a conflict between Napoléon and Chateaubriand. 1810. Courtesy of the Bibliothèque de l'Opéra.

47. Portrait of Madame de Staël and her lovely daughter Albertine, by Elisabeth Vigée-Lebrun, Courtesy of the Chateau de Coppet, Geneva.

48. P. L. Débucourt (1809), *La Dansomanie*. The postrevolutionary dance craze led to the opening of many dance halls and inspired Pierre Gardel's 1800 ballet. Gaston Vuiller, *History of Dancing* (London: Heineman, 1898), p. 189.

49. M. Beaupré in *Paul et Virginie* (1806). Domingo finds himself fascinated by his image in a mirror. Courtesy of the Bibliothèque de l'Opéra.

50. *L'Enfant Prodigue* (1812). *The Prodigal Son* presented an array of figures from the Bible. Costumes by François-Guillaume Menagéot caught the physical feel and texture of the times. Courtesy of the Bibliothèque de l'Opéra.

51. The beauteous Mademoiselle Bigotini in *Le Carnaval de Venise* (1816) wearing a lovely, if skimpy, confection. Imagine what the Bishop of Durham would have said about this costume. Courtesy of the Bibliothèque de l'Opéra.

52. "A Bath Ball or Virtue in Danger" (1820). The assembly rooms at Bath were the site for many balls of great social importance. The popularity of décolleté dresses caused much conversation. Courtesy of the British Museum Print Collection.

53. Mademoiselle Bigottini elaborately dressed in her costume for *Clari, or The Promise of Marriage* (1820). The gold trimming, crown and elegant line emphasized the wealth of her position. Courtesy of the Bibliothèque de l'Opéra.

54. Costume for Victor danced by Mademoiselle Bigottini in *Les Pages du duc de Vendôme*. The tradition of women in men's roles became very

popular and lasted throughout the century (1820). Courtesy of the Bibliothèque de l'Opéra.

55. The costume designer Auguste Garneray dresses Madame de St. Ange of *Les Pages du duc de Vendôme* in elaborate materials and ornamentation. Courtesy of the Bibliothèque de l'Opéra.

56. Mademoiselle Brocard in a sky-blue transparent tunic dotted with stars, in the opera *La Mort de Tasse* (1821). Garneray flourished in an atmosphere that encouraged his talent and innovation. Courtesy of the Bibliothèque de l'Opéra.

57. Costume design by Garneray for a female soloist in *Aladin: ou La Lampe Merveilleuse* (1822). The jeweled embroidery gives the costume its "oriental" character, although the skirt closely follows street fashions.

58. La Fée Mélise in *Cendrillon* (1823). This attractive and romantically exciting ballet still attracts large audiences. Courtesy of the Bibliothèque de l'Opéra.

59. Les Trois Divinités du Jour, Modes de 1830. Extravagance rules fashion aesthetics in the style of the day with wild hair styles, balloon sleeves, and bouffante skirts. Courtesy of the Cabinet des Estampes.

60. A fashionable lady wearing outrageous hair and sleeve styles. And what is that strange scarf around her neck? Courtesy of the Cabinet des Estampes.

61. Caricature of corset tight-lacing, W. Heath, "New Machine for Winding Up Ladies," 1827. Courtesy of the British Museum Print Collection.

62. Marie Taglioni endorsed the amazing product, the mechanical corset, which allowed women to lace and unlace themselves automatically. This illustration is from *Le Petit Courrier des Dames,* March 25, 1833, p. 130.

63. Sketch of Fanny Ellsler's toe shoe from the Vienna State Opera Museum. "The dotted lines are meant to show double rows of stitching. The shoe is soft, made of pink satin. The stitching probably follows the hem of tape or ribbon inside the shoe, and the total effect, like quilting, gives structural support so that the toes do not splay as they normally would in a very high demi-pointe." Courtesy of Monica Moseley, Dance Collection of the New York Public Library.

64. Marie Taglioni's pointe shoe, held by Dame Alicia Markova. Unlike today's shoes, Taglioni's shoe was unblocked and had no shank. Ribbons emphasized the close relationship with the early nineteenth-century dress shoe. Photo by Gordon Anthony. Courtesy of the Theatre Museum, London.

65. Emma Livry's pointe shoe, early 1860s, reproduced from Cyril Beaumont, *Ballet Design Past and Present* (London: The Studio, 1946), p. 55. As in Taglioni's day, the shoe was unblocked and the pointes and sides strengthened by darning.

66. In the ballet of the opera *La Muette de Portici* (1828) by Auber, La Femme Espagnole dansant La Quarache, Spanish woman dancing La Quarache. Here the costume designer Lecomte offers charm as well as regional color with a distinctive headdress and long scarves that move with the body. Courtesy of the Bibliothèque de l'Opéra.

67. Costume for Mademoiselle Noblet in *La Belle au Bois Dormant* or *Sleeping Beauty* (1829). Though Lecomte's name is not indicated, this looks like his work. The Renaissance design for her dress is typical of the period, while her grandiose hat echoes exotic influences. Courtesy of the Bibliothèque de l'Opéra.

68. Marie Taglioni was the hit of *La Belle au Bois Dormant*. Her beauty and grace mesmerized an otherwise unimpressed audience. She emerges from the depths of the ocean in Naiad-like ball dresses. Courtesy of the Bibliothèque de l'Opéra.

69. *Manon Lescaut* evoked the excesses and ornamentation of eighteenth-century ball gowns. Courtesy of the Bibliothèque de l'Opéra.

70. Third act ballet scene from *Robert le Diable,* portraying nuns who come alive from their tombs. It was the sensation of the season with Taglioni as the Abbess. Courtesy of the Bibliothèque de l'Opéra.

71. The ballet from *Robert le Diable.* Painting by Edgar Degas (1876). This production was a careful re-staging of the original Ciceri and Lamy designs and presents a dream-like version of the Bacchanale scene. Courtesy of the Metropolitan Museum of Art.

72. The role of Abbess Hélène initially played by Taglioni, in a habit that, when torn off, exposed the ballet gown dress worn during the bacchanale scene that followed. Courtesy of the Bibliothèque de l'Opéra.

73. No single costume is more important than that worn by Marie Taglioni in *La Sylphide* (1832). Lami's conception led to the archetypal design for the tutu worn by all ballerinas. Courtesy Bibliothèque de l'Opéra.

74. Marie Taglioni partnered by Joseph Mazillier in *La Sylphide* (1832). Courtesy of the Bibliothèque de l'Opéra.

Acknowledgments

Writing this book has been a grand and satisfying experience. My understanding of both the world of fashion and ballet costume design has expanded and deepened. Without the generosity of many friends, colleagues, and institutions, it would have been much more arduous.

First and foremost, I am grateful to my beautiful family—getting larger every year. They believed in this project and permitted me the time, space, and travel to finish it.

I cannot thank enough two women who walked me through this text many times, editing and suggesting—Melinda Jordan and Barbara Palfy. Their commitment to this work and to me was undaunting. Barbara contributed her solid and staunch editing while Melinda's wonderfully fresh approach to editing and visualizing the final text gave me courage. Early on discussions with Ruth Steinberg and Ann Tyler were also of great assistance.

For a fine eye and help with the French translations, I am indebted to Claude Fouillade with whom I went to graduate school and who remains a close colleague.

Friends who provided much appreciated advice and encouragement as well as bibliographic suggestions include Jennifer Predock-Linnell, Noel Pugach, Malcolm McCormick, Flora Clancy, Christopher Mead, Susanne Backmann, Mariel McEwan, Linda Tomko, Judith Milhous, Lynn Garafola, Claude Conyers, Sheila Hannah, Marvin Weil, Sally Banes, and Marilyn Hunt. The staff in my department, Patsy Morris, Marvin Archuleta, Chris Squire, and Sarah Lentz, generously gave me some free time to work on this manuscript. Finally, my graduate assistant, Bridgit Lujan, offered unwavering and wonderful last-minute support.

One of my strongest supporters was Ivor Guest, who spent hours going over material and ideas with me. He and Ann Hutchinson Guest were warm hosts during our stay in London.

A number of libraries, museums, and costume collections provided tremendous help with sources and gave me the necessary time and access to materials. They were the Bibliothèque de l'Opéra, where Romain Feist was my chief contact; the Costume Institute of the Metropolitan Museum of Art, where Stephane Houy Towner was of great assistance; The Arsenal, where Simone Drouin was my guide; the Bath Museum of Costume, where Rosemary Harden showed me beautiful examples of late eighteenth-century and neoclassic designs; the Royal Academy of Dancing, where Mandy Payne brought out books and pamphlets that shed light on rehearsal clothes; the dress collection of the Victoria and Albert Museum, where Susan North spent time showing corsets and dresses and discussing fashion developments; the print collection of the British Museum, where Mary Bagulay was most helpful; the Wellcome Institute for the History of Medicine, where Roy Porter made some valuable suggestions about books to read; the Courtauld Institute of Art, where Aileen Ribeiro was kind enough to respond to a number of my questions; the dance collection at the New York Public Library of the Performing Arts, where my dear friend Monica Moseley directed me to many illustrations and manuscripts and also sought out information, especially on early pointe shoes; and, finally, the Theatre Museum of the Victoria and Albert Museum in Covent Garden, where Sarah Woodcock was my ciceroni and never too busy to listen to my queries. In my town, the librarians at the University of New Mexico—Barbara Rosen, David Hertzel, and Kate Luger—cheered me on with much bibliographic help. The costume historians, Mariel McEwan, Louise Coffey, and Sydney Jowers, responded warmly to my questions.

Finally, I am very delighted that Richard Carlin at Routledge, an old buddy, decided to take a chance and publish this book.

Preface

VIOLETTE VERDY

Judith Chazin-Bennahum's historical discussion of fashion and ballet describes a Paris that remains amazingly familiar to all of us who love that city of light. To be able to live in a great city like Paris is to live in a living museum, where every monument, garden, and street delivers views and perspectives that constantly remind one of beauty, the proportions of the human condition, and a longing for harmony. As a young child, I lived through the Second World War and its aftermath. The conditions during the war were so harsh and scary. The cruelty and injustice reconfirmed my deep desire for peace. As a young dancer in pursuit of the ideals of art and ballet, peace seemed the ultimate purpose of life. The world and its obstacles were calculated to make one want more clearly and strongly that which I saw as good and intrinsically true.

I remember in that gray time my first elegant costume from the haute couture of Jeanne Lafaurie, and later, especially Pierre Cardin. And even though at the time my obsession was for the acquisition of technique and artistry in ballet, I almost reluctantly had to admit to myself that to be well dressed was part of the continuation of the same artistic search to please the public on and off stage.

The thrill of working with great scenic artists and costume designers, the inspiration and excitement to be either better than or, at best, totally transformed from the ordinary to the magical, were irresistible. That pleasure provided more discovery and imagination for each role so that they literally fed each other. I believe that stage artists in France have continuously carried the ritual and formality of presentation to the highest possible level on stage.

Life is reconfigured to represent a variety of moral, social, and artistic circumstances. Working at the Paris Opéra was even more completely the *summum bonum* of all these ideas; if the look of things appeared simpler, the intricate concerns had not really changed. The numerous elements of each ballet were carefully considered, cared for, and prepared. France is a peculiar country in that philosophy, art, and beauty are of such importance to both the artist and the audience.

Your book, dear Judith, covers all the ingredients in such a rich, abundant, and sometimes unexpected cornucopia that it is more than one could dream of—it is a total revelation of the history of the times chosen. On reading it, my thoughts turned to Balanchine, and the contrast seems extreme. His decisions of choosing only certain elements from all that theater and dance can deliver were, as we know, based on necessity, which for him was indeed the mother of invention. For him a great score, great dancing, and great lights meant that plot construction and décor were insignificant. He was driven by a desire for perfection, naked rather than disguised, but totally recognizable. Though a suspicious instrument, the body for Mr. B. was transformed without the seductive effects of ornamental costumes, lighting, and décor.

For you, Judith, the "Lure" becomes a search, a butterfly that does not always burn its wings—vanity reduced, the quest is on! That core, heart of it all, is the one that forever welcomes all aspects of talent, invention, and creative expression. Originality can appear then, as the proof of freshness, in candid, surprising recognition. Judith's book is a joy in which the past calls to us and we rediscover our memories and our future.

The Lure of Perfection

Fashion and Ballet, 1780–1830

O Mightiest Fairy! Goddess of Fashion
Demon, Devil or Sorceress!
How we all stream to your altar
Where you are enthroned with submission
Presiding over human will
Sometimes with strength, other times with cunning
And every fancy you excuse as mere folly
For you are nothing but folly itself.[1]

For many years, I have wanted to create a narrative about stage costumes and street wear, including a discussion of the various social, artistic, and, political influences that shaped the design of clothing and costume and, specifically, how they affected French ballet in the late-eighteenth to mid-nineteenth centuries. I wondered why dancers wore skirts that were in some cases full and bouncy and at other times narrow and lithe, short, long, or heavy. Why were they asked to wear a low, décolleté bodice or a wig, or to apply thick globs of makeup? Of course, they wore tutus with layers of tulle that floated about their bodies, but why was the traditional tutu such a rigid and corseted structure? And what is our understanding of the evolution of dancing shoes that were often tortuous to wear, whether character shoes for peasant roles or toe shoes for the ballet?

I find fashion to be a dictating force. My perception is that we cannot track the progression of dance costume design independently from the study of fashion on the streets. Although we know the names of choreographers and people who designed costumes at the Paris Opéra, it is interesting to note that we do not know the names of many street clothing designers.

1

Instead, we learn much about fashion from the "costume plates" that fashion houses used to advertise their clothing.

The study of fashion brings insight into many areas of our lives. Influenced by nature, literature, art, economics, and politics, fashion changes the way we view ourselves and our place in society. And it can take on an extraordinary life of its own. Why, for instance, is a painterly description of the body designed to look small or large, short or tall, slim or wide, or divided into two or more parts? In fashion, what part of the body is displayed? Does the skin show at the neck and torso, on the back, or at the hips? Why is a face veiled or the legs hidden?

Clothing acts like a screen between the wearer and the body; it allows a complex flow of sensations to reach the body that are sent back out to the space and surrounding viewers. The material we wear, whether on the stage or the street, contains personal imagery that reveals more of our inner nature than we realize. Attire often heralds new ideas and generates inspiration. The flower children of the 1960s not only floated in a haze of drugs but also wore loose, easily removed, shimmering, and psychedelic clothing; it conformed to their visions of a liberated nature unrestricted by rules of social behavior.

Every generation needs to explore and express its ideas, and fashion is one way of helping us to paint the pictures in our imaginations, just as stage costumes lead us into visual realms that tabulate a scenario's meanings. Fashion refines and defines itself and offers an interpretation of our own existence and our world. As we change the shape of the body and its parts by the way we dress, we become works of art. Envisioning the silhouette has mystifying consequences, and variety enhances all aspects of sartorial aesthetics. In his "Fashion System," Roland Barthes describes "the rhythm of changes in fashion as both unpredictable and systematic, regular and unknown, aleatory and structured."[2]

To some extent fashion erases the past, but it also insists on the past's omnipresence. "In framing the body, however precariously, dress contributes to the symbolic translation of materiality into cultural images or signifiers. As a mediator between the carnal dimension of existence and the abstract laws of the symbolic order of language and institutions, dress aids the constructions of subjectivity as representation."[3]

As fashion enriches and gives shape to our lives, it can also become detrimental to our well-being. In his book *The Dress of the Period in its Relations to Health* (1884), physician Frederick Treves bemoans the dictatorship of style over rational people. In a positive sense he sees costume or fashion as "a reflex of the national mind and the popular dress of any age that is often the finest exponent of its tendencies and of its social and moral tastes."[4] However, he says that no dictatorship is more blindly obeyed than the laws of fashion, and its influence is despotic, with no regard for personal judgment. At one time fashion "decreed that a woman should wear an excrescence on her head and a bump upon her back, and the order has been carried out . . . there has been the time of hoops when women appear to have endeavored to clothe themselves with a balloon as a garment." Revealing the secret of who is responsible for a particular fashion would furnish little excuse for the blind and unquestioning manner in which fashion is pursued.[5]

It is to be lamented that *plus ça change, plus c'est la même chose* [the more things change, the more they remain the same]. Although the corset went out in the flapper era, it never really disappeared. According to Mary Lynn Steward and Nancy Janovicek, the importance of stays has chased women throughout the twentieth century until the present. How, you will ask, if women are no longer wearing corsets? Because women are clothing themselves as if they were obsessed by eating less and less. The slim figure from the late Renaissance continues. However, now it is with diet and exercise that we achieve that line.[6]

Furthermore, women flappers were engaged in a passionate exchange of roles as the market for sexually explicit displays expanded considerably. Women in the theater, as well as women's clothing, received enormous attention. Many words were spent in journals, newspapers, and magazine articles remarking upon the dangers to women that fashion and the theater engendered.[7]

As unhealthy emotionally or physically as wearing a particular design of clothing or costume may be, women in daily life and on stage willingly engage in this endeavor. In exploring changes in fashion, one increasingly notices how deleterious and sometimes dangerous this sport is, for it is competitive and the drive to emulate is usually self-serving.

Concepts of the dance costume have been explored by dance historian Carole Rambaud. In her introduction to the catalogue for the 1989 exhibition "Costume à Danser," which took place in Boulogne-Billancourt, she speaks about the dance costume and how in singling out this one element of the choreographic spectacle, the costume becomes a plastic witness to the spectacle and uncovers a specific artistic expression of its creator. The costume designer not only works with the choreographer but also considers the movement as well as the dancer's body. The texture and tactility of the costume enter into the choreography in an imaginative way. The costume becomes accompaniment to movement and to energy. Also writing about dance costume, Geneviève Vincent suggests that once the dancer is dressed, an imaginary discourse ensues that tells the viewer about meaning in movement. The costume travels through space, evoking unsuspected sensations.[8]

Pondering the mysteries of stage costume led me to ideas about fashion and its governance over the many aspects of life in different historical periods. While I was writing my dissertation on ballet during the French Revolution, I discovered that the costumes, movements of the dancers, and the tales told on stage revealed insights into the aesthetic conscience of the time. Revelations abounded, not just in the way characters related to one another during stage action but also through subtle gesturing, steps, and rhythmic patterns in space, and by the shapes of the costumed bodies, their profiles and silhouettes. Spectators also wore special clothing for these occasions, which gave them their own identity. Thus, theater became a framework for shared diverse cultural narratives.

This book centers primarily on France and proceeds chronologically from the years leading up to the French Revolution through the first third of the nineteenth century. Thus, my period of interest is approximately from the 1780s through the Empire and the Restoration to the neo-revolutionary movements of the 1830s, Romanticism, and the Industrial Revolution. The book ends with the beginning of the Victorian era, when the seeds of Victorian thinking were already in the wind in both France and England and were to effect changes that predicted late-nineteenth-century fashion and morality.

I speak of the brilliant writers and artists who contributed to their time and who brought about new ways of understanding the human experience in terms of the clothed body. The sites for these observations are in both France and England, but I concentrate primarily on Paris, the cynosure of fashion. I do not exclude male fashion, but my focus is on women's costume.

In France the word costume, or *la mode*, also means fashion, dress, or suit, and in one way or another all clothing in France was connected to fashion, whether one was a milkmaid, a queen, or a sylph. For centuries, forces of fashion and the reigning taste of the time determined how people were dressed on stage at the Opéra or at the King's Theatre. When the aristocracy ruled, stage costumes mirrored court fashions in their opulence. Women in court dress might be compared to moving fortresses, and dancing in such devices demanded not only a sense of dedication to court etiquette but also the conviction that you are what you wear; otherwise, why would one choose to move around with so much width and weight?

It is essential to recognize how the French court affected all aspects of the stage and how fashion in the corridors of Versailles impacted the way ballet costumes were designed. In order to better understand the monolithic power of the French aristocracy who, according to the cultural historian Norbert Elias,[9] controlled the civilizing process and its influence over its own population as well as its neighbors, I discuss the middle and last years of the French court and its aesthetic paradigms and consider how the fresh ideas of the *Philosophes* brought social and aesthetic changes, including new attitudes toward fashion. We shall see how a member of the court, Marie Antoinette, unwittingly subscribed to a less rigid costume that ultimately symbolized the monarchy's collapse.

The demise of the court and therefore court dress ushered in the French Revolution. Fashion that represented different currents, such as the revival of Greek ideals with a relaxation of daily costume, became popular. Vast changes brought about the gradual democratization of a society steeped in the absolutism of monarchy and church and prompted new attitudes about the body politic and the individual female body. One result was that women began making their own decisions, however futile and premature, about their lives and fashion. Giving women the right to show their bodies, especially the lower half, occurred during the period of neoclassicism, lasting approximately from the 1780s through the early nineteenth century. It was a remarkable and brief moment in which the bonds of clothing that restricted and impeded movement and desire were relinquished.

After the radical strategies of the Revolution had collapsed, conservative forces quickly took back control during the course of Napoleon's reign, which reinforced the rigidity of court costume. Although it was a male-dominated society where men controlled politics and fashion, paradoxically, some women still decided to wear more relaxed clothing, symbolized by classical Greek attire. They opted for an idealized body that represented what they envisioned as a free and rational society. The white transparent tunic of Greek statuary draped easily over the body, and the female body walked with freer foot and with ankles and legs that were visible to the passerby. However, these lovely, statuesque creatures looked much alike, and it is disturbing that the new imperials wanted their women to look like white marble statues.

No doubt women's legs had been imagined, but certainly not seen, in the western world since antiquity. What did that mean? It meant a great deal to a dancer, and this is the crux of what happened on stage during this period. Dancers, especially women, were urged to explore what they had been heading toward for some time—a much more vigorous use of space and a daring expansion of their physical abilities. This was unimaginable before the Revolution.

By the nineteenth century, the cry for more equality under the law, driven by a growing population of workers who longed to become members of the middle class, ushered in the Industrial Revolution. Middle-class values tended to be conservative, mirroring in France the growing prudery that England acquired when Victoria became queen. The Industrial Revolution brought both tremendous advantages and disadvantages. Ideas about fashion spread rapidly to a large population of women who wanted to be as chic and exciting as the fashion journals told them to be. Mass consumption was becoming a reality and, as the women of Paris changed fashions, they changed their personas—all hoping to appear like the rich and powerful. They, as well as their stage sisters, enjoyed the exotic ornamentation that had come from conquered nations as well as their local communities.

Industrialization also allowed the corset to be manufactured in greater quantities. Cost and fashion conspired to spread its use to larger groups of men, women, and children, causing greater constriction of movement and, in some cases, gross deformities. In addition, the Industrial Revolution brought less distinction and individuality to fabrics, styles, and colors. It degraded and polluted working and living conditions, while increased profits prolonged the institution of slavery that produced the necessary cotton for neoclassic fashions.

Industrialization had an unfortunate impact on the conceptualization of the ballerina's body. It perpetuated what choreographer Jean-Georges Noverre decried in the eighteenth century—dancers paid more attention to technique than to expression. Management now treated the dancer as if she were a machine, an extremely beautiful and fanciful one but, nevertheless, a machine. Diverse changes in ballet technique streamlined and enhanced the female body and its performance on the stage. In the mid-eighteenth century, philosopher Julien Offray de La Mettrie wrote a treatise, *L'Homme Machine*, or *Man a Machine* (1748). He proclaimed that the "human body is a machine which winds its own springs. It is the living image of perpetual movement."[10] The body was seen as an object that worked efficiently and created an effective product, and strict standards were established that had to be adhered to in order to manufacture the best possible commodity. The tutu and the early version of the toe shoe are examples of the industrial age's discoveries.

As an antidote to the Industrial Revolution, the arts sought a return to nature and the romantic and mystical contemplation of beauty. Inspired by the philosopher Rousseau, the Romantic Age brought a suspicion of abstract or rational thinking, and the "Age of Reason" gradually gave way to a change of ideas about emotions. People took refuge in Romantic novels and performances that helped them to escape the mundane, harsh realities of the changing nineteenth-century environment: cities, factories, and dirty coal mines. Perhaps the image of the Romantic ballerina in her tutu epitomized the prevailing desire for lightness, fleetness, and ethereality.

The Romantic Age birthed the ballet as we know it today, and this is where my book ends. Although I have tried to fill in as many gaps as I could, a troubling aspect of this book is that it centers mostly on the upper classes. While I do call attention to the dress and costumes of "national origins," the urban and rural poor are barely addressed. When I asked

Richard Martin, the late curator of the Costume Institute at the Metropolitan Museum of Art, about eighteenth-century workers and what they wore, he responded that, lamentably, "we do not have examples of their clothing; they wore them to death."[11]

I also recognize that many writers on fashion have taken notice of the vital periods of history between the late eighteenth and mid-nineteenth centuries. They helped me to understand the issues generated by the interaction of forces that have affected the different time periods and their people, the streets, and the stage. Their books shed light on human motivations and psychological drives as well as historical and theoretical approaches to dress. And while I agree with many of their premises, I do not believe that they fully explain why and how people chose to clothe their bodies and how those choices affected the French ballet. This has been my fascination and my purpose.

CHAPTER 1

Setting the Stage

Aristocratic Fashion and Baroque Body Politics before the French Revolution

The Baroque period began with the era of Louis XIV's reign (1661–1715) and extended beyond his death to the French Revolution in 1789. The period evoked images of great opulence, panoply, and sensuousness in which fashion and ballet followed a carefully coded vocabulary. The Baroque aesthetic had to change in order to yield to newer ways of conceiving women's clothing.

For more than four hundred years, the chief purpose of decorative clothing in Western Europe and colonial countries had been the differentiation and division of people according to birth and wealth, which the nobility between the fourteenth and the eighteenth centuries had secured by numerous sumptuary laws and edicts. Fashion rules the world, but who rules fashion? At every age there have been a few men and women who have stood out as the dictators in manners of fashion, and occasionally these were not the most outstanding leaders in other phases of life. Sumptuary laws, or codes that regulated how people dressed, created a fashion system assuring that only rulers, clergy, and court lieges could dress in certain kinds of clothing. It is important to realize that although the aristocracy represented a tiny portion of the population, this privileged group reigned supreme over taste and manners.

In the late eighteenth century, the aristocracy fancied itself at the center of the world, reviving the image of Louis XIV's Sun King, around whose glaring radiance everything revolved. The concept of the Sun King came from Louis XIV's early foray into ballet, when he danced the role of the sun in *Le Ballet de la Nuit* (1653). After all, from the king's bright light came financial and political support that fueled all activities in the country. Opera, ballet, and theater followed suit. The vivid colors and rich fabrics such as silks, velvets, and embroideries of court clothing reflected the importance of the aristocracy in their everyday lives. The French court deemed itself terribly advanced in style and presentation, but the courtiers often wore unwashed clothing; most materials were not washable but were occasionally spot-cleaned. Nor were their heads and hair clean under their extravagantly tall wigs which, on the eve of the Revolution, became increasingly massive, ready to tilt and fall into the guillotine's *La Lanterne* basket. Headgear rose so high that women could not use ordinary sedan chairs for transport.

Diaries and novels of the period were revelatory about manners. An extremely insightful description of the quality of life at the high levels of French society may be found in the novel *Letters from a Peruvian Woman*, by Françoise de Graffigny: "The men and women wear finery so splendid and so covered with useless decorations . . . I cannot help but think that the French have chosen superfluousness as the object of their worship; they devote to it their arts, which are so far above nature."[1] Graffigny makes it clear that the French desperately needed to appear wealthy:

> The great pretense among the French is to appear lavishly wealthy. Genius, the arts, and perhaps even the sciences all relate back to ostentation and contribute to the destruction of fortunes . . . I have it on their own authority that they contemptuously turn their backs on those solid, pleasant objects produced in abundance by France itself, instead extracting from all parts of the world, and at great expense, the fragile, useless furnishings that decorate their houses, the dazzling garments with which they are covered, and even the very food and drink of which their meals are composed.[2]

Never before had Europe seen as magnificent a setting as the royal European court, and especially Versailles, for conspicuous leisure. But Versailles was a decidedly uncomfortable place, hot in the summer and cold in the winter. It was built not for ease but for glory, the life of unproductive labor in its purest form. The many levels of courtiers presupposed a complex pecking order through which one rose by wit, grace, and clever politics. The witty but earnest seventeenth-century *précieuse* and *honnête homme* would have been lost in the decadent Versailles of gambling, gossip, and ridicule. The court at Versailles was always referred to, by those who belonged to it, as "ce pays-ci," this country, and it did have a climate—a manner of speech and body, as well as a moral code—all its own that penetrated all its activities. Why in this environment was fashion so decidedly important?

Fig. 1 Comtesse d'Artois, 1780s. This extravagant court costume began to lose favor toward the time of the Revolution. The Countess was a walking advertisement for outrageously conspicuous consumption. Courtesy of the Cabinet des Estampes, Bibliothèque Nationale.

The courtly woman became a center of self-interest and self-importance. In looking back at the fashions of upper-class women just before the Revolution, one immediately notices that the clothing of the richest, most powerful, and influential symbolized an *outré*, excessive, nearly grotesque covering of the human figure, what Quentin Bell called "conspicuous outrage." Court costumes were especially exaggerated, implying that courtiers performed for one another in a grizzly game of one-upmanship in opulence.

The eighteenth-century woman took up twice as much space as the man. "In the French fashion plates, the feminine figure is filled out with fichus (lacy shawls), ballooning skirts covered with ruffles and garlands, and mountains of frizzed and fluffed hair. The whole cloud-like ensemble is enhanced by the movement of thin veils and ribbons that catch the air as the lady walks. . . . "[3] Walking and especially dancing became treacherous feats, as wearing heels impeded all natural movement. "During Louis XIV's reign, heeled shoes entered the ballroom for court dancing . . . heels were colored red in order to distinguish courtiers from other would-be aristocrats. This restriction implied the wearer's elite status."[4]

Women studied how to glide along with tiny steps when moving through the hallways, attempting to appear to float as they displaced volumes of space with their clothing's width and decoration. Could these floating fortresses possibly be the ancestors of the nineteenth-century ball gowns that inspired the tutu design of the 1830s? Certainly, the male partner of the Romantic ballerina had to adjust constantly to the billowing skirts of the woman he lifted high into the air, just as the eighteenth-century courtier made way for his lady counterpart.

As Richard Martin revealed in his study *The Ceaseless Century*, cinematic and stage performances create stunning images of the French court by presenting the highly ornamented and hand-painted dresses that represent the authority of eighteenth-century style.[5] The wide vertical and obstructional shape of the pannier served the purpose of exhibiting the rich, jeweled materials a woman wore, sometimes fifty-five inches of display. If two women bumped into one another in a narrow hall and one fell down on her back, like a turtle, she had to be raised to standing by several people.

There was a reason why aristocratic and upper-class women of the eighteenth century dressed in clothing that was so cumbersome it disabled them: they were not supposed to work. Fashion was a weapon of power for women, a way to demonstrate and hold authority. Women needed money and control of money; fashion and sex appeal gave them hegemony, or control of financial power. Novels and journals of the time faithfully recounted the sufferings, conquests, and greed of the French court at Versailles that reiterated the need to be powerful and rich.

Covered as she was, the mystery of the late eighteenth-century aristocratic woman symbolized a government that these women represented, one whose functions mystified the people but whose sensual grandeurs and festivities were deeply attractive. The eighteenth-century woman as an active participant in creative activities of the court is difficult to portray. Her role as a controlling person in terms of taste found its focus and center in the salon, where she wheedled, gossiped, and cajoled her favorite artist or writer into some sort of stardom. Jean François Marmontel, an encyclopedist, wrote in his *Mémoires* that Madame de Tencin advised him to befriend women, "for, it is through women, she used to say, that one obtains what one wishes from men."[6] Salon women patronized young artists and lobbied the intelligentsia to support their proteges.

Fashion and ballet fused when one was presented at court. The performance proved as important as any show in the ballet or theater. Hundreds of rules of etiquette, arbitrated by court dancing masters, framed the entrances, exits, and behaviors of the aristocracy. In her *Memoirs*, Madame de La Tour du Pin narrates a teenage visit to the queen. She made a special trip to Paris in advance in order to visit her dancing master, M. Huart, so that he could give her "two lessons in the curtsey":

> It is impossible to conceive of anything more ridiculous than those rehearsals of the presentation. M. Huart, a large man, his hair very well dressed and white with powder, wore a billowing underskirt and stood at the far end of the room to represent the Queen . . . he showed me just when to remove my glove and bow to kiss the hem of the Queen's gown. He showed me the gesture she would make to prevent me. Nothing was forgotten or overlooked in these rehearsals which went on for three or four hours.[7]

Madame described her dress of wide panniers with a long train, the layers of lace on her sleeves, and the eight rows of diamonds that the queen lent her. "The day of one's presentation was very embarrassing and exceedingly tiring. It meant being stared at by the whole Court and being torn to shreds by every critical tongue."[8] Madame de la Tour du Pin's diaries remain as important commentaries during the late eighteenth century.

Sometimes a court rehearsal for presentation took several days because of the amount of training needed. A young woman had to adjust to the pain of a whale-boned bodice that cut into the upper arms. Her costume, to which a long cloth train was attached, had to be manipulated repeatedly with little kicks to move forward, and after curtsying low several times, the wearer had to retreat backwards from the royal presence without tripping. The length of the train was proportionate to the rank of the wearer. The presentation outfit was usually black, but if the courtier were in the later stages of mourning, white was the preferred color.[9]

As the eighteenth century came to a close, the middle classes began to assert themselves with greater force. Their increasingly opulent lifestyle nonplussed aristocrats who cultivated and retreated behind an invisible

Fig. 2 Chapeau à l'Anglaise. Spencer à l'Anglaise, 1810. English influences pervaded French society despite political conflicts. From Horace Vernet's collection of fashion illustrations, in his *Incroyables et Merveilleuses Costumes et Modes d'Autrefois Paris 1810–1818.* Courtesy of the Irene Lewisohn Costume Reference Library, the Costume Institute at the Metropolitan Museum of Art.

social barrier of manners rather than wealth. Elegant movement was an art that could not be purchased; it required time and practice. One could achieve it with three things: dancing masters, etiquette books, and fashionable attire. The look of status always outweighed one's desire for physical comfort in order to become a work of art.

England's Effect on the French Court

In England, the court wielded less influence, tempered by regular meetings of the House of Lords and the House of Commons. The rich and privileged in England remained on their rightful estates, creating, in theory, a greater sense of security for both lords and their ladies, while at Versailles, the king, mindful of the dangerous *Fronde*, or rebellion against Louis XIV in the mid-seventeenth century, took them from their lands and forced them to live in Versailles.

After the defeat of Cromwell, the radical Puritan leader (1599–1658), the English tradition of wearing austere clothing remained concomitant with its conservative values. The place of religion is significant. The British are Protestant and did not approve of frippery, while the French are Catholic and enjoyed flaunting their decorations and finery. The English associated popery with feminine sexuality and with France and Italy as centers of passion, sensuality, and superstition as well as decayed feudalism and diabolical Catholicism.

The tensions between England and France have an age-old history. But their geographic proximity, as well as similar philosophical interests in governmental freedoms and creative scientific thinking, brought the English and the French into an odd love–hate relationship. Parisian women read English novels and fashion magazines, while English women followed every twist and turn of Parisian styles.

French women differed from English women in the objects they owned and revered. In *An Elegant Art: Fashion and Fantasy in the Eighteenth Century,* which describes the life and manners of eighteenth-century aristocrats, we learn from personal diaries and novels that the two most important items in an English lady's boudoir were her writing desk and her bed; in France, they were the bidet and the bed.[10]

By the 1780s, the English responded to the more practical, outdoorsy, relaxed look, and portrait painters placed their models in natural surroundings rather than in the stiff drawing rooms preferred by the French. The English penchant for living a more rural, country life was called *à l'Anglaise* by the French. For the high-minded French and English moralists, the blurring of class distinctions in dress created the problem of upstanding women looking like prostitutes and vice versa. "Prostitutes had no special way of dressing, and by the end of the century high-class kept women were the leaders of fashion."[11] The analogy of dancers as courtesans or prostitutes became a common assumption at the end of the eighteenth century and grew throughout the nineteenth century.

The appeal of dresses in the English style centered on what became known as *le fourreau*—a dress of one piece with a bodice that is drawn up, tightened, and laced up the back, and a closed skirt in front—which represented a reaction against the tyranny of the blown-up body. Elizabeth Vigée-Lebrun painted the actress, Dugazon, the title character in *Nina ou la Folle par Amour* in such a shape, and the young Marquise de La Tour du Pin in 1786 ordered, from England, one of these *fourreaux* in white gauze. In 1768 *Le Courrier de la Mode* recommended even for dancing "les habits anglais à manche serrée, à sabots garnis de gaze, avec le petit chapeau orné de fleurs," or "English clothes with tight sleeve, clogs garnished with gauze, with the small hat adorned with flowers." This simple dress reflected Rousseau's ideas on "l'amour de la campagne," maternity, and rediscovered nature. In addition to *le fourreau,* the French adored the English penchant for sports, for the redingote (riding-jacket dress) that they wore for horseback riding. The redingote was distinguished by a tapering lapel, large oval buttons made out of English steel, and an open skirt over an underskirt.[12] Interesting to note is that Gravelot, the son of a French tailor, spent twenty years in London. He published in 1744 *Des études d'hommes et de femmes dessinés d'après trois mannequins,* which had been written in England. He brought to his work a taste for straw hats, flat dresses (*robes plates*), and white cloth. Writing on the eighteenth century, Alice Browne reaffirms the English approach to movement and dancing. She explains that the English danced in order to improve their posture, as it was an important marker of class. Manuals of conduct from the time include illustrations showing how to hold oneself and where to put one's hands.[13]

The hat was one of the most important borrowed fashions from England, used mostly by very elegant women. The Duchess of Devonshire, a tremendously popular and seductive public figure, was immortalized by Gainsborough in a hat of her own design. She was instrumental in perpetuating the wide-brimmed picture hat dramatically ornamented with a wide sash and drooping feathers.[14] It was Devonshire who introduced the muslin gown to English women. What started as an intellectual fashion—anglomanie, also known as *philosophisme*—became a matter of style in dress, sports, and entertainment. "Women, especially, were avid readers of the English romances, and they sported high bonnets, which bore such romantic names as 'stifled sighs' and 'bitter complaints.'"[15]

Apart from ceremonial events, Frenchmen echoed Englishmen's preference for the conservative. The English tended to wear dark and unassuming suits. Middle-class businessmen, as well as lawyers and administrators who lived in cities, adopted this costume as their uniform. Cities were dirty, and black, or a dark color, suited any occasion, just as it does today. The sophisticated court-centered formality of French dress could no longer be tolerated, so that egalitarian English styles associated with England's greater social freedoms were more suited to the new French.

One of the prominent French supporters of English style was the brother of Louis XVI, Philippe l'Egalité, the Duc d'Orléans, who wore short jackets, pantaloons, and a round hat, with a handkerchief tied sailor-fashion and loose around the neck. Unafraid to stir up trouble in the French court, he befriended the English Prince of Wales and championed revolutionary politics. These outward expressions did not protect him as he, too, died on the guillotine not long after the king and Marie Antoinette. In an anti-English move, Rose Bertin, Marie Antoinette's coutouriére, created a style celebrating the American Revolutionary War as a reaction against England which, besides being the traditional opponent, also supported the French monarchy during the French Revolution.

Of course, not all Frenchmen relished the idea of copying styles from across the Channel. The annoyed French dramatist Pierre de Belloy said, "Should one suppose that by imitating, good or bad, their carriages, their card games, their promenades, their theater and even their supposed independence we should merit the esteem of the English? No, love and serve our *patrie* as they love theirs . . ."[16]

At the end of the eighteenth century, but French and English fashion not only followed the idiosyncratic desires of the court, it also responded to changing attitudes toward the body, as important writers and philosophers brought fresh ideas of democracy to popular attention. Performances in the theater and at court catered to stunning women in search of power and fame. As English styles penetrated all levels of society, less ornate and freer-moving dress became the norm.

Marie Antoinette

The quintessential moderators of fashion and the arts were, naturally, the heads of the court—the king and queen. Marie Antoinette's celebrity was criticized as a sybaritic influence from the time she married Louis XVI in 1770 until her demise on the scaffold in 1793. She arrived at a time when the French court indulged itself in all manner of pleasures and frivolities.

Marie Antoinette provided the spirit and panache that the French people both loved and hated. Part of the simmering dislike for the queen stemmed from her Austrian background and her powerful Austrian mother, Maria Theresa. Marie Antoinette spent her young years at her mother's imperial court in Vienna, where she studied with great artists: singing lessons with Sainville, music lessons with Gluck, and dancing lessons with Jean-Georges Noverre, the great ballet master.[17] Her early studies with Noverre inspired her to help install him as ballet director at the Opéra in 1776, the locus of European ballet tradition, when she became queen. Even when she was a

Fig. 3 Painting of Marie Antoinette in lustrous court attire by Elisabeth Vigée-Lebrun found in the Chateau de Versailles et de Trianon. Courtesy of Alinari/Art Resources, New York.

child dauphine, she and her young sisters- and brothers-in-law entertained the young Louis XVI.

The queen's persona haunted the court. The entrance of the mystical Marie Antoinette to her court caused all eyes to gaze upon her and remark upon her latest fashions. Marie reveled in her clothing, jewels, laces, and even shoe buckles. Nodding to and fro, the feathers that garnished her beautiful wig delicately swayed as she moved through the crowds in the halls of Versailles.[18] Madame de Campan, a chronicler of Marie Antoinette's reign, disapproved of her excess of fashion, noting that "monstrous headdresses were erected over extremely light heads."[19]

The queen's couturière, Rose Bertin, one of the first celebrated woman fashion designers, was expected to create a morning dress, an afternoon dress, and an evening dress for Marie.[20] In order to demonstrate that France was first in fashion, she made 171 dresses for the queen. Bertin, known as the "Minister of Fashion," is described in the memoirs of Baroness d'Oberkirch as being "puffed up with conceit and she regarded herself as equal in importance to the Princesses."[21] Bertin ran a famous dressmaking establishment to fulfill the needs of the aristocracy and she dreaded anyone else's talent for design. When she sensed that another designer might subvert her power over Marie Antoinette, she confronted her in the halls of Versailles by spitting in her face, a crime for which Bertin was fined.[22]

Marie Antoinette's average dress account in the early and mid-1780s was 100,000 *livres* per year (100,000 *livres* in the 1780s would be equivalent to more than a half million dollars today); in 1791–1792, 36,000 *livres*; and 18,000 *livres* in the last year of her life. Her *grand habit de la cour,* or court costume, had a heavily boned bodice, layered lace sleeves, a heavily trimmed skirt worn over a vast hoop, and a long train. The other court dress, or *robe de cérémonie*, was called the sacque dress; it was a less formal, elegantly trimmed gown with big hoops. Her dresses without hoops were called *robes à l'anglaise.*[23]

An interesting aside to the relationship between Bertin and Marie Antoinette was perceptively noted by the cultural historian Simon Schama:

> Marie Antoinette's dress maker, Rose Bertin, who had created the loose muslin à la Gaulle outfits for the Queen, had been criticized by both the friends and the enemies of the monarchy for her presumption in talking to her sovereign like an equal. When the artist Elizabeth Vigée-Lebrun painted portraits both of herself and of the Queen wearing Bertin dresses, and exhibited them for public admiration in the biennial Salon, the golden triangle of couturier, patron and illustrator was formed.[24]

With the spending of such extraordinary sums of money on clothing, Marie Antoinette came to symbolize the abuses, callousness, frivolity, and licentiousness of the *ancien régime*. She also represented the public female, the woman whose meaningful presence in the world both attracted and fascinated public attention, much like the actresses and dancers of her time.

Performing in plays and operas became a passion for Marie Antoinette, as it was for many French people, both aristocrats and the middle classes. Adolphe Jullien recalls that "Le Théâtre, c'est une rage, une fureur, une folie de se divertir et de se produire" or "Theater is a rage, a furor, a folly to amuse oneself and to act."[25] Women of the upper class learned to act, dance, and sing for their friends, thereby developing an audience for their frivolities.

Marie Antoinette felt that part of her role as queen to the king of France was to perform for him as an actress and a dancer. She was haunted by the enduring memory and influence of the beautiful and talented consort of Louis XV, Madame de Pompadour (la Marquise Antoinette Poisson), who also set court style for dress fashions, theatrical entertainments, and opulent decors. Under the influence of the rococo, Mme de Pompadour's style of dress was characterized by gaiety and soft colors. The surface of her dresses was broken up with frills, ruffles, and padded robings. The air of playfulness and frivolity was enhanced by tiny headdresses made of flowers, lace, and feathers. Late rococo (1770–1789) fashion embodied the wealth of a dying aristocracy, inclined to idleness, who lived on the income of their properties.[26]

The development of amateur theater in the second half of the eighteenth century may owe its strategies to Madame de Pompadour, who used the theater to achieve additional power by having all eyes set on herself. The excitement of performance entranced La Pompadour, and anything she displayed or wore became iconic. The theater offered the illusion of comedy, backstage life, and the enchantment that seduces the public. For each play, the starlets rehearsed for six weeks, took six hours to put on costume and makeup, and, in order to appear lithe, fasted for twenty-four hours before the show. La Pompadour's theater was as beautiful as the Opéra.

At Versailles, able to draw upon the royal treasury as well as her own talents, La Pompadour created a first-rate theater. She recruited actors and dancers from suitable, exalted ranks, but only those with previous experience could perform. She herself was one of the best of the salon actresses, and she saw to it that her group was well rehearsed by celebrated professional actresses such as Dumesnil and Gaussin. All was well disciplined; schedules were maintained and understudies trained. The orchestra was top quality, as were the costumers, wigmakers, and decorators. The king was spending more than 230,000 *livres* per year on her Théâtre des Petits Cabinets. Performances were in mid-November after the court returned from Fontainebleau. Women were not present as spectators during the first two years, and admission was a coveted perquisite. Rousseau's mélodrame *Le Devin du Village* was presented at Versailles at a cost of 115,000 *livres*, while wages of workers in the chateau were suspended. The theater did not reopen after 1753; it had lasted a mere six years.

In the late eighteenth century, the theater reflected French society's growing passion for liberation as well as its adoration of opera, music, and dance. In the theater one was free, and despite censorship, which held little sway in the private domain, theatrical entertainment often mirrored fresh attitudes toward politics and social issues. Within the new spirit of liberalism, aristocratic women wanted to be seen on stage: court life was so prescribed that the need for a more expansive experience found its expression on the stage. French aristocratic women also lived to seduce, and playing on the stage was another form of seduction.

During Louis XVI's regime some of the most radical activity—satirical, risqué, innovative—took place on private stages at private residences. The emergence of women as organizers and animators of "*théâtres de société*" (private salon theaters) became responsible for some of the most interesting theatrical activity of the century. These unofficial playhouses, country chateaux, Paris townhouses, and the royal court had become all the rage—and entry to the salon theaters was by invitation only. When Marie Antoinette was at the Petit Trianon, no one could force her to be at the mercy of court etiquette, "elle vivait dans une indépendance entière"—she lived a completely independent life.[27]

Marie turned to the stage as a distraction in the face of impending disaster. In 1780 the queen began to act and dance on stage in her theater garnished with cupids, garlands, and blue velvet. Initially there were forty spectators, all royalty. Then the troupe enlarged its audience, sometimes by as many as 260 invitations. At the opening, she played a soubrette in Sedaine's *La Gageur Imprévue.* Later she assumed the roles of a bourgeoise and the heroine, Colette. Her stage appearances culminated in the role of Rosine, the saucy charmer in the *Barber of Seville* (1785), in which her costumes conformed to a free picture of the young woman in search of love, not necessarily of an aristocratic husband. In the unrest and scandal of the time, this role was viewed as an act of astounding *maladresse.* The value of these acting personas was that they helped to soothe her disenchantment: "to divert her from the distressing role she played as queen, she adopted the character of a soubrette on stage. The king assisted by encouraging these games . . ."[28]

The great English writer and politician Horace Walpole praised Marie Antoinette for her grace and charms as a performer: "whether she is standing or sitting, she is a statue of beauty. When she moves, she is Grace incarnate. One would say that if she danced off rhythm, it would be the rhythm that was wrong."[29] Not pleased with Marie Antoinette's showmanship, some judged her mediocre at best, saying that she suffered in comparison with her rival, Madame de Montesson, mistress to the Duc d'Orléans.

Regardless of the quality of their performances, the very wealthy looked for recognition and pleasure in role-playing. Marie Antoinette lived in the public eye and, like La Pompadour, desired to find meaning through performance. She became a romanticized version of the happy peasant, a stage role that many a corps ballerina has enjoyed throughout the nineteenth

Fig. 4 Self-portrait of Elizabeth Vigée-Lebrun. Her luminous paintings portrayed courtly figures such as Marie Antoinette with an idealized and tender beauty. Courtesy of the Cabinet des Estampes, Bibliothèque Nationale.

and twentieth centuries. The queen found solace in the free atmosphere of the little Trianon, with its charming gardens and streams where she and her entourage dressed as stage shepherds and shepherdesses.[30] There, she and her guests would find large jars of cream which they would beat into butter or give the impression of doing so. On Sundays she gave a ball in the gardens and welcomed anyone dressed in a simple, unaffected way; there she danced the contredanse to show her affinity for what was popular.[31] Almost everything she did bordered on performance.

In the 1780s, under the influence of Marie Antoinette and the court painter Elizabeth Vigée-Lebrun as well as English style, the chemise dress came into fashion. Revolutionary in its simplicity, in its early form the chemise was merely a tube of white muslin with a drawstring at the neck and a sash at the waist. The light color gave the shape and quality of draping a lovely aura. "Coming from the French West Indies (where indigo grew, giving the dresses a bright bluish-white hue), it was popularized by Marie Antoinette and from her court spread all over Europe."[32]

Several English aristocrats were regular visitors to the French Court. Yielding to the influence of English fashions on local gossip and chatter, in 1783 Marie Antoinette rebelliously asked Vigée-Lebrun to paint a portrait of her with her hair unpowdered and unwigged, and wearing a simple muslin blouse. The result of this portrait was the style *chemise à la reine*, when its bluish-white color came into popularity in the 1780s. Vigée-Lebrun did twenty-five paintings of Marie Antoinette. She recalled in her memoirs first encountering the queen in the gardens of Marly-le-Roi "walking in the park with several of the ladies of her court. They were all in white dresses, and so young and pretty that for a moment I thought I was in a dream."[33]

As a sad epilogue to this story, Marie Antoinette spent her last days with her children and sister-in-law in the prisons of Le Temple and, finally, in La Conciergerie. From 1792 until her death on October 16, 1793, Marie Antoinette was under arrest and suffering indescribable deprivation. Nine months after Louis's death, the Republicans sought her execution and treated her without mercy. Jacques-Louis David sketched her as she was led to her death in a cart. Unforgiving, the picture showed her internal misery, her totally changed appearance: a lined face and scraggly gray hair covered by a peasant cap, emphasizing her age and desperate situation. All her life seemed to be compressed into the last degrading and terrifying days of imprisonment. Anticipating the guillotine, she developed traumatic menstrual bleeding. On that final day she wanted to wear a white dress, the color of royal mourning, but it was drenched in blood. The gendarme refused permission for her to change her clothes out of his sight for fear she might escape. She crouched in a tiny space between the bed and the wall with a maid standing between her and the gendarme in order to hide her nakedness. She was ashamed to leave her soiled linen for people to see, so she hid her chemise in a crevice in the wall behind the stove. Her bleeding served as one of her final punishments.[34]

Fashion Influences from Other Countries

Fashion from other countries where travelers journeyed also affected contemporary trends. Foreign markets developed in Western and Eastern Europe as well as China, India, and other colonies. Beautiful fabrics, new dyes, unusual designs, and materials from other lands all sparked interest in novel modes of clothing the body. When Louis XV married a Polish princess, Marie Lesczynzska, an appetite for exotic Polish styles arose that continued under Louis XVI, especially during the years 1776–1787: flattened sleeves inserted at the elbow, a shortened ruffle in a shoe-like shape. The *Polonaise* dethroned the French *robe de cour,* and its popularity continued into the late nineteenth century. Hooked at the neck, the *Polonaise* tunic spread over an underskirt and billowed out at the back, the central piece being the longest. The narrow-waisted underskirt flared at the sides and back with pads or bustles in the back, lifting up the overskirt and arranging it in three swags of material. It was suggested that the three panels represented the carving up of Poland in 1772.

In addition, there was a Russian element added to fashion, especially copying Peter the Great, who wore a big fur hat. Rousseau, upon his return from Armenia, wore a fur hat as well—probably a very practical idea.[35] From 1775 onward, there was a succession of exotic fashions—*à la Polonaise, à la Circassienne, à la Lévite, à la Levantine, à la Turque, à la Sultane.*

There were voyages to Turkey by ambassadors and artists who then adopted Turkish ways when they returned to France. In England, Lady Montague's husband was ambassador to Turkey. In addition, a number of plays and operas contained Turkish themes. Apparently, in the Turkish fashion the singers and actresses of the Favart comic opera company did not wear corsets underneath their oriental outfits; women in the audience were fascinated.

The Ottoman Empire, in decline since the seventeenth century, opened up to European travelers who sought the fantasy of harems, balloon pants, and the secret, exotic court of Constantinople. Turkey also exported its beautiful silks and embroideries to Venice.[36] In 1779, the capture of the island of Grenada by the Comte d'Estaing was responsible for the creation of the *chapeau à la Grenade,* decorated with pomegranates.

One other "oriental style" that interested fashion followers was *la Lévite,* in part due to the great success of Racine's *Athalie,* which played in Paris in the late 1770s. Athalie wore a Jewish costume consisting of a straight dress with a shawl collar and pleats in the back, held with a loose scarf around the waist (*à col châle et à plis derrière, seulement retenue à la taille par une écharpe lâche*). Marie Antoinette wore this costume *à la Lévite* when she was pregnant in 1778. It was considered quite radical for the period.

At the same time, dresses in the Indian or Creole style found admirers looking for supple and simple forms similar to *la Lévite*. With the popularity of the American revolutionary cause, there was also a dress called *à l'insurgente* to excite the fashion hunters. It was simply a dress in the English style with lapel lining of a different color: "*qui n'était d'ailleurs qu'une robe à l'anglaise dont la pointe du devant relevée formait un revers de couleur differente*"[37] (Boucher, 1983, 296). The presence of a remarkably fascinating American ambassador to Paris, Benjamin Franklin, added to the allure of politics. Also, the departures of Lafayette and Rochambeau for America created styles in decorations for clothing.

Clothing and Fashion that Affected Dance

Stage costumes before the eighteenth century mimicked extravagant court dress with the addition of characteristic symbols sewn onto the costumes or carried by hand to give some indication of the performer's role. Emblematic signs satisfied the audience's need to follow the script and lessened the distance between the audience and performers since most wore court costumes. When there were mythological characters associated with fantasy or the underworld of Hades, their costumes, as well as their movement, were represented more imaginatively.

Fashion played a large role in some of the stylistic and technical provisos that guided people's dancing. Although it is uncertain whether clothing actually determined the creation of these dance principles, the relationship must be taken very seriously.

The corset (which contains the French word *corps* or body) became an important artifact in the development of dance principles. It began to be used during the sixteenth century when rules of social dance were the driving force of court life. With its lacing, the corset provided a slimmer line and, at the same time, provided support for the breasts. The shape of the corset changed during the course of many centuries, depending upon the way women's bodies were viewed. The corset may have originally been invented as a means to correct certain back problems. The first important period of the corset came with the widespread Spanish fashion of the late Renaissance, the mid-sixteenth to the seventeenth century, which suppressed the breasts with stays that were stiffened with wood, metal, or whalebone, a flattening that essentially deformed the female figure. Portraits of Queen Elizabeth I and others of her period display the female body as abnormally thin and elongated. Beatrice Fontenel describes the kind of underdress that suited Renaissance dresses, which became heavier and more rigid: "The basquine which derived from the Medieval cottes, consisted of a tight-fitting, sleeveless bodice worn over a shirt and laced at the back. To stiffen it, the

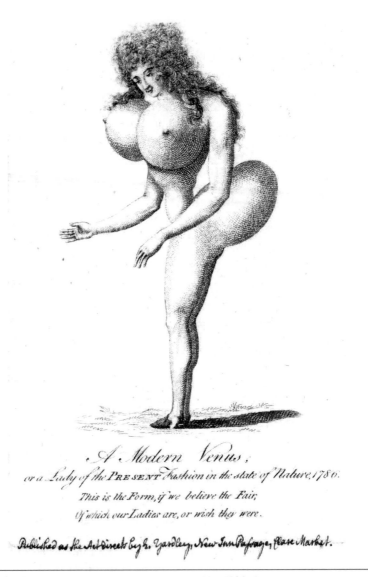

A Modern Venus,
or a Lady of the PRESENT *Fashion in the state of Nature, 1786.*
This is the Form, if we believe the Fair,
Of which our Ladies are, or wish they were.

Published as the Act directs by G. Yardley, New Inn Passage, Clare Market.

Fig. 5 "A Modern Venus," fashion and nature collide, 1786. A strange way to create the S-curve on the fashionable body. Courtesy of the British Museum Print Collection.

basquine was lined with prepared cloth, and even reinforced with brassware."[38] A brilliant surgeon of the sixteenth century, Ambroise Paré, described his autopsy of a young woman who died of an unknown disease: she had an extremely narrow waist and her ribs were overlapped. He deduced that the corset was responsible for her untimely death.

As the corset developed in fashion, it took on various shapes and attributes. At one point, a horsehair pad was sewn in the back of the corset at the lower back in order to project a woman's silhouette outward at the rear. This created the S-curve or shaped body. Lacing was usually up the back, with a buskin or a stiff piece of bone or metal in the front. If a woman were heavy, there might be two or three sets of lacing. After the mid-seventeenth century, breasts were once again emphasized, with French fashion leading the way. Short-waisted in the seventeenth century, the corsets became longer, more pointed, and cone-shaped in the eighteenth century, often covered with rich materials.

In 1753 the artist William Hogarth posited a fascinating analysis of beauty based upon the S-curve. The S-curve inserted itself as a spatial design for the costume in the ballroom as dancing couples swerved and swayed, creating an S pattern on the floor. People began to walk, stand, and gesture in S-curve patterns.[39] Hogarth had the idea that beauty could be identified as a gently curving, serpentine line, an S-line that stood for nature and against deformity and extremes. Hogarth did not want corset stays to be too curved or too straight; there should be a happy medium.[40]

The physical constraint of the corset assisted the aristocrat in appearing contained and controlled. During the Renaissance, spontaneous gesturing was considered a grave fault and disorderly. Moderate behavior signified a virtuous person. The body behaving in a controlled and contained fashion became a marker for that which is virtuous.

How did clothing help to constrain and create an aura of moderation in dancing? The values of standing up straight and looking tall were basic standards of comportment that began in the Renaissance and carried over into the eighteenth century: the neck long, the torso lifted, the waist held in carefully below a long, straight back. Dancing masters perpetuated the beauty and necessity of this corseted look:

> In dancing [the dancer] could not be expected to have very much forward or backward flexion in ribs or waistline, but she could execute subtle and expressive épaulement—twisting and tilting the upper torso on the spinal axis . . . From the restrictions imposed by the structure of corsets a manner of holding and using the upper torso, arms and head evolved, and affected conventions around the stylistic execution of steps and patterns of movement.[41]

The corset was the central means of encouraging a very erect, carefully balanced, kinesiologically efficient posture that distributed the great weight of the clothing precisely around a central axis, in order to reduce stress resulting from curvature in the alignment of body parts.

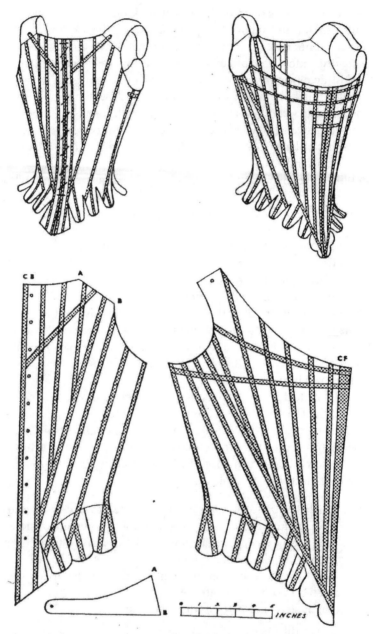

15. Pattern of stays from Diderot's *L'Encyclopédie*, "Tailleur de Corps". It is a half-boned stay, cut from six pieces only, the shaping being given by the direction of the bones. It would have the extra busk and the shaping bones across the front and across the shoulder blades. It might also be fully boned *(1776)*

Fig. 6 Pattern of stays or corset from Diderot's *L'Encyclopédie* (1776). The corset was the primary means of encouraging an erect and elegant posture. Courtesy of *Dictionnaire Raisonné des Sciences. des Arts, et des Métiers,* 1966, Stuttgart-BAD Constatt, Fromann.

Considerable problems for movement resulted with the tight stays. A letter written by the Duchess of Devonshire in 1778 said that her new French corset caused her much pain, especially under the arms, and that its tightness and discomfort made it impossible for her to lift her arms.[42]

Tight sleeves made it difficult to move or swing the arms, keeping them in the dance and, in life's activities, fairly close to the body, which gave the woman an air of totality, composure, and containment. The slim bodice and sleeves dictated that the arms would never straighten but, rather, passed through stated planes along the front of the body and to a medium height, softly bending and reaching as if carrying garlands in each hand, forming the double curves of an S. The protruding bosom emphasized the woman's sexuality, reaffirming her role as a gorgeous ornament, rather like the clothing accessories that could only be afforded by an exceptionally wealthy or powerful person.

A woman could bend to the side and a bit backwards, but basically she was stiff as a board from the stays, which were rammed up along her chest, ribs, and back. In addition, the corset might extend beyond the waist onto the hips, and crossing one thigh over another could cause serious harm. There are illustrations that show women sitting on the edge of their chair, or reclining sideways or backwards with the elbow on a table for support. If a woman dropped a handkerchief or a fan, a servant or gentlemen had to pick it up.[43]

Another article of clothing that hindered free movement was shoes, which traditionally lacked arch supports. The eighteenth-century shoe made the muscles of the feet and ankles work hard. When the shoes had three-inch heels, the weight of the body tipped toward the balls of the feet, causing difficulty for the stride. When the heel was narrow, the ankles would wobble. French women tended to enjoy higher heels more than the more sober-minded English women.[44]

The pannier, or wide skirt, was treated by the aristocracy as a necessary female property, the wider the more elegant, and the unhurried (how could you hurry with all that material?) long carriage of the body lifted above the skirt gave the woman an air of floating dominance and confidence. In order to move smoothly in a wide skirt and petticoats, a woman could not take steps too large or too small while walking for fear that her head might bob up and down, and her skirts would bounce unceremoniously. On the dance floor, the skirt drew attention away from the hips and legs. Lifting the legs high, turning in different directions or jumping easily were of diminished importance while wearing the heavy skirts. It was the feet and the intricacy of their exciting moves that caught the eye.

There were three skirt shapes—round hoop, panniers, and bustle, each of which enlarged some aspect of the lady's hips. Panniers were the ultimate status symbol, sometimes causing traffic jams in the streets, riots in the theater and supreme irritation in parks, ballrooms, and church pews.[45] Women had to turn their bodies sideways to pass through doorways and, in order to avoid danger, had to think far in advance what their next move might be.

Another twist on the women's long and large skirts in the ballroom was expressed by the dancing master of London's Haymarket Theatre, Giovanni-Andrea Gallini, who tells us that there may have been a positive side to the skirts that women wore: "The female dancers have also an advantage over the men, in that the petticoat can conceal many defects in their execution [of the dance]; even, if the indulgence due to that amiable sex did not only make great allowances, but give to the least agreeable steps in them, the power of obtaining applause."[46]

The fashionable eighteenth-century aristocrat found other ways to impede her movement. She enjoyed the disguise of wearing a mask—for festivals, for balls, for surreptitious rendezvous, and for the stage. Like her fan, the mask might be highly ornamented with jewels, feathers, and other adornments. On stage it was traditionally worn by leading characters in court ballets, as well as at the Opéra, and created a uniform picture of dramatic characters, which in this era were often mythological heroes. They were *de rigueur* for the leading artists in a ballet company until the choreographer and dancer Maximilien Gardel decided to dispense with them, no doubt realizing that their purpose was no longer valid and that they not only impeded the way one moved but also hindered the display of real feelings.

Finally, the last piece of clothing distinguishing the elegant courtier that limited the quick and natural movement of her head was the wig. Overblown hair creations were important signals in the index of fashion; the eighteenth century began with a fairly large shape to the aristocratic lady's head and ended up with such a huge peruke that it sat dangerously on her coiffure. Any noteworthy occasion spurred changes in hairstyles. When the sloop *Belle-Poule* held off the enemy English's *Arethusa* in 1778, the coiffure "Belle-Poule" was launched with miniature ships bobbing on waves of powdered curls.[47] The same stunning disproportion was fashionable on stage, and in an August 19, 1778, *Journal de Paris* article, the author described how he responded to this effect:

> The height of the women's hairstyles and the fear of accidents that might occur in the event of a collision forced them to stoop too low and fall into awkward attitudes that break the rhythm, are lacking in grace and make the audience wince.[48]

The peruke was worn by members of the court, the upper classes, and stage artists. Whether layered with ornamental shapes of curls as high as several feet, or held close to her own head, the wig proscribed swinging around too rapidly. If heavy, its effect on the body's movement was also deleterious, causing the body to tilt forward or backward, depending on which way one's weight shifted. In the ballroom or on the stage, the head could not initiate a sudden turn or move; it followed the calculated advances of the entire torso. However, if a stage artist did not wear a powdered wig, it was considered an affront to the court. There was an occasion when Larivé, the great tragic actor, caused a ruckus by appearing in the royal presence without a powdered wig and with bare arms.

The Dancing Masters

Fashions brought changes to the technique of dancing, both socially and on stage. The person who determined how the canon expanded was the dancing master, whose profession became important centuries earlier. The grace and elegance, lift of the torso, and turnout of the feet demanded from the dance master became a display and indicator of one's rank at court.

Some dancing masters primarily taught the upper classes in their residences. They were also attached to opera houses or various theaters as choreographers who managed to find time to give social dance lessons on the side. Wherever they worked, they were beholden to the upper classes and the rich, while the rich understood that learning from the dancing master was an essential occupation and became a political statement.

Social dancing was perhaps the perfect display of aristocratic sang-froid. It required long hours of practice from an early age and, in addition to the dance steps themselves, it taught people the simplest but most highly considered ways of gesturing.

> Movement impulses within this code were to be veiled, as well as emotional responses. . . . The lady practiced moving quickly without changing level so that she appeared to float weightlessly with no expenditure of energy. . . . The forearms, wrists and fingers, the lower legs and feet were highly decorative. They performed fluttering embroideries on the periphery of a controlled and tranquil center.[49]

The reverences, sitting down and getting up, passing bows, taking the hat on and off, greetings and good byes, and using the fan—these gestures all required meticulous attention. Couples performed for as long as ten minutes to the various musical forms that were learned in the classroom, with the minuet the favorite eighteenth-century show dance.

The dancing master was one of the most important figures at court and in the social life of the late seventeenth and eighteenth centuries. He prodded and harangued his willing, suffering pupils into learning how to be the graceful champions of the world that they were. Just a small part of his enterprise was concerned with dance. Much of his work involved teaching the movements and gestures associated with greetings and good behavior. As tutor of the dances that pleased the court, he assumed responsibility for defining "current and socially correct behavior."[50] It is Molière, attached to Louis XIV's court, who presents his dancing master as a comical character of exceptional arrogance and posturing, trying to buy his way into the upwardly mobile life of M. Jourdain and his family. In *Le Bourgeois Gentilhomme*, le Maître à Danser applauds the place of dance in world cosmology: "All the misfortunes experienced by men, all the disastrous setbacks with which stories are filled, all the blunders of politicians, and all the derelictions of duty of the great captains, all have come to pass because people did not know how to dance."[51] Dancing represented, indeed epitomized, the aristocratic life. By wanting Jourdain to acquire taste in dance, the dancing master continued to uphold the "naive belief" that dancing can lead to social changes.[52] True or not, the upper classes, including the wealthy and aristocratic, looked to the dancing master for lifesaving instructions about manners and courtesy.

Dancing masters of Louis XIV's reign, an epoch of illustrious men, codified and taught the dance technique in the late seventeenth and early eighteenth centuries that came to be known as Baroque throughout European courts. The principles of this social and theatrical dance form were derived from centuries of Italian and French teachings. It really took root in the French aristocracy when the Italian Catherine de Medici was brought to Paris to marry Henri II (1533), and there it was refined and practiced both on and off the stage. Renaissance dancing masters initiated the style and technique of court dance as it would be practiced for centuries. Louis XIV decided to create an Academy of Dance in 1661, thereby institutionalizing the training of choreographers, dance teachers, and dancers.

Echoing Renaissance principles of harmony and aplomb, Michel de Pure, a commentator on the arts during Louis XIV's reign, described good dancing, saying that "one must remain graceful and natural at all times . . . but that demands great care. One must not outrage the rules of nature. Beautiful dancing consists in a certain finesse of motion, in one's bearing, how one takes a step, and carries one's entire body in a way that cannot be expressed verbally or taught."[3]

Adapting and expanding on de Pure's instructions, the Abbé du Bos published a book on dance in 1733 with many suggestions derived from the dance of the ancients. He speaks of dance as "attitudes and movements that only serve to perform gracefully."[54] Grace is the pure intention of all dance; therefore, the element that must not show is effort or tension as one is executing the steps. The aristocrat ruled the world and had to give the appearance of lyric control.

Pierre Rameau, who served as a dancing master at the Spanish court, wrote that "there is hardly a Court in Europe where the dancing master is not French."[55] Standards of grace for European aristocracy coincided with Rameau's instructions and confirmed the way in which fashion adjudicated behavior. Rameau saw the dance as a means to a healthy life and noted that if dancing were limited to the theater, it would not divert many people. Everyone should dance; "dancing adds graces to the gifts which nature has bestowed upon us, by regulating the movements of the body and setting it in its proper positions."[56] Rameau dedicated attention to the use of the arms in the course of moving through the various patterns. He made it clear that the arms served to "harmonize" and "adorn" the body. Calling attention to the intricate and dangling lace, the arms moved from the elbow and the wrist, turning and bending them in opposition to the feet and according to form.

Another early writer on the dance, Charles Batteux, wrote *Les Beaux Arts Réduits à un même Principe* (1746),[57] or *The Fine Arts Guided by the Same Principle*. Batteux stipulated that all of the arts must be seen as reduced to a taste for nature adorned gracefully. The word grace was not be taken lightly, for it was the highest of all virtues. Following Aristotle, Batteux sought attention to the imitation of nature, where gesture would be involved as a valued part of movement. However, gestures must be driven and inspired by feelings—real feelings. As a predecessor of Romanticism, he also influenced Noverre and cared deeply about expression and the clear presentation of feelings.[58] He emphasized the value of restraint and discouraged all dancers from showing tension or effort in dancing, to "create easy and simple" movements.[59]

In 1779, the dancing master Gennaro Magri, in his *Theoretical and Practical Treatise on Dancing*, described the well-placed and well-trained social and stage dancer. The development of social dancers became more demanding, and they had to spend many hours training. Although they dressed in the same heavy and elegant materials of the court, Magri felt entirely unconstrained by the clothing of his time. Coming from an Italian tradition that was far more virtuosic and gestural, he prophesied the training of French and English opera dancers. His treatise included a number of the *grotteschi* dance combinations and steps, having himself been a professional dancer and choreographer.

Magri's careful and often elaborate instructions about ballet and social dance technique illustrated a new emphasis on movement and on the great strides ballet was making. The importance of carriage, posture, fluidity of style, and grace were mentioned, but other issues came to the fore, such as the freer use of the legs and arms, greater flexibility of style, multiple beats and pirouettes, and the increasing use of the instep and foot for line and gravity.

Magri emphasized the way the foot should look, which in the later Romantic ballet took on new aesthetic value. He explained that in the basic walk in the ballroom, the *pas marché*, one must point the toes and arch the instep, and the toe of the foot must only just touch the ground.[60] He described the "Pliant movements of the insteps" in the *Pas de Marseilles*.[61] Although the social dancer did not jump, he or she still had to master a complex foot technique. Announcing a far more limber stage dancer, especially one who wore lighter clothing, he spoke of the legs during a *battement* reaching as high as the shoulder or head.[62]

The stage dancer in the late eighteenth century and early nineteenth century had to have many tricks in order to attract the public. As a stage performer, he could accomplish at least nine pirouettes. The great dancers of the day, Vestris and Pitrot, were able to shock the audiences with "extraordinary feats of balance or aplomb."[63] Like many of this writer's forebears, he praised the dancer who moved his audience with meaningful attitudes or touching physical expression with the quality of sensibility and feeling that motivated gestures.

Jean-Georges Noverre (1727–1810), the great writer, choreographer, and director of the Paris Opéra Ballet (1776–1781), was also a renowned dancing master who devoted his life to the art of ballet. Noverre insisted on truth, simplicity, harmony, and the imitation of nature, and believed that the perfection of dance technique actually prevented ballet from achieving its full potential. A focus on the technicalities of movement tended to mechanize performances, resulting in a lack of warmth or expression of inner emotions. Noverre was intent on creating realistic characters in his ballets whose being, gestures, and demeanors paralleled reality and would tell us about ourselves. He was a proponent of the power of pantomime to convey ideas and emotions through gestures and facial expressions.

Noverre usually linked the word "nature" with "belle" and maintained that "the artist must make choices in order to correct the defects of nature and embellish his subject sufficiently to arrive at a noble or picturesque effect. He encouraged intelligent poetic license, which contributed to the perfection, elegance or variety of presentation."[64] He was aware that one's work habits greatly affected posture, movement, and gestures, and he urged his students to be alert for subjects taken from daily life and all strata of society.

CHAPTER 2

Reformers and *Philosophes* as Forerunners of the Revolution in Fashion

Sans costume, point d'illusion.

—Noverre

Stage dress continued to reflect contemporary court fashions throughout the eighteenth century, although there were moments of true reform. In the mid-eighteenth century, theatrical and dance artists began to initiate discussions about costumes. Clothing had serious meanings that resonated throughout court and opera life. Theaters catered to the court, often the source of their *privilèges* and subsidies. Everything connected to the public theater had some link to the aristocracy and could be manipulated. The costume, a minor ornament, related to the fashions and tastes of the moment. It took several broad-minded and informed theatrical and boulevard artists, some in England as well as in France, to discover the value of a knowledgeably conceived production. Costume reform, or the use of clothing on stage consistent with the period and concept of the characters and drama, began more significantly on the acting stage, before it came to influence opera or ballet.

Seminal Theater Reforms

After 1760, there was a reaction against the use of court dress. Costume designers introduced simplicity and truth in dress. Both performers and spectators became aware of the glaring discrepancies between the garments actually worn in antiquity and those worn by theatrical performers purporting to represent the ancients. Reform was inevitable.[1] The elaborate and gaudy clothing of mythological heroes and heroines, Turks, or Chinese characters began to look absurd. Towering feathers and embroidered brocades struck a false note, especially in the austere and profound neoclassic tragedies.[2]

The actress/singer/dancer Madame Favart at the Comédie-Italienne (often a source for radical ideas) was a reformer and dressed in a woolen villager's dress and wooden shoes—with unadorned hair and bare arms and legs—when she played in *les Amours de Bastien et Bastienne* at the Opéra-Comique in 1753. Her attire suggested changes from previous depictions of peasants that had often included diamonds in coiffures and long gloves. However, it took years for this breakthrough to occur in traditional theaters.

The great actress La Clairon (1723–1803) tried to reform the costume in 1766. She eliminated the *panniers*. The desire to take control over her roles, no matter how great the social and professional pressures, endowed Clairon with a strong sense of individuality. "Her style of acting and her costume reforms, allowed her to claim authorial rights over her public persona, removing 'editing' privileges from the influential all-male audience which stood in the orchestra, or parterre section of the theatre."[3] Clairon's intellectual bent led her to write her thoughts on theatrical expression and stage clothing in her *Mémoires*, written in the eighteenth century but not published until 1822. She thought that "Les draperies d'après l'antique dessinent et découvrent trop le nu" (the Greek garments are too revealing) and seemed to be better for statues and paintings of statues than for actresses. However, she believed that one should preserve the line and the intention of a particular time and place, as in antiquity. She warned actresses not to add ornaments to costumes that were unknown before commerce with the Indies and the New World. "La seule mode à suivre est le costume du rôle qu'on joue. . . . On doit surtout arranger ses vêtements d'après les personnages; l'âge, l'austérité, la douleur, rejettent tout ce que permet la jeunesse, le désir de plaire, et le calme de l'âme." ("The only fashion to follow is the costume of the role one plays. . . . One must especially wear the clothes of the character, his age, his austerity, his sadness and reject all that youth can do, the desire to please and the calmness of soul.")[4] Perhaps the most cogent remark Clairon made was saved for her last sentence: "The audience's first glance of an actress must prepare them for the character she wishes to develop."[5]

The encyclopedist Marmontel befriended Clairon and wrote about visiting the actress when she was about to play Roxane in *Bajazet* at Versailles. "For the first time," he observed, "I found her in sultana's dress, without panniers, arms half exposed and in true Oriental costume."[6] Apparently, the audience was amazed and impressed by the innovation. Several days

Fig. 7 Madame Favart, actress from the Opéra Comique, was known for her refreshing and radical ideas on stage costuming. Courtesy of the Bibliothèque de l'Opéra.

Fig. 8 La Clairon, a celebrated tragic actress, brought reform to costuming as well as the status of actresses in society. Courtesy of the Bibliothèque de l'Opéra.

later, Clairon played the part of Electra and once again abandoned court attire, wearing instead a simple slave's habit; her hair loose and long chains on her arms. The elimination of the *hanches,* or panniers, which for years had forced the great actresses to use the mincing gait of the eighteenth-century salon, led to a more natural way of walking.[7]

Clairon's actions defined the nature of the public roles women assumed in the decades before the Revolution. Her public appeal depended on attracting masculine attention and, like hostesses of the intelligentsia or salon, she facilitated the dissemination of enlightened ideas.[8]

Another influence on costume was the great French actor François Talma. Born in Paris in 1763 and trained in England, he was unrivaled as an exponent of strong and concentrated passion on stage. When he visited London as a young man, Talma made the acquaintance of the actress George Anne Bellamy and the actors Charles Macklin and John Philip Kemble, all of whom were interested in authentic costume. These English actors brought a new sense of truth to the English stage and, by their example, actors attempted to depict their characters with an immediacy and honesty not found in the formalistic and histrionic habits of classical training. For example, Bellamy, like Clairon, wrote memoirs that bemoaned the fact that costumes were unhistoric. She recounts that her rival, Mistress Furval, was supposed to play Cleopatra and foolishly wore a rich dress of the eighteenth century because she wanted to outshine Bellamy.

Aided by his friend, the painter Jacques-Louis David, Talma was among the earliest advocates of realism in costume and scenery. He did research on the period of his plays and "was seen studying assiduously in the libraries and studying monuments of different ages and then showed on the stage the results of his research."[9] At David's bidding, Talma appeared in 1789 in the small role of Proculus in Voltaire's *Brutus* looking like a Greek statue, with a toga and Roman headdress, much to the surprise of an audience accustomed to eighteenth-century costume. "When Talma entered backstage with short hair and dressed in a simple cloth tunic, while everyone else was wearing the usual wigs and expensive silks, actress Madame Vestris looked him up and down and said, 'But Talma, your arms are bare!' He answered 'Roman arms were bare.' She said 'But Talma, you have no breeches!' He said 'The Romans wore none.' 'Swine!' was her response."[10]

Further development in costume and makeup was evident in Talma's stage portrait of Jean-Jacques Rousseau (1790), as he was pronounced a wonderful likeness in *Le Journaliste des Ombres.* He also appeared in Chénier's controversial *Charles IX* with black, unpowdered hair, dressed simply but strikingly in a black velvet coat decorated in gold, stockings of white silk, and a white gauze ruff."[11] His partner Madame Vestris also succumbed to wearing a similar historical costume. With Talma's initiatives, by

Nº 58.

Costume de TALMA, dans CINNA.

Théâtre Français   Tragédie de Racine

A Paris chez Martinet Libraire rue du Coq Nº 15

Que Rome se déclare ou pour ou contre nous,
Mourant pour vous servir, tout me semblera doux

Acte Iᵉʳ Scene IIIᵉ

Fig. 9 François Talma in a Roman costume for his role in *Cinna*. He was among the early French advocates for realism in both scenery and costume.

the end of 1791 authentic costumes and interest in the study of period dress prevailed.

Dance Costume Reformers before the Revolution

During the period before the Revolution, choreographers did not think it mattered that dancers were not wearing costumes in the period of the story. In fact, the term *choreographer,* someone who oversaw the ballet and all its parts, did not really come into usage until the *ballet d'action,* or ballet pantomime, in the nineteenth century. Prior to that there were *maîtres de ballets,* or ballet masters, and the program would indicate that the ballet was "de la composition de Gardel ou Dauberval." Costumes were not historically correct, nor did they accurately mirror the character's region or profession. Ballet did not look objectively at itself as an independent art form. It lacked a strong sense of identity.

Philosophically, the ballet costume before reform projected an illusion of fantasy rather than reality and facilitated the evasion of the daily constraints of banality and monotony. It offered the possibility of poetically imagining all that is strange, sumptuous, and unexpected.[12] It was subject to contemporary taste and was, therefore, in a sense, a slave to fashion. Until reform, the necessities of ballet still resided in aesthetics and in technique.

Accuracy in costume was a pressing issue during reform: a mythological hero deserved different clothing than an eighteenth-century lord. The dancer in the eighteenth century carried enormous amounts of weight and materials on his body. For example, in ballet, he or she wore what might be worn at a fancy dress ball, with some accoutrements that would emblematically suggest a certain character or theme. The recognized costume for that eighteenth-century male dancer in the noble or serious style was the dress of a Roman officer seen through the eyes of eighteenth-century artists. It consisted of a tight-fitting body like the Roman cuirass carried out in fabric, with sleeves reaching to the waist that were puffed out from shoulder to elbow. The base of the body widened out into a short skirt made to assume a hooped shape by being stretched over a light frame; the skirt was called a *tonnelet,* for *tonneau,* or cask. Noverre pointed out the absurdity, as well as the inconvenience, of dancing in such outfits: "If the style of a ridiculous costume annoys the dancer so that he feels overcome by the weight of his clothes to the extent of forgetting his part, how can he act with ease and warmth . . . ?"[13]

The ideals of each epoch governed attitudes toward dance and costuming dance. For years ballet costumes were ruled by the notion of genres that were divided into three categories: noble, *demi-caractère,* and comic. The genres evolved from a long series of developments in the ballet technique as well as stories of the dances. For the most part, mythological tales and their characters, including those found in anacreontic plots, affected the style of the costumes. Individuals became famous for specific roles, such as Pierrot, Scaramouche, and Columbine. The three genres of the French ballet stage satisfied different historical influences. If dancers were playing noble or heroic roles, their costumes would automatically require ceremonial and elegant attire with feathers adorning their wigs. Their moves were steady, slow, and grave. Demi-caractère dancers fell in between the noble and comic, as their costuming was not overly formal but, at the same time, it did not have comedic ornaments or shapes. The demi-caractère dancer prided himself on his nimble capers and jumping style. The comic dancer had a more rustic look: short and heavy. He was expected to spin, jump, and amuse with daring and grotesque moves.

Despite the work of innovative and intelligent actors, changes in these genres were slow in coming; there was a repetitious tedium of costume design until the mid- to late eighteenth century. Cooks and shepherds in silver *tonnelets* had to be dressed luxuriously if they were in the presence of aristocrats, as the audience was supposed to envision an idealized beauty of even the most lowly characters.[14]

Dancers at the Opéra aligned themselves with the aristocracy. For example, the famed Gaetan Vestris, "le Dieu de la Danse," and Jean Dauberval (the distinguished choreographer of *La Fille mal gardée*) refused in 1779 to appear on stage in Armide wearing the costumes of a bourgeois, believing that such clothing belittled their reputations. Auguste, the son of Gaetan, was then asked to appear in his father's place. Gaetan ran to his son and threatened that if he danced, the father would prevent him from using the great family name, Vestris. Auguste dutifully obeyed and they were all sent promptly to Fort-l'Évêque, all for a costume that the dancers deemed the enemy.[15]

In another contretemps that succeeded and led to reform, the elder Vestris was supposed to dance Apollo in *Castor et Pollux*, wearing a big black wig, a mask, and a great golden armor with a sun on his chest. Vestris did not show up, and actor Maximilien Gardel came to take his place. However, he, too, eschewed the traditional garb of the heroic Apollo and chose to appear with long blond curls and no mask. From that day forward, the soloists gave up their masks and other courtly attire. Simple, light tunics became the required mythological garb.

Listening to the calls for reform, the dancers themselves, who had more at risk, were keen to make changes. Significant strides were made by Marie-Anne de Cupis de Camargo (1710–1770), a Paris Opéra soloist known for her exceptional work as a jumper and fast mover and as a brio dancer. She

Fig. 10 La Camargo (1761), famous for her brilliant "batterie," or jumping beats. They were more easily seen and applauded when she cleverly shortened her skirts. Courtesy of the Theatre Museum, London.

was the first to perform steps previously relegated to men, such as *entrechats* and *cabrioles*. She is famous for having shortened her skirt, thereby giving her more freedom to execute her complicated *petit allegro* and *batterie* and allowing the audience to actually see these steps. She also saw to it that her dancing shoes were made more pliable in order to facilitate her *batterie*.[16] Her fame reached the most elite social circles and, as often happens, a number of French food dishes were named after her, such as *Soufflé Camargo*.

Brought up in Brussels, her dancing-master father arranged for her to work with the celebrated professional dancer Françoise Prévost. In Paris, Camargo first danced the same ballet for which Prévost had become known, *Les Caractères de la danse*. Her name quickly became famous: "When she jumped minutes passed."[17] At the time that she decided to shorten her skirts, the public asked what she wore above her knees. Nothing? A *maillot* (tights)? Or *Caleçons* (bloomers)?

The vision of a woman's ankles and even more received a terrible jolt when, in 1754, le Sieur Clément de Genève wrote an impassioned letter about actresses without underwear. The origin of his outcry was an accident at the Opéra-Comique: an actress fell down after being hit on stage by a branch from a tree. When they tried to lift the broken tree branch from her body, it caught and pulled up her skirts, revealing nothing on her bottom, and she raced like lightning to get off stage. This odd event brought about a policy insisting that women wear some sort of tights or bloomers.[18]

During the same period that Camargo danced, one of Camargo's most serious rivals, Marie Sallé, was also known as fiercely defiant because she had the courage to completely abandon the court costume and to put on the tunic that was appropriate to the Greek myth of the ballet. The newspaper *Le Mercure de France* in 1736 extolled Sallé for having daringly appeared in London practically undressed when she played Galatea in *Pygmalion* (1734), "without panniers, without a skirt, without a corset, and without any ornaments on her head . . . in a simple muslin robe draped in the style of a Greek tunic."[19] Sallé had great success in the ballets *Pygmalion* and *Bacchus et Ariane*, according to contemporary accounts. Her extremely sensuous scenario for Pygmalion was recounted in the April 1734 edition of *Le Mercure*:

> Pygmalion enters surrounded by many statues one of which greatly attracts him; he looks at her, he considers her and sighs; he carries his hands to her feet and waist; he examines them and observes all her contours as well as her arms and neck, which he adorns with precious bracelets and an expensive collier; he becomes passionate and expresses his inquietude and falls in a reverie, after which he throws himself at the feet of Venus begging her to bring to life this gorgeous statue; Venus responds to his prayer with three beams of light and gradually the statue comes alive and notices where she is; Pygmalion is amazed by her elegant attitudes; he dances and she imitates him and inspires his greatest tenderness.[20]

The king, the queen, and all the court asked for this dance to be presented at a benefit for Sallé. Barton-Baker of the *London Stage* newspaper wrote that Covent Garden had a terrific crowd. Actor David Garrick remembered the furor even though he was only seventeen years old. And the romancier, l'Abbé Prévot, wrote that Sallé had the talents to open a thousand purses.[21] Sallé did not rush to return to France; she renewed her contract with the entrepreneur John Rich for the next season, taking chances once again with her costume. She did her *Caractères de l'Amour* and played a male part, Cupidon, which seemed to disfavor her and was the cause of some disgrace.

MLLE. ALLARD AS HEBE

Fig. 11 Mademoiselle Allard as Hébé Boquet's elaborately delicate designs characterized the mid- to late 18th-century costume designs at the Opéra. Courtesy of the Bibliothèque de l'Opéra.

As the eighteenth century progressed, it continued to see the rise of some extremely talented and strong-minded dancers. One of the most intense and individualistic women, Marie-Madeleine Guimard, became the center-piece for many ballets and opera-ballets. Her interest in fashion and in creating fashion on the stage grew as she became more renowned. Guimard (1743–1818) held one of the most powerful positions in the Paris Opéra, not only as principal dancer, but also as a political force—driving the politics of the administration and the direction of the ballet.[22]

Poems and *éloges* sang of Guimard's exciting presence. M. Duplain wrote, "She mixes perfectly the transparent with the nude, force with elegance. Nothing shows effort. If she rises into the air, her élan is a flight and her fall is a stroke of lightning."[23] She openly quarreled with Noverre when he directed the Opéra dancers, challenging him as well as the directors of the Opéra to take her seriously, no matter how whimsical her wishes. And they did. François Métra, the anonymous author of the gossipy and informative *Correspondance littéraire*, called La Guimard "La déesse de Goût," or "The Goddess of Taste." Her taste cost the Opéra a lot of money: in 1779, 30,000 *livres* (many thousands of dollars) were spent for her costumes.

In his biography of Guimard, Edmond de Goncourt discussed her intriguing power at court and in the theater. He sought to understand how she presented herself on stage as well as in public and posited that ballerinas, in and of themselves, were mythological and fantasy figures because of their graceful and lyrical movements. He agreed with the illusionistic way that dance was costumed in the eighteenth century because he did not feel that ballerinas needed to be costumed in a realistic manner.

> One must say that dance cannot have the same exigencies as tragedy or drama. The ballerina, no matter what she dances: a nymph, a warrior, a shepherdess, a fairy—is always a graceful chimera, lets the spectator voluntarily imagine himself to be in the middle of fantasy, and, not at all, reality.[24]

Under Louis XV, the court designer for the Opéra, Louis Boquet, created designs that the king would approve of as he was paid by the Director of the Menus Plaisirs, a special department that oversaw entertainment, especially for the court. Goncourt clearly described Boquet's designs for Guimard, costumes that no doubt she advised him to create for her pronounced persona. She sensed the need to "dress down" and reveal a simpler mode for movement. Goncourt poetically sketches Guimard's attire:

> In this temple of flashiness and showy rags, one feels in the grand dancer a taste for simplicity, a search for clear radiance, a predilection for the color white, that is shown by the repetition of the same motif

at the bottom of the costumes of Mademoiselle Guimard: All white (. . .) glazed with silver . . . very bright.[25]

Designs for Guimard revealed how well the eighteenth century translated visions of fairylands. Ballet costumes expressed ethereal visions from antiquity, from southern and northern poles, and of fictional characters in moral allegories. Actors wore silky armor decorated with serpent scales, striped cloaks with leopard skin vests, capes with enormous sleeves and net embroidery, clover-colored tunics with clouds of gauze and peacock feathers—a wonderland of shimmering, flowing fabrics.[26] On the stage beautiful phantoms rather than realistic dance figures emerged.

Guimard created some of her own styles, such as the *robe à la Guimard* in 1771, which was named for a dress that looked like one of her ballet costumes and prefigured the dresses of Marie Antoinette's weekend jaunts to her farm. In Vestris's version of Noverre's ballet *Jason et Médée* (1770), Guimard attired herself as a simple shepherdess, which started the vogue for using an overskirt that was hitched up so that one could see the underskirt of another color. In addition, she abandoned the use of the *domino*, a large, cape-like garment that covered up the whole dress during Carnival season, which caused others to do the same. When seen in the streets, Guimard followed the fashions of Marie Antoinette and the court, but occasionally she would disguise herself as a man in order to hide her identity.[27]

Dance historian Léandre Vaillat attributes Eugène Lamy's discovery of the beautiful tutu for *La Sylphide* to Guimard's costume as Princess Créuse in the ballet *Jason et Médée*. Her dress, which seemed to hold itself up without need of panniers or other rigid hoops, had a shortened and bouffant skirt initiating the romantic model. The costume maintained its shape with the help of a muslin crinoline, leaving the dancer totally free to move. This extraordinary costume assured the dancer that she need not fear for her modesty, since she was wearing tights underneath it all.[28]

Besides advising the designer Boquet, Guimard also counseled her tailors at the Opéra, Delaître and his son. In all the costumes designed by Boquet and realized by the father and son Delaître, Guimard saw no interest in innovation or in "local color." That was promoted by the Comédie-Française and brought to the Opéra by the woman singer Antoinette Saint-Huberty. Guimard thought she looked more beautiful in pale colors and white, and wanted clothing with the least cluttered line. She was known both as L'Araignée, or spider, and La Squelette, or skeleton, because of her very slender body, enhanced by the simple line. In 1781 Guimard convinced Delaître that he was not being paid enough, which was probably true, but her meddling incensed the directors of the Opéra.[29]

Mlle GUIMARD dans le ballet du Navigateur.

Elle unit les vertus, l'efprit et la bonté
À la grace plus belle encor que la beauté.

Duterbre pinx.   Janinet

Fig. 12 La Guimard's flowing, soft skirts and bodice gave the impression of a fairy-like heroine, whose "grace was more exquisite than beauty itself." Courtesy of the Bibliothèque de l'Arsenal.

In the role of Mélide in *Le Premier Navigateur* (1785), Guimard's appearance was distinctively romantic. Her hair hung freely; she wore a white tunic with a blue waistband that flowed behind her. The fervent sentimentality of the Salomon Gessner poem on which the ballet was based created a libretto that called for the extreme emotions of young love and its potential loss. Critics praised her brilliant characterization and claimed her talents as a passionate actress were moving. A poem by Dorat celebrated Guimard in the role of Mélide. He called attention to the floating waves of her hair ornamented by a scalloped headdress, to her fluttering dress, to that romantic overpowering sensibility that English and German poets exulted in and that was soon to grace the stages of Romantic ballet. He extolled the beauty of her dancing: "Let your brilliant steps release a flight of pleasures."[30]

Guimard was invited to London, where her popularity gave her great confidence and enriched her coffers. The English respected her style and the fact that she was the creator of fashionable attire and fashion in general. Guimard's fame as a beautifully dressed woman preceded her; she was assaulted by clothes merchants and tailors who begged her for her opinion on the latest English fashions, and she frankly told them what she thought.[31]

Guimard was also sought by the aristocracy. In a letter of 1789, she spoke of spending her time with the famous ballet lover and supporter, the Duchess of Devonshire. Guimard was also summoned by Marie Antoinette to give her opinion on the shape of the neckline and the height of the hair of the ladies-in-waiting. Marie Antoinette respected Guimard, as she had heard that Guimard was an ardent benefactress, offering clothing and money to the poor.[32] Guimard was sent to Fort-l'Évêque prison for some misdemeanor, a not-uncommon event for recalcitrant dancers and actresses, whereupon she said to the queen's lady-in-waiting, "Dry your eyes Justine. I have written to the queen, telling her of a new coiffure I have just invented and depend upon it, I shall be at liberty before nightfall."[33] Fort-l'Évêque was a royal prison for debtors, especially actors and performers. Prisoners were able to bring their servants and silver with them and were also allowed to leave the prison in the evenings to play their parts in the theater.

Guimard often gave dinners described by Bachaumont, the author of *Mémoires secrèts*, as the most amusing in Paris. On Tuesday evenings she invited people of the court, on Thursdays, important literati, and on Saturdays, a motley assemblage of wits, actresses, and "viveurs." Guimard also had her own theater, where there were presentations of pieces that were known for their salacious stories.[34]

Guimard's unique approach to stage apparel drove ballet fashions in new directions that lasted for some time. She was also known for her talent for applying makeup that gave her an eternally youthful quality, something she

Fig. 13 Mademoiselle Guimard as Nicette in *La Chercheuse d'Esprit* (1787), wearing a charming costume with a lifted skirt for which she became known. Courtesy of the Bibliothèque de l'Opéra.

needed as she spent many years at the Opéra, having made her debut in 1762 and not retiring until 1789. Aside from her extravagant and self-interested sense of style, she also sensed the Rousseauistic desire for simplicity and naturalism. No doubt she also read the Encyclopedists, who called for a truer, more rational approach to the necessities of life, including fashion, whether on the stage or on the street.

Great Writers and the Philosophes

Great thinkers and writers of the eighteenth century were very attracted to social dance and court ballet. French upper classes relied on the Salon as a socializing force, where taste and politics mingled. The *Philosophes* also depended on the Salon as the place where their ideas and writings were promulgated. They wrote profusely on the subject of dance, calling for more critical and theoretical study that extended beyond movement to costuming, as well. Activities at the popular boulevard theaters and fairs sparked interest in more realistic presentations of ballet. Plots that touched the spectators and amusing incidents characteristic of the Italian comedians brought a true-to-life atmosphere to the stage. The Philosophes, or "Encyclopedists," of the eighteenth century included Jean-Jacques Rousseau, Denis Diderot, François Marie Arouet Voltaire, Louis de Cahusac, and, although he was not an official contributor to the *Encyclopedia*, Jean-Georges Noverre.

Rousseau (1712–1778)

Rousseau's thoughts and writings reflected a plea for returning to nature and the simpler outdoor life. The "back to nature" philosophy he championed was a reaction against formality, luxury, elaborate clothes, etiquette, the suppression of simple human sentiments, and ignorance of the innocent pleasures that were the hallmark of Versailles and the world of fashion. Rousseau's insightful understanding of the power of individual emotions, which he insisted must be given free reign both inside and outside, reflected each person's will. Rousseau, like other theater writers of the period, was intrigued by the English novel of sentiment that undermined neoclassical literary traditions. The novelist Samuel Richardson's *Pamela* and *Clarissa Harlowe* exerted a strong influence over Rousseau, who produced a similarly epistolary romance, *Julie ou la Nouvelle Héloise* (1761). Centering on Julie, the female heroine, Rousseau's novel explored the young girl's and her tutor's worlds of sensations and feelings and thereby changed the course of European thought. Perhaps more than any other person, Rousseau affected the future of fashion.

As a Swiss citizen, Rousseau lived with the angry pressures and limitations of a Calvinist upbringing, which preached the depravities of human beings. In contrast, Rousseau spoke of the goodness of human beings, especially if they are close to nature. Sensibility came with contempt for urban life and the conventions of civilized society, such as business and legal activities, and its aesthetic tastes. Furthermore, love for the simplicity of rural life and the solitude and beauty of the countryside heightened the individual's potential for good and virtue. In the setting for Rousseau's sentimental fiction, emotions, sighs and palpitations, tears, ecstasies, and swoons abound; restraint receded into the background. Nature became a reflection

Fig. 14 Portrait of Jean-Jacques Rousseau (1761) in a painting by Sir Allen Ramsay. He's wearing his famous fur hat. Rousseau's powerful voice reflected a plea for returning to nature and the simpler outdoor life. Courtesy of the Chateau de Coppet, Geneva.

of (or response to) the emotional state of the hero or heroine. The artificial and corrupt life of Paris evoked contempt compared with living in nature. This free-wheeling nature reflected a moral attitude, a virtuousness made more virtuous by the open expression of one's passions, as extreme or florid as they might be.

In *Julie ou La Nouvelle Héloise*, Rousseau was quick to praise the English, although he spent barely five years in England, and to criticize the French, especially French women. He spoke of the English as being able to rise to fortune by more honest methods because "the people having more share in the government, public esteem is there as a greater means of distinguishing oneself."[35] He noted that French women were "slender rather than well-proportioned; they do not have a good figure; thus they readily prefer fashions which disguise it."[36] Rousseau diminished the French women's basic qualities, calling them frivolous, guileful, false, heedless, flighty, given to idle chatter, all characterized by their outward dressing of rouge and hoop petticoats. He did, however, find them soundly educated and said that their fine education was of better service to their judgment.

Rousseau's opinion of women can best be described as backward and in keeping with traditional religious suspicions of what was perceived as women's essentially deceptive character. In *Émile*, Sophie, the wife-to-be counterpart of Émile, is brought up to attract and please men. Not well educated, she knows enough to be modest and to appear innocent. Certainly she needs to dress in a pleasing way and to be clever enough to conquer Émile's heart.[37] The girl-child has no place outside the home and no place in an intellectual world where ideas are discussed and discovered. *Émile* achieved widespread notoriety, mainly for its wholesome approach to motherhood, a condition necessary to bring tenderness and love between the child and the mother who enjoys nurturing and coddling the soon-to-be "citizens" of the world.

Rousseau insisted that the institution of the family was absolutely essential to achieving order and eliminating chaos that might result from a world without boundaries, a world without law. Love in the family fostered love of state. A good husband, father, and son made a good citizen. He emphasized women's reproductive role. He linked nursing to morality and regarded population as a matter of major importance. In such a world, women's infidelity was the greatest crime. Speech was what Rousseau feared most, as well as the "cackle" of women's societies and their interminable gossip. He explained that a woman's role is contradictory: she is there to manipulate and seduce, and to curb man's unlimited desires. Women must be in their proper place, in the back rooms. (It is interesting to note that Rousseau abandoned several (if not all) of his children and gave them up for adoption.)

According to Rousseau, if a mother and child are separated and the mother begins to play an active role in society, away from hearth and home, there ensues a breakdown resulting in the ultimate destruction of the ties that hold community together. He equated the eighteenth-century cosmopolis with an excessively feminized place, a politically absolutist state where excessive softness and sensuality reigned.

Rousseau continued, "There are no good morals for women outside of a withdrawn and domestic life . . . when they seek men's looks, they are already letting themselves be corrupted by them."[38] He looked back to the ancients, affirming that in Greek and Roman society the women were kept inside, away from view and certainly not seen publicly. He gave the example of ancient Greek women who occupied a separate seating section in the theater, the kerkis, where it was convenient neither to see nor to be seen, and he appreciated the fact that the ancients lived in a very segregated fashion.[39]

At the same time that Rousseau preached the need to contain women's behavior, he also understood that their bodies were severely hindered by their corsets and heavy skirts. Rousseau and other philosophers pronounced that young people should not be tied up in adult corsets and constricting clothes.[40] Young girls started to wear dresses that were close to the body, high-waisted with a low neckline and tiny sleeves. Boys wore simple suits. Adults also copied this relaxed look.

Clothing also gave permission to feeling. Loose clothes suggested a freeing of instinct and emotions. When Rousseau's hero, Saint-Preux, enters Julie's bedroom, he identifies everything, including her clothing, with her glorious person:

> All the parts of your scattered dress present to my ardent imagination those of your body that they conceal. This delicate headdress which sets off the large blond curls which it pretends to cover; this happy bodice shawl against which at least once I shall not have to complain; this elegant and simple gown which displays so well the taste of the wearer; these dainty slippers that a supple foot fills so easily; this corset so slender which touches and embraces . . . what an enchanting form! . . . in front two gentle curves . . . oh voluptuous sight . . . the whalebone has yielded to the force of the impression . . . delicious imprints, let me kiss you a thousand times! Gods! Gods! what will it be when . . . Ah, I think I am already feeling that tender heart beating under that happy hand![41]

The tradition of a lighter skirt had begun in the 1760s. It was a style that prefigured the nineteenth-century tutu: "Transparent overskirts came into vogue as an interesting innovation for ballet costumes. They were frequently worn on ball gowns with pleated frills and gathered ribbon."[42] Of course, a number of petticoats were worn underneath the transparent tulle covering, but this may have been one more of the developments that led to the layered, puffy look of the Romantic ballet costume.

Rousseau's resonating opening lines to *The Social Contract* applied as well to this arena. "L'homme est né libre et partout il est dans les fers." ("Man is born free but everywhere he lives in shackles.") According to Rousseau, the women's corset and the baby's swaddling clothes were dangerous practices that sought to crush individuality by harnessing the body. Images of great symbolic value are carved on Rousseau's tomb in Ermonville (he died in 1778): an enactment of naked children burning whalebone stays and swaddling clothes. It is unfortunate that Rousseau's radical thinking about the corset and swaddling clothes did not extend to his preference for keeping women in the back room and away from the public eye.

Rousseau's stringent statements about clothing affected many writers, including those in England. Walter Vaughan's *Philosophical and Medical Essay Concerning Modern Clothing* (1792) tried to address problems of deformity and the unhealthy aspects of dress. Vaughan criticized the dress of his time for producing "inability, disease and death."[43] Like Rousseau, he felt that fashion was a corrupter of virtue and a masker of vice. The common mode of clothing altered the natural form of our bodies; he wanted all clothing to be suitable to every age and sex, constitution and country.

In his *Letter to M. D'Alembert*, Rousseau, a Calvinist, suggested that the theater and women are one, and that the corruption and duplicity of living in society may be equated with being on stage:

> It is modern public women . . . the actresses of the stage, the salon-going women of the capital cities, and the illicit women of the court—who in their person and in their speech best symbolize the evils of an excessively spectacular existence. These vain and independent women show themselves off—tempt the looks of all men—in a public fashion.[44]

Echoing Plato's criticism of the theater, Rousseau saw the actor or actress as a charlatan who puts on another character and basically lies about everything. Moreover, the actress symbolized all the evils of a public existence. In denying women the opportunity to be on stage, Rousseau was exercising a harsh opinion, for a stage career was one of the very few professions in which a woman of his era could hope to earn a living, practice a craft, and achieve some measure of social acclaim.

Rousseau's novels were widely read in Europe by virtue of many translations. Romantic love and the powerful emotions that drove couples together provided hot fare for impressionable young women. Mary Seidman Trouille presented a series of important intellectual womens' opinions of Rousseau's concepts. For example, Madame de Genlis, passionate royalist and tutor to

Louis-Philippe, "while a firm advocate of the Rousseauian ideals of enlightened domesticity and motherhood . . . rejected Rousseau's limited view of female capabilities and insisted on the liberating force of a solid education for women."[45] As noted, Rousseau recognized the value of a good education; he just did not think a woman needed it.

Neither did the late-eighteenth-century aristocracy see much value in women's education despite a few notable exceptions such as Madame de Genlis. Rather, young women indulged in Romantic reveries such as those portrayed in novels by Rousseau, Bernardin de Saint Pierre, and Chateaubriand. They began to unleash their highly calculated sense of love and longing by releasing their tight clothing and relinquishing various ornaments and hairdos. Clothing became expressive of the personal self, permitting one's individual physical characteristics to show. The trend toward large, imposing court uniforms gradually faded. It was an age of reverie, sentiment, and melancholy, of country *fêtes* and pastoral pleasures.

Most people are aware that Rousseau wrote brilliant political and social polemics as well as extensive treatises on music. Less known is that he not only composed music for ballets but also designed their stories and wrote various articles for the *Encyclopedia*. Rousseau criticized the way ballet trivialized its themes. He viewed gesture, movements, and pantomime as a mysterious language, beautiful and occasionally startling in its virtuosity. He believed the language of movement should be viewed separately from the world of words, song, drama, and opera. Ballet must have its own reason for being.

In his novel *Julie: Ou La Nouvelle Héloise*, Rousseau noted that ballet is often the most brilliant part of the performance, or opera, with wonderful spectacle and magnificent dancing. However, in spite of its glitter, the impact of the opera suffers from too much dance.

Rousseau decried the entrance in each act of the ballet, where important action is suspended in order to present the dancers to the seated singers as a delicious dish. The activities of the hero and heroine have been forgotten. If the prince is happy, all are happy and dance. If he is unhappy, he is cheered up with dances—all this while the fate of the crown remains in splendid oblivion.[46] What most perturbed Rousseau was the destruction of dramatic continuity in a musical sense when a certain emotive equality had been established and promptly shattered by the inclusion of senseless figured dances (somewhat like the musical films of the thirties). Thus, not only does opera or drama suffer, but also the dance is harmed since the choreography does not dedicate itself to serious themes.

Rousseau created several unsuccessful ballets, but his luck changed when he wrote the music for *Le Devin du Village* in 1752. Madame de Pompadour played the romantic male lead in its first performance at court. What was unusual about this opera-play was the central scene in pantomime that evoked and heightened the conflict and the drama of the story. Thus, movement was utilized in order to carry on the plot of the story. Diderot lauded the value of such an addition to the libretto of an opera.

Diderot (1713–1784)

Diderot, principal editor of the *Encyclopedia*, attempted as a theorist and playwright to break the grip of convention in the rule-ridden and static French theater. He applied the same critical reasoning to the ballet of the time. The "truth of nature" that was sought in the theater was also pursued by Diderot in his search for the "natural man."

Diderot spoke for the "pathos" of life, everyday life that had as much value as the great moments of heroism associated with classical mythology and theaete. The *Troisième Entretien sur le Fils Naturel* describes this view:

> A twist of fate, the fear of ignomiry, the consequences of misery, a passion which drives man to his ruin, from ruin to desperation, from desperation to a violent death—these are not rare events; and you'd imagine that they would never affect you as much as the fabulous death of a great hero, or the sacrifice of a child at the altars of Athenian or Roman gods?[47]

In his *Entretiens*, Diderot not only justified a new type of theater with sentimental plots and middle-class characters, but he also wished to launch a theater aimed "at the people." Diderot consciously sought to proclaim the theater an agency of social reform and to entrust it to the gospel of philanthropy. Although the execution of his dramatic works *Le Fils Naturel* (1757) and *Le Père de Famille* (1758) fell short of his aims, they contained a unique fermenting element.

In *Troisième Entretien* (1758), the two protagonists, Diderot-Moi and Dorval, argue and exchange opinions about this new poetic prose theater. They discuss the lyric theater and the pantomime. Moi asks the question, "And what should become of our ballets?" A serious response is given by Dorval: "The dance? The dance is awaiting a man of genius; it is mediocre everywhere because it is cliché-ridden."[48] Dorval goes on to criticize the constant use of minuets, passepieds, rigaudons, allemands, and sarabands, where certain patterns are traced on the floor. Diderot questioned the significance of these court dances that were beautifully done but abstract and cold. He likened the dance to a poem that requires the collaboration of the poet, the painter, the musician, and the pantomimist. This poem also has a subject that may be expressed through dramatic gesture, often informed by feelings of unusual human power. Lui of Diderot's *Rameau's Nephew* echoes this refrain in his conversation with Moi concerning lyric poetry on the stage: "It is the animal cry of passion that should dictate the melodic line."[49] Diderot then describes Rousseau's dance opera *Le Devin du Village*, in which there is an interlude or ballet done by villagers in the eighth scene. In the piece, the peasants create a lovely pantomime and rehearse it for the performance: "Walking and pantomime which are not in time to the music are the recitative of dance. If the dancer does not know how to act, everything is lost."[50] Moi then asks whether the seventeenth century left anything for the eighteenth century to accomplish in the theater. Dorval responds that, yes, there would be created the domestic and bourgeois tragedy. Also, the pantomime would be linked closely to the dramatic action, and then there is the ballet, "to be reduced to poetic form, to be designed to be separated from any other imitative art."[51] Thus, the ballet with a plot, or the *ballet d'action*, is supported and given credibility by Diderot.

Diderot's art criticism in his celebrated *Salons* (1759–1781) also promoted a fresh approach to the portraiture of the time. He pleaded for a more sensitive and sentimental style. His writings contributed to an enlightened attitude toward the body, what it wore, how it expressed itself, and how it was perceived by painters. He looked for a more reasonable, day-to-day vision so that clothing portrayed a more realistic picture of the person. It was an attempt to found an aesthetic based on the morality of emotions. Pictures, Diderot preached in the *Salons* (which could be regarded as the first example of art criticism), were good only if they taught moral lessons.

During his career, Diderot experienced the paintings of a number of important artists, many of whom agreed with his thoughts on art, although many did not. Pastoral pleasures abounded in the idealized and sensual paintings of François Boucher and Jean Honoré Fragonard, which appeared superfluous to Diderot. They capitalized on mythological illusions, heaping angels upon sensualized angels, while painter Antoine Watteau created sweet dreamy incidents of joyous afternoons spent dancing and cavorting. Fragonard achieved official recognition by painting (against his nature) pictures that had the cachet of official approval. Afterward, he returned to the more frivolous masterpieces that reflected his own taste and the spirit of the previous generation.

On the other hand, Jean-Marc Nattier, following Diderot's instructions, abandoned his mythological portraits to paint sitters in modern clothing. Jean-Baptiste Chardin devoted his genius to the illumination of humble persons and quiet domestic manners. More popular, and in keeping with the new climate of emotion, were the melting beauties of Elisabeth Vigée-Lebrun and the insidious little innocents of Jean-Baptiste Greuze, a finer painter than was commonly recognized.

Diderot's favorite paintings told documentary stories, like those of Greuze and Chardin. In his Salon of 1763 he extolled Greuze's work: "First of all, the genre pleases me. It is moral painting . . . Courage, my friend Greuze, create morality in your painting and always do it! When I see an elegant and pathetic old man, I feel my soul soften and tears readily come to my eyes."[52]

Diderot wished to uphold the values of the new middle classes and of domestic life rather than those of kings and princes, such as Fragonard and Boucher painted. He wanted sitters to look real, to avoid pretentious poses and to shun aristocratic symbols, such as the court costume that dressed nobles like "dolls in wigs." The clothing that one wore in portraits breathed a truth and reality where the thinking, emotive person lives:

> Natural beauty, which is nothing more in our mores than the obser-
> vation of essential beauty in our behavior, relative to what we are
> amongst the beings of nature; as concerns the writings of the mind, it
> is nothing more than the imitation and faithful depiction of the pro-
> ductions of nature in all its variety; as concerns harmony, it is nothing
> more than submission to the laws that nature has introduced in sono-
> rous bodies, their resonance and the conformation of the ear.[53]

Diderot wanted actors to look at paintings, thus expressing the emergent notion that the total stage picture, clothes included, might serve a function, the way a painting does—to help reveal the truth about life and to express a particular vision of that truth.[54]

Influenced by the swings of fashion as well as current philosophical dia-
logues, Diderot paid attention to what was happening across the Channel. Subjects of English paintings displayed people outdoors, in more practical fabrics, and with occasional imitations of working-class clothing. Focused on the court's activities, the French seemed in less harmony with nature and preferred paintings that were formal, with indoor scenes of luxury, contrary to Diderot's declamations.

Voltaire (1699–1778)

One of the perpetrators of English influences and Anglomania was the philosophe extraordinaire Voltaire (1699–1778). His correspondence described his experiences in England, where he lived from 1726 to 1728, and was first published in 1734; ten editions appeared by 1739. The French Parlia-
ment ordered the work to be burned as scandalous and disrespectful and the author to be arrested. The letters extolled various aspects of English life and government and brought attention to the advantages of living as an Englishman. Although the letters dealt primarily with philosophy and politics, they cast a strong light on a more democratic and egalitarian country

seeking to be ruled by enlightened and rational principles. If Voltaire admired the enemy across the Channel, why not other Frenchmen?

In addition to his interest in England's government, he was a formidable tragedian and writer of theater and ballet performance. Voltaire greatly valued technique and was critical of extravagant subject matter in dance. He found superficiality and lack of social purpose to be major defects in ballet. He was also a catalyst for reforming costuming in tragedies. When Voltaire handed over the text of his *Orphelin de la Chine* to the Comédie Française troupe, Clairon decided that it would not suffice to play the Asian heroine in the hoops and frilly French dresses she and other actresses customarily sported: she aspired to a model truer to the Chinese culture. Voltaire apparently waived his royalties in order that "they might be passed on to the actor to purchase costumes more in keeping with the spirit of his tragedy."[55]

Writings of the *Philosophes* influenced not only their readers but also each other. Relationships formed between them and an especially strong bond developed between Voltaire and Noverre. Many letters passed between them, exchanging ideas and expressing their respect for each other. When Noverre sent Voltaire a copy of his *Lettres*, Voltaire thanked him: "The title of your book may only indicate dance, but you shed a great deal of light on all the arts. Your style is as elegant as your ballets have imagination."[56]

After expressing his regrets for being unable to see one of Noverre's ballets, Voltaire added: "I think that your talent will be much appreciated in England, since they love the truths of nature there. But where will you find the acting dancers capable of executing your ideas?" Six months later, Voltaire reaffirmed his high opinion of Noverre: "I find that all you do is full of poetry; painters and poets will argue with one another as to whether you are a painter or a poet."[57]

Voltaire's correspondence with Noverre highlighted a common thread between them; both felt their abilities were not appreciated in France, and they went elsewhere to discover their fame.

Cahusac (1700–1759)

One of the most articulate and versatile writers on dance and its principles was the encyclopedist Cahusac. In the *Biographie Universelle*, Cahusac is described as having "a lively character, insecure and too demanding of his friends, very sensitive about his reputation, and of a sensibility that could create imbalance in his mind, and might perhaps shorten his days."[57] In other words, he was neurotic and intellectual.

Although Cahusac was primarily interested in opera, his deepening interest in ballet corresponded with the writing of his article "Ballet" for the *Encyclopedia* in 1752. In it he noted that eighteenth-century choreographers had been experimenting with a new dance form, the *danse en action*, that established the independence of ballet as an art both in its structure and content. It required that ballet have an intelligible story that ends suitably, and that dance be integrated with dramatic action. Cahusac noted the significance of the *ballet d'action* and defined it as an observer and a libretist:

> In our time, we have introduced the 'merveilleux' [magic] into the ballet; we've created the danse d'action; it is that dance is essential in enhancing an idea or subject. This type of dance . . . pleases the public, thanks to its novelty, and offers greater possibilities of amusing the spectators. By utilizing similar devices applied in poetry, painting, and music, the riches of the art are expanded.[59]

In his historical treatise on dance of 1754, Cahusac substantiated the importance of grace in earlier aesthetic comments on the dance:

> In order to be a fine dancer, one has to know how to move one's arms gracefully, to keep one's balance in all positions, to form one's steps in a flowing and light manner, to develop the energy and elasticity of the body in rhythmic measure; and finally all those things that are necessary for the grand ballet as well as simple dancing—these are the alphabet of theatrical dancing.[60]

Cahusac also insisted on the value of *le geste,* or the swift essence of a movement that sums up and furthers action more effectively than a discourse in words. In successive movement pictures, each moment of expression was to be performed with great animation. Thus, a dynamic play of emotion enhanced this type of ballet.

Cahusac also compared painting and the visual arts to ballet. He contended that not only painting but also dramatic dialogue was unable to compete with ballet in terms of expression: "[A] painting has only one moment that it can express. Theatrical dance has a succession of moments that it wishes to paint. The dance's progression proceeds from tableau to tableau, to which movement lends life. In painting it is only imitated, in dance it is real."[61]

Cahusac's intellectual discourses on ballet helped strengthen the progression of the art form toward a more dynamic expression of the body that, in turn, forced the necessary changes in costume to accommodate these new movements.

Noverre (1727–1810)

In his *Lettres sur la Danse,* first published in 1760, choreographer and writer Noverre recognized that a tremendous interest in the ballet pervaded all of Europe; sovereigns felt obliged to decorate their spectacles with dances. In his view audiences clapped for nothing—for mediocrity. He cried out that

Fig. 15 Portrait of Jean-Georges Noverre by Jean-Baptiste Perroneau (1764). Noverre's *Letters on Dance and Dancing* became one of the most important texts on eighteenth-century ballet. He was considered the dance encylopedist though he did not have any articles in the famous publication. Courtesy of the Bibliothèque de l'Opéra.

he lived in an age with old and worn-out methods and ancient copies of steps. And, he asked, "Where are the passions?"

> Children of Terpsichore, renounce your cabrioles, entrechats and the steps that are too complicated; abandon the sham expressions that bring your sentiments, naive graces and expression; entertain theuse of noble pantomime. Don't forget that this is the soul of your art; put wit and reason in your pas de deux; let voluptuousness and genius abound in all situations . . . be original, create a new genre after much

research; copy, but only copy nature. It is a beautiful model that never strays from truth.[62]

Noverre entreated choreographers to make ballets with a clear plan: write it down, divide it into scenes, read it over a hundred times, make sure one scene follows another, avoid ballets that are too lengthy, make dancers dance and let them be aware of their importance, let them be good mimes and make their passions metamorphose at every moment. If faces and bodies displayed what their souls were feeling, the work would be inspired. These were Noverre's instructions for the *ballet d'action*.

How did Noverre regard pantomime? He reiterated Diderot's words—in seeking to create a real experience on stage, the choreographer must rehearse a scene until the movements belong to the dancers and "till the moments become the dancers and finally those who execute them discover the instant of truth in nature common to all men; a precious moment that always presents itself with so much force of truth when it is inspired by true feeling."[63] How did the dancer train to produce these natural moments? Perhaps by learning the pantomime that brought the ancients the most noble tradition in theater. Noverre wrote in his *Lettres* that the pantomime in Rome was similar to the gestures of the deaf mutes of the eighteenth century, a system taught by the priests who cared for them. They used quick hand movements to signify something specific. However, Noverre cynically pointed out that the authors of antiquity and our unfaithful translators wrote about declamation, music pantomime, etc., but one book contradicted another and often the exaggerated praises caused one to pause. In other words, the miracle of Greek and Roman pantomime was quite overrated. Noverre thought that dance in the eighteenth century was probably more interesting and varied because of the addition of highly developed foot and hand vocabularies. He noted that the ancients used masks as part of their pantomime, thereby denying a very important part of the body's potential for expression.

Perhaps it was Noverre who best represented the *Encyclopedia*'s philosophy in regard to a rational costume reform. One of the precursors of his reformist ideas was Saint-Hubert, who wrote *La Manière de Composer et Faire Réussir les Ballets* (1641). It briefly guided the choreographer in costuming ballets:

> One should seek, not so much lavishness as fitness, since a buckram or a frieze costume, well related to the subject, will be finer and better than an inappropriate silk one. It is not by spending more but by carefully observing a ballet's organization that one will make it more pleasant.[64]

Noverre was a stickler for the subtlest and most nuanced fabrics and shapes, but he did not succeed in affecting old-fashioned ideas at the Paris Opéra. Noverre had unpleasant battles with the opera administration and costume designers. When costumes became the issue, he lamented, "The costume designer no longer consults anyone; he often sacrifices the clothes of an ancient people to the fashions of the time or to the capricious desires of a famous dancer or singer. The dancing master has no influence."[65] Soon, though, Noverre's ideas began to penetrate those hallowed halls.

The reformers' and *Philosophes*' cries for change were heard in the *ballet d' action*. Choreographers began creating ballet scenarios, or *livrets* that had complete, well-knit story lines, and they infused their academic ballet vocabulary with expressive pantomime. Dancers learned to become actors with sincere attention to the roles they were asked to dance. Emphasis on lifelike representation of human passions brought larger audiences and a serious prestige to ballet. Choreographers and dancers in Paris who played at the boulevard theaters before they were employed at the Opéra pleased a more popular audience with less attitudinizing and more honest dramatic or comic portrayals in scenarios that appealed to the new tastes of the bourgeoisie.

Audiences relished the excitement of seeing the human body push beyond the virtuosity of a former age. With a freer body no longer restricted by corsets, brocades, wigs, masks, and high heels, broader possibilities for dramatic and dance expression emerged. The physical eloquence combined with a new sense of stage space forced the dancer to jump higher, spin faster, and grandly flow from one part of the scene to another. Men and women were able to dance more closely with one another and to begin to seriously engage in the technique of partnering. This was the moment when ballet would begin to look like what it does today.[66]

CHAPTER 3

The Moderate and the Outrageous

Dancer In An All Day, All Night Festival for the Revolution, Paris 1794
Judith Berke

Was this why I learned to dance
with a straight back, and my feet
turned out, and my arms
like stems, like flowers?
This wasn't dancing, Citizen,
it was marching. We who were
dancers: a hundred of us. A thousand.

The smell of incense
was food enough, Citizen Robespierre said.
The women watching wore the same costumes
as we: One breast
exposed, like his statue that stood
for something.

When all along it was freedom
I wanted.
As a flag is free, but not the pieces
of the flag, torn and sewn
together.

But what is all this to the wind,
Citizen?

Revolutionary History and the Politics of Style

The first symbolic act of the Revolution was the storming of the Bastille prison on July 14, 1789. Angry mobs forced their way in to free the prisoners, an event that unleashed revolutionary ardor and fury. The most redoubtable of state prisons, the Bastille was synonymous with injustice and the crushing of liberties of ordinary citizens. Many illustrious persons were confined there, as well, including Voltaire.

The Reign of Terror began in 1793 with a law ordering the arrest of anyone suspected of disloyalty to the Revolution. It ended with the fall of Robespierre, the "architect of the Revolution," in 1794. Suspects were tried and almost invariably condemned by the *tribunal révolutionnaire* and, during the worst period, were executed en bloc without trial. One of the first victims was Marie Antoinette (October 16, 1793).

The rapid swerves and tastes of Paris fashion during the Revolution (1789–1799) were influenced by political winds and clearly affected all dance and public performances. Even time was negotiated by politics: a Revolutionary calendar was adopted in order to distinguish the old era from the new. It began in 1793 and lasted until 1802.

The political structure of French society had been established for centuries as having three groups, or three estates (*états*) as they were called. Each estate dressed according to its strictures. When power shifted to the third and largest estate, this signaled the end of the *ancien régime*.

At the time of the French Revolution, the First Estate, the clergy, consisted of nearly 130,000 people, half of whom were regular clergy and the other half of whom were secular. All of these church workers were exempt from taxation, which infuriated the rest of the population. The Second Estate consisted of the nobility, approximately two hundred thousand in number—*the noblesse d'épée* (original feudal aristocracy) and the *noblesse de robe*, the judicial and financial offices of the kingdom. They dominated the *parlements*.

The Third Estate, which had not been called to meet since 1614, comprised bank workers, peasants, and the bourgeoisie. As these were the people who were most heavily taxed, they had a special interest in tax relief. Two-thirds of the men in France were literate, and one-third of the women could read but a little in 1788. It soon became clear to the realistic leaders of the twenty-five million French population that representatives of the people had to be elected; twelve hundred deputies would soon deal with tax reform and the abolition of feudal rights. Pamphlets and papers touting diverse political opinions were published as the pace of events quickened.

The dying *ancien régime* desperately tried to revive old sumptuary laws. Two months before the storming of the Bastille, Dreux de Brézé, Master of Ceremonies to Louis XVI, "produced an ancient order dating from 1614 which referred to the dress of the various estates and ordered, or rather attempted to order, the third estate to dress 'very simply' in black so that they might be distinguished from the prelates in their purple and the nobility in their gold-embroidered, lace-trimmed garments."[1] For the May 5, 1789, opening session of the Estates-General, people were required to wear cere-monial dress distinguishing one estate from the other, adhering to the soon-to-be-abolished sumptuary laws. The First Estate wore scarlet silk, while the Second Estate wore a vest of black silk and lace decorated with gold braid, matching cloak, white stockings, a lace cravat, and a hat with feathers in the fashion of Henri IV. They also carried swords. Members of the Third Estate were dressed in simple suits of black cloth with tail coats, and short knee breeches (also called *culottes*); some wore short cloaks, a plain muslin cravat, and a black three-cornered hat, but they still wore powdered wigs and did not carry swords.

A new ethos of dress according to function had to replace such social distinctions, but politics affected everyone and, on May 20, 1790, the National Assembly voted to have all mayors wear a tricolor sash.[2]

The National Assembly also voted to abolish the antiquated laws, and the democratization of fashion became a legally established fact. The Third Estate regulated fashion, with the deputies at the National Assembly wear-ing black tail-coats and tall hats. For a time they continued to wear pow-dered wigs, but eventually the American-style ponytail and natural hair color became common. Many men preferred not to wear a sword except when being presented at court. The lower classes followed suit, and no one could stem the tide of this fashion. "Thus a tradition of the French nobility that was centuries old was summarily abandoned."[3] This was the moment when men were no longer interested in being beautiful. It was unsuitable for a *citoyen* of the Republic to adorn himself with embroidery and lace and per-fume himself.[4]

In 1794 an official committee of the Revolutionary government, the Société Populaire et Républicaine des Arts, began to discuss costume and how it represented the values of the moment—a person ready to fight and to be a useful citizen. Painter and designer Jacques-Louis David submitted designs for officials, civilians, and the military, some of which were quite outrageous. He developed ideas for tunics, either long or short, with open-sided mantles. He copied what he promoted as a passable imitation of clas-sical antiquity, as was worn on the stage. Swords and plumed toques or hats were accepted, but not the bare legs; people were too used to wearing knee breeches or pantaloons. The clothes of classical antiquity were most popu-lar, but occasionally they looked somewhat like sixteenth-century costume. David's costume sketches at that moment resembled the "old Spanish dress,

FIN TRAGIQUE DE LOUIS XVI

Execute le 2/ Ianvier 1793 sur la Place de LouisXV

Je meurs innocent des crimes dont on m'accuse.
Je n'ai ramais desire que le bonheur de mon peuple,
et mes derniers vocax sont que le Ciel lui pardonne ma mort.

A Paris chez les Marchands de Nouveautes.

FINE TRAGICO DI LUIGI XVI

Eseguito li 2/Genaro 1793 nella Piazza di Luigi XV

Io muoio innocente dei delitti di cui m'accusano.
Io ho sempre desiderato la felicita del mio popolo,
e gl'ultimi miei voti sono che il Cielo li perdoni la mia morte.

In Loreto per gl'Eredi Sartory.

Fig. 16 The tragic death of Louis XVI on January 21, 1793. His last words were, "I die innocent of the crimes for which I've been accused. I never wished but for the happiness of my people and in these last vows I hope that God will pardon my death." Courtesy of the Cabinet des Estampes.

consisting of a jacket with tight trousers, a coat without sleeves above the jacket, a short cloak which may either hang loose from the left shoulder or be drawn over both; a belt to which two pistols and a sword may be attached, a round hat and a feather."[5]

The French Revolution shook European society; it changed political and economic situations and had a profound effect upon fashion. Even before the king was executed in 1793, there were few embroidered coats or brocaded gowns, few wigs or powdered hair (white flour was considered more important for culinary purposes). No more elaborate headdresses, no more *talons rouges* or red high heels, that were worn by aristocratic men. Clothes became more practical and comfortable, and fashion extended its sphere of influence to more sections of the population. Even before the storming of the Bastille, hoop skirts and pigtails had seen their day. Rousseau's call for simplicity and Voltaire's rationalism were echoed in dress.

Ah ça ira ça ira.

Fig. 17 Figure of a working woman dancing to one of the most important revolutionary songs, "Ah we'll win, we'll win" (1791). The song was sung during the Terror in all the theaters. In addition, people would report lists of the soldiers who fell during the campaigns. Courtesy of the Cabinet des Estampes.

The drive toward a simpler way of dressing affected the economics of textiles and clothing. *Marchandes des modes,* the shopkeepers responsible for selling unique designs and fashions to those willing to spend the money and whose establishments were places to meet and gossip, were the fashion magicians who touted trimmings and ornamentation and taught their clients how to be chic. These vital individuals fled Paris during the Revolution as fashion was under attack. In addition, many women in lace and silk factories were put out of work as the demand for luxury goods declined.

At no other time in history have politics and dress been so closely entwined. Just as there were political pamphlets and flyers appearing daily, so the fashions of the times received the attention of publishers who produced guides and explanations of what to wear and how to wear it. The tone was moralistic and ideological rather than the usual prattle of the fashion journals. Numerous costume plates or illustrations of costume designs inform us about the meaning and importance of change in fashion. However, during the Terror of 1793 to 1794, there were no journals of fashion such as *Le Journal de la Mode et du Goût.* The Puritanical Jacobins, or "liberals," and their sympathizers saw no reason to encourage interest in such trivialities, especially since the wars were sapping financial resources. Dress was a serious affair.

Approximately twenty thousand people were killed in France during the Revolution, mostly soldiers on the battlefield. However, many of those who died were aristocrats. In order to sustain the war, 870,000 Frenchmen were drafted into the military by 1794. A passion for uniforms and uniformity spread throughout the nation. When Napoleon came to power in 1799, men in uniforms replaced men in court dress with the same symbolic and ritualistic meanings. Roman virtues such as youth, courage, and valor were associated with the change of clothing.

Red and blue became the colors of the city of Paris; the color white had been associated with the Bourbons, the family line of the king and queen. The three colors maintained their popularity as the major colors of the Revolution. There were means other than wearing certain colors to demonstrate support for Louis: when the king and queen were under siege, the aristocracy demonstrated their sympathy by cutting their hair.

One of the more symbolic accoutrements to aristocratic clothing was the shoe buckle. The beauty and complexity of their interwoven, jeweled designs stunned the observer, as they practically lit up a room. The *Journal de Paris* in 1789 announced that all aristocrats should donate their valuable shoe buckles for the benefit of "la nation."[6] Dressing as a serious *citoyen,* in 1792 Minister Roland visited the king wearing shoes without buckles, a clean head without powder and without a hat, in an old suit. This was a revolutionary gesture![7] Only in France was there a special dress for the citizen. During these dangerous and chaotic times, the life of fashion became the life of politics with the politicization of clothing, dress, and costume design. You were what you wore.

Beaumarchais was the most successful author to influence fashion, with his *Mariage de Figaro* and *Tarare*. The two works produced enormous numbers of jackets à la Suzanne, *caracos à la Chérubin*, costumes au grand Figaro, and hats *à la Tarare*. The skirts of men's waistcoats offered the ideal surface for embroiderers to create scenes, such as the bust of Voltaire and Rousseau in a forest of poplars. Naturally, the Revolution bred all sorts of innovative depictions of the great event. Perhaps the most successful category of accessory that made reference to current events was the Revolutionary fan. The pleated paper bore a colored print on one side and a song on the other. And there were commentaries on various events. Thus, women covered their faces and fanned themselves with moments from the great sweep of French history.[8]

Those who supported the Revolution wore their hair unpowdered, not only because Talma, the actor, had created a veritable fad for the coiffure "à la Titus" when he played the lead role in Voltaire's *Brutus* but also because the trend away from ornament had begun. Clothing for government officials emphasized the shape of the body, with dark suits, pantaloons, or woven tights to show the contour of the leg.

During the Terror, scrappy street rebels and the leading radicals dressed the opposite of aristocrats—the *carmagnole* vest, red bonnet, and *sans-culottes* (trousers) were associated with *le peuple*. The word *sans-culottes* became known and began to be used in September 1789 at a meeting of the National Assembly. Radical women in the audience were making a great deal of noise and someone was heard to say, "Mr. President, please ask the *sans-culottes* to be quiet." From that time on it was associated with zealous political behavior.[9]

Children of aristocrats who were killed during the Terror were called the *Incroyables*, a term coined in 1796. They moved about Paris removing Republican slogans from public buildings and parks. They were immediately recognizable as they carried sticks and wore tight-fitting *culottes,* or breeches, a greatcoat, a starched cravat of huge proportions, and long hair with a comb in the back to look like the guillotine blade. "Few more bizarre silhouettes have ever been seen than those of the French *Incroyables* of the 1790s."[10] Those known as *Muscadins* (which means scented with musk) powdered, primped, and paid attention to their toilette but were frowned upon for their personal vanity. Illustrations of the time show these young men looking exceptionally slim in long, striped jackets. Their posture connoted languor

Fig. 18 Incroyable et Merveilleuse. A characteristic article of clothing was a broad cravat that virtually covered the mouth. The frockcoat of unusual cut was worn with a flowered waistcoat with wide lapels and knee stockings with tassels. The girl, a Merveilleuse, wears a hat with a soaring brim. Courtesy of the Cabinet des Estampes.

and they were often called effeminate. These counter-revolutionaries wore green, a color that symbolized resistance to the Revolution. It is a grand irony that Robespierre, the architect of the Terror, continued to wear a powdered wig and to appear in elegant, if not prissy, attire.

These agitated young people also participated in odd rituals; for example, they held *bals à la victime* at which they wore black for mourning. Some women wore a red ribbon around their neck, symbolizing the cut made by the guillotine. Occasionally women would cross scarlet ribbons over their bodice called *croisures à la victime*, indicating that the wearer would sacrifice everything for her lover. *Incroyables* danced with strange movements of the head, bobbing to and fro as if it were about to topple from the neck. Red shawls were also common, a reminder of the red sheet that was thrown over executed murderers like Charlotte Corday, who killed the notorious revolutionary writer of *Ami du Peuple*, Jean-Paul Marat.

The *Incroyables* displayed other bizarre manifestations of the tensions of the time. For example, extreme delicacy appeared in the ideas and conversations of those who wished to be in the fashion. The letters *R* and *G* were considered harsh and purged from the language. A favorite exclamation was *En véité, c'est incoyable!* T'uly, it's inc'edible![11] Other counter-revolutionary clothing was manifested at this time. A woman's *costume catholique* appeared, one which connoted that the wearer was against the Revolution. Had this been worn during the Terror, it would have been grounds for reprisal or death. It consisted of a Pierrot jacket, a white linen skirt, a black bonnet with white feather, and a red-and-black shawl—all symbols of the *ancien régime*. Gradually, black became one of the most important colors, not only because of its basic simplicity but also because it meant that those who had lost loved ones openly showed their distress by wearing the color of mourning. Costing more than other dyes, black reflected a sincere expression of sympathy.

Women of the Revolution

The styles of women who were imprisoned and guillotined during the Revolution were described by many journalists and chroniclers. The leading female aristocrat was, of course, Marie Antoinette.

No clothing could have been more vivid, more startling than Marie Antoinette's wardrobe; however, that, and everything about her, disturbed the French more than ever at the time of the Revolution. Marie Antoinette's body became a symbol of immorality and objectification.[12] Many pamphlets, flyers, and stage plays that circulated in the late 1780s and 1790s told the story that she had poisoned her Bourbon men: the king by her infidelity, her son by her incest—the toxins of her evil, physical appetites. Her beautiful clothing, they said, masked a deeply repugnant and evil soul. Her body had to be destroyed and made to disappear. Revolutionaries made sure that Marie Antoinette's body could not be recovered after her death.

The queen's power in the kingdom reflected upon how women threatened society as autonomous individuals during the Revolution. She was the emblem (and sacrificial victim) of the feared disintegration of gender boundaries that accompanied the Revolution.[13] There was great fear that women might acquire the same rights as men. When Republican women established their own *Société*, they were vilified for imitating their brothers when they wore the traditional red bonnet and cockades. For the Republicans, aristocratic degeneracy was associated with femininity. Because of their potential for acquiring power, Marie Antoinette, playwright Olympe de Gouges, and Madame Roland, writer and lover of literature who conducted a celebrated salon in Paris with political influence, were grouped together by the *Moniteur Universel* as examples of unnatural women. Women who wished to participate actively in the French Revolution were caught in a discursive double bind; virtue was a two-edged sword that bisected the sovereign into two different destinies, one male and one female. "Male virtue meant participation in the public world of politics; female virtue meant withdrawal into the private world of the family."[14]

The radical renovations of the Revolution ought logically to have furthered women's liberation, yet October 1793 saw the defeat of revolutionary radical feminism, as the feminists were beaten by the proletarian *poissardes* (fishwives). The Convention or National Assembly from 1792–1795 went on, early in November, to order the closure of the women's revolutionary clubs.

The most public women of this time, who were household names in France and dictated the world of fashion either died on the guillotine or suffered mental breakdowns: Marie Antoinette (1755–1793), Charlotte Corday (1768–1793), Olympe de Gouges (1755–1793), and Théroigne de Méricourt (1762–1817). The murderess Corday's death has been movingly described: "Nature seemed to connect itself with human passion, and a violent storm burst over Paris. . . . The reflection on her red dress heightened, in a strange and fanstastic manner, the brilliant effect of her complexion and eyes. . . . The young girl reappeared at the moment when the executioner took off her neck-handkerchief; her modesty suffered; she advanced as if anticipating death."[15] Charlotte Corday assassinated Jean-Paul Marat, a revolutionary who instigated the September massacres—priests and felons were bludgoned to death. Also imprisoned, but for much less time, was Madame Roland (1754–1793), who went to her death saying, "Oh Liberty, what crimes have been committed in your name." She went to her death wearing a white muslin dress trimmed with yellow and a black velvet sash.

The famed woman leader and writer Théroigne de Méricourt, who had the courage and charisma to lead the third corps of the Faubourg army in Paris, in an illustration of "Françaises Devenues libres" wore a double-breasted riding habit, boots, a plumed wide hat, and a short skirt. She looked properly aggressive holding a lance, her stance firm. This was considered male attire. At other times she was pictured holding a pistol, with a sword dangling from her belt. Her dress at the time of her death in 1817 was a

Fig. 19 Théroigne de Méricourt, famed woman revolutionary who fought in the third corps of the Faubourg army in Paris, wore virtually male attire. The title of this illustration is "Frenchwomen have become free." Courtesy of the Cabinet des Estampes.

simple gown without properties of warfare. De Méricourt also spoke out in passionate pleas for women's rights. She wrote dramatic criticism and, as a Girondist (moderate revolutionary) heroine, she was called *L'Amazone de la Liberté*. Her deeply intellectual, political diatribes captured audiences of the revolutionary National Assembly. Unlike de Gouges, she was known as a great beauty. Jules Michelet imagined her as a very seductive creature: "We recognize her coat of red silk, and her large sabre of the 5th of October . . ."; actor Desmoulins cried out: "It is the Queen of Sheba, coming to visit the Solomon of the districts."[16] Unfortunately, de Mericourt suffered a sad demise: she went mad and was sent to an asylum, where she died in 1817.

Olympe de Gouges has recently received a great deal of attention. Her demise on the guillotine amused and dismayed many of her followers as, in an effort to be treated with clemency, she pretended to be pregnant when that was not the case. Dressed in rags, she was a sorry sight. It was sensational that de Gouges, a monarchist Girondist, also used the language of rights and the principles of republican virtue in *Les Droits de la femme et de la citoyenne* (1791). She was the illiterate daughter of a butcher, who had to dictate her plays. An actress and political organizer before becoming a playwright, she was swept into the vigorous debate that occurred during the Revolution. Discourses of the *Philosophes* and *Encyclopédistes* raged during the eighteenth century. Committed women, such as de Gouges, participated in dialogues about natural rights and religion. She completed approximately thirty works, many with radical themes. One, the anticonventual play *Le Couvent, ou les Voeux Forcés* (1790), proposed an unlikely reform program that demanded legal sexual equality, admission for women to all occupations, suppression of the dowry system, and an end to the forcing of young women into convents. She wanted education for girls and especially the opening of all careers. De Gouges wrote with great prescience: *The Droits* went much farther than Mary Wollstonecraft's *Vindication* in that by emulating the terse form of the Declaration of the Rights of Man of 1789, it actually formulated the rights that should be specifically guaranteed to women based on a philosophy of natural rights. "The spirit of de Gouges' work is encapsulated in the first principle: 'Woman is born free and lives equal to man in her rights.' Social distinctions can be based on the common utility."[17] For actresses and women playwrights, she encouraged the establishment of a national theater in which only plays by women would be performed. Unfortunately, Olympe de Gouges' plays were considered disastrous, as audiences found them unbearably vulgar.

The most important female public icon of the Revolution was the mythic Marianne. She represented common woman, was a metaphor for Mother Earth and Liberty, and appeared everywhere, as did La Liberté, who resplendently rode on the moving wagons of Revolutionary Festivals. Marianne, symbol of the people, galvanized crowds and graced public spaces. She appealed to the rich and poor as a Greek goddess, as a mother, and as an ideal citizen. She wore close-fitting, flowing robes and occasionally was seen in contemporary dress with her breasts bared. "The exposed breasts revealed the nurturing powers of women when breast feeding."[18]

Those who held the coin or picture engraved with Marianne were also said to absorb her unconditional love. Her beauty and calm, enhanced by her lightly wrapped body, contrasted with the many contemporary caricatures and pornographic illustrations of the other Marie—Marie Antoinette. Since the queen's immature character and appetite for gaudiness incensed the French revolutionary public, Marianne's body illustrated a new popular attitude, one that embraced the real body that nursed everyone regardless of class, "giving a collective meaning to motion, flow and change within the human body, flowing and freeing movement now nurturing a new kind of life."[19]

Revolutionary Festivals

Bringing Costumes to the People

Politics, ideology, dance, and fashion became even more intimate when government leaders decided to present the *Fête Révolutionnaire* or the Revolutionary Festival.[20] Although not normally conceived of as either ballet or pantomime, the grand processions were choreographed in the tradition of ancient Greek festivals.

Young Jacobins knew Greek history, especially those events that contributed to democratic rule. In December 1792 Jean-Paul Rabaut, author of *L'Histoire primitive de la Grèce*, faced the Convention and asked how all Frenchmen could be enthusiastic about liberty, equality, and fraternity. He suggested that Cretan and Spartan means of public education might succeed and proposed that each canton or district build a national temple to be used as a school building and as an assembly hall where on Sundays citizens could gather, listen to lessons in ethics, and sing in honor of liberty, equality, and fraternity. In fair weather, they engaged in public games, gymnastics, and military exercises. The aim was to make Spartans out of Frenchmen, a seeming impossibility with the Frenchman's taste for good food, wine, and love. In a utopian dream, all Frenchmen would live in health, dress alike, and be active in natural exercises. To excite their love of country, they would be required to read Plutarch and, while they were reading, would listen to war-like marches so that the institutions of Lycurgus might be better engraved on their hearts. The Committee of Public Instruction cited Rousseau as its prophet, since he had recommended that one's time be filled with physical exercises, gymnastics, and dances set to warlike music.

And since, as in Sparta, girls as well as boys were to be educated, the boys with their female contemporaries would go through the evolutions of a Pyrrhic dance while the girls would respond with a virginal dance which would recall the ancient festivals of Diana.[21]

In the "Procès-verbaux du Comité d'Instruction publique de la Convention Nationale," Rabaut de Saint Étienne presented a National Education Project. Having read Plutarch's *Life of Lycurgus* about Spartan society, Rabaut sought to have the legislative body determine what mode of dress should be worn, as all aspects of societal experience were to be legislated by the ruling parties.[22]

The celebrated painter Jacques-Louis David was pronounced by the Jacobins the "couturier of the Revolution." He attempted to create a standard and ethical construct for clothing. As early as 1784, he painted *Oath of the Horatii*, in which he displayed men in helmets wearing short Roman tunics and sandals. David sketched out new clothing for citizens of the Revolution as though the revolutionaries were actors in a giant presentation that took to the streets when everyone gathered for the various festivals.

To replace devotion to the church and king, David was mandated to inaugurate a series of indoor and outdoor festivals. The outdoor street-theater demonstrations were intended to arouse patriotic virtues, encouraging all to participate. Various scenes from hallowed moments of the Revolution were recreated on moving platforms, with choruses and dancers placed in careful *tableaux vivants*. A lot of drapery fell on these floats. The festivals helped to promote the notion of French national costume by bringing to the attention of the government the potential propaganda value of a distinctive form of dress, such as women wearing white dresses and tricolor sashes.[23]

In a rather propagandist gesture, the *Journal des Théâtres*, on August 18, 1794, proclaimed, "Of all the institutions that produced our revolutionary genius, those which create the national festivals are beyond a doubt the most worthy of republican attention." Such was the thinking of revolutionary patriots in the years after the taking of the Bastille. Large outdoor celebrations encouraged popular participation and fraternal feelings. David played the role of Cecil B. DeMille, and the foremost dance director in France at this time, Pierre Gardel, was called upon to conceive the movements and symbolic gestures that filled these massive festivals.

Dancers, especially those from the Opéra, traditionally were associated with the aristocracy; their lovers and their supporters came from the wealthy classes. How were they to continue working and keep everything as part of the status quo? Denunciations were widespread and most artists had to proclaim their loyalty to the new radical government and to plays, ballets, and

Fig. 20 Homage to Liberty. Revolutionary festivals were common during the Revolution. They stirred deep nationalistic feelings meant to replace old attachments to the *ancien regime*. Courtesy of the Cabinet des Estampes.

operas that promoted "Republican" and Jacobin politics. "Anyone with an ounce of political acumen spoke of his love for liberty and fidelity to the Republic."[24] The festivals, boring pseudo-Greek processions, or stories of *sans-culotte* heroism were small-enough payment for the privilege of continuing to work in one's profession in a time of surprising bestiality.

Ballet master to the Paris Opéra, Pierre Gardel worked hard to sustain his position at the Opéra, not only by making himself an important part of the large festivals but also by producing the mythical ballets that diverted and distracted a terrorized and exhausted Parisian audience. Gardel's relationship with David solidified when he worked on *Fête de la Fédération* in July 1790, on the Champ de Mars. The celebrated playright Marie-Joseph Chénier wrote the words for this vast event. During this festival, even Marie Antoinette had to wear tricolor feathers. The festival was launched at Notre Dame and continued through the streets until it reached the Champ de Mars, where four hundred thousand spectators watched, undoubtedly one of the largest live public spectacles in history.

In 1792 Gardel arranged the dances and movements to music by Christophe Willibald Gluck for heroic festivals bestowing honors on fallen young men. An excerpt from the scenario describes the event:

. . . forming six groups, artists from the different theatres will march in the following order: the first group will be composed of musicians, the second of a male chorus, the third of male dancers, the fourth of a women's chorus, the fifth of female dancers, and the sixth of poets who will recite the verses they have composed in honor of the young heroes. . . . When the urns have been placed on the altar, the young danseurs will perform funeral dances of the most intense sorrow, and lay branches of cypresses on the urns; at the same moment, musicians and singers will deplore the ravages of fanaticism which have taken these young lives from us.[25]

These festivals were the agit-prop of the time, giving news of battles that Frenchmen were fighting in Belgium, Prussia, Italy, and Austria. Songs and dances touted the heroism of their soldiers, often in settings that imitated the noble antique past.

Perhaps the most startling and ominous festival exhibition, *Fête de l'Etre Suprême*, on June 8, 1794, called upon all the resources of the city of Paris in a futile effort by Robespierre to initiate a new religion. The libretto exhorts: "The true priest of the Supreme Being is Nature, her temple is the Universe, her cult is truth." David, remembering the Greek processions as recounted in Abbé Barthelémy's *Voyage du Jeune Anacharsis,*[26] and Gardel once again designed these exercises with *Scènes patriotiques* by Marie-Joseph Chénier. One of the more rousing moments took place when "Robespierre set fire with a torch handed to him by David to a huge cardboard figure of Atheism, which went up in flames, exposing to view a rather smoky statue of Wisdom, after which the whole of the Convention, and delegates to sections, ascended an artificial mountain where appropriate ceremonies were performed."[27] Latter-day Nazi celebrations surely referred back to these revolutionary pageants.

Some women and children were dressed in the simple long white tunics and sandals, while others wore the omnipresent red bonnet, a *cocorde*, and carried the French flag. "Even rich and poor were to be alike in some fashion in the festivals. The program for the Festival of the Supreme Being called for young ladies to use powder with restraint and to bunch up their skirts in the Roman style."[28]

Two costume paradigms were displayed at these festivals. Depending upon the choreography and the scenario, prominently exhibited goddesses were clothed in traditional Greek and Roman tunics, while the citizens who grouped around them were dressed in common attire, that of the everyday street person who hungered for the freedoms that these festivals promised. Not uncommon were men dressed in the uniform of the moment, those

Fig. 21 *La Raison*, or Reason, is presented as a new god with a *bonnet rouge* suspended above her head. No longer were people to worship in a mystical and unknowing way; they were free to choose their destinies. Courtesy of the Cabinet des Estampes.

losing their lives on the battlefield for the sake of liberty. The frequency and importance of the festivals diminished after Robespierre's death.

Dance and Costume

After the Terror, court costume was eliminated on stage. When revolutionary parties mirrored the heroes in Jacques-Louis David's antique paintings, fashions on stage became Spartan or Roman. In several performances of Voltaire's *Mort de César*, the murderer of Caesar, as well as a bust of Caesar, wore the Phrygian cap. The Phrygian bonnet served as a symbol for the *sans-culottes*, or aficionados of Republican thought. Never before had there been a hat of such iconic value; *sans-culottes* ratified "its adoption as part of a type of Revolutionary uniform."[29] *Sabots*, or wooden shoes, accompanied this garb. The bonnet, worn by freed slaves in ancient Rome, went along with trousers and the tricolor cockade. The carmagnole was the name of a dance that represented a rather wild, ecstatic expression of a call for governmental freedoms. Occasionally, the carmagnole was performed after some poor aristocrat was caught unaware and beheaded. Numerous times during the Revolution there occurred spontaneous, bloody spectacles with dances and singing in a bacchic orgy. This frightening demonic atmosphere during the Terror was vividly described by Charles Dickens in *A Tale of Two Cities*.[30] Even frightened aristocrats were caught up in the passions of the Revolution. Madame de Genlis is described as dancing "Ça Ira" and wearing the tricolor stripes.[31] Illustrations showed women wearing the mandated tricolor cockade with jackets and skirts and simple shawls à l'égalité during these ritual street dances, while the men in the streets looked shabby and disheveled.

At the Opéra, ballet scenarios reflected not only the political events of the time but also stories of contemporary novels, comic operas, and the theater; they brought with them a melodramatic pictorialization of the moment, a revived interest in local manners and customs of rural life, as, for example, in Dauberval's *La Fille mal gardée ou il n'est qu'un pas de mal au bien* (1789). Although this ballet premiered far from Paris at the Grand Théâtre in Bordeaux, reverberations of its radically different scenario, décor, and costumes were felt at the Opéra. Dauberval's stormy career at the Paris Opéra began in 1761 as a dancer; he became dancing master in 1771 but found more welcoming environments in Bordeaux and then London. In London at the Pantheon Theatre, rival to the King's Theatre at Haymarket, Dauberval sought to produce money-making spectacles that brought in large audiences. He had specific ideas about textiles and designs that were inspired by his stay at the Paris Opéra. The prevailing color of his costumes was white. They were embellished with colored trimmings common to a

Fig. 22 In the ballet *Le Déserteur*, uniforms were the starring attraction and meant to instill patriotic sentiments for the armies fighting abroad. These are costume illustrations of a restaging in 1824. Courtesy of the Bibliothèque Nationale.

particular couple in the story, so that Magdeleine Louise Catherine Théodore and James D'Egville wore similarly colored trimmings to look as if they were teamed together. This convention also served as a forecast to partners who marry in the traditional happy ending. As was true in the Paris Opéra, differences in dancers' status might be indicated by the trimmings or careful fit of a costume rather than by changing its basic fabric. Dauberval followed Noverre's stipulation that lighter materials such as lustring, a glossy silk fabric, worked better for dancers.

The recently discovered Bedford Opera Papers describe in detail Dauberval's costumes for the April 30, 1791, London production of *La Fille mal gardée* two years after its Bordeaux debut.[32] Since these costumes were made from scratch, one cannot assume that they were exactly like those in Bordeaux, but it was likely that Dauberval would not have changed the original designs.

The libretto of *La Fille mal gardée* tells the story of a *fermière du château*, Ragotte, who works to bring in the harvest and also to arrange a proper marriage for her daughter, Lison. Despite Ragotte's wishes, Lison rejects Alain, a dunce-like character, and falls in love with Colas, a charming and handsome neighbor. What was striking about the ballet, which premiered two weeks before the French Revolution, was its rustic setting and references to daily work, such as churning butter and harvesting. The characters also came from quite humble backgrounds. Regardless of the librettto's modest characters and seeming simplicity, Dauberval wanted satin and silk costumes. Colas (Charles Didelot) wore a dark gray, rich silk coat and breeches with a gaudy waistcoat striped yellow, red, and white—anything but a peasant's attire. Fialon and Vigano, playing Alain and his father, respectively, wore gray stuff (wool) suits and gray worsted stockings. (No program of this ballet has been discovered. Consequently, scholars rely on newspaper articles and informed guessing.) Both had scarlet stuff waistcoats. Vigano had a second waistcoat of red and white striped lustring. All the men had round hats and silk handkerchiefs. The stage peasants, or *figurants*, wore jaunty pink stuff jackets trimmed in blue, blue breeches with black sashes, and black straw hats bound with blue ribbon. Lison (Madame Théodore) wore jackets of "mazarine blue" Irish poplin, ribboned hats, striped petticoats, and an apron. The color of her stripes matched Colas's. Two other women wore colors similar to Lison, intimating that they were her friends. Other characters representing wealthier friends were attired in silks, satins, and embroidered stomachers. Dauberval's propensity for elegance and the look of class suggests that in this ballet he had no intention of displaying peasants as they really were. Rather, he found a charming story for his exceptional abilities as a dramatic choreographer and was

En Liberté comme toi
La République frań. d'accord avec la Nature
l'ont voulu : ne suis-je pas ta Sœur?

Fig. 23 "Liberated as you are, the French Republic has deemed it necessary. Am I not your sister?" The French freed the slaves in Santo Domingo (Haiti) in 1791, but soon Napoléon reassumed hegemony and tyranny when Haiti's hero Toussaint L'Ouverture was imprisoned and died. Courtesy of the Cabinet des Estampes.

rewarded with the stamp of history.[33] *La Fille mal gardée* is still in the repertoire of many ballet companies. It continues to amuse and touch audiences around the world.

In early 1796, the very popular ballet *Le Déserteur* at the Opéra was criticized for its lavish uniforms, and, not wishing to offend soldiers of the people, national uniforms that were less gaudy were quickly substituted. Dauberval's *The Deserter* (his version was originally performed in the 1785 Bordeaux production) thoroughly excited and pleased audiences in London during the 1791 season, perhaps owing to the realism of men in uniform fighting wars in foreign lands. A variety of more than seventy military uniforms appeared, from the highest ranks to the common soldiers. Only eight costumes were designated for dancers. In the third act, there was a review of the troops that was the visual highlight of the ballet.[34] Most of the uniforms were scarlet trimmed with gold lace and metal buttons, depending upon the rank. Some officers' coats were blue, white, and yellow; Hussars' jackets were trimmed with fur. Dauberval, in the role of Skirmish, wore scarlet cashmere with blue lining, a white waistcoat and breeches, and a light helmet covering a red wig. Dauberval's display of military maneuvers brought panache and glamour to this ballet and, while the costumes were made less opulent, they still attested to Dauberval's desire to see life through rose-colored glasses.

Apart from the Revolutionary Festivals or specific plays dealing with political enthusiasms of the time, several theatrical and opera scenarios containing dances demonstrated a passion for liberty, equality, and fraternity. These ideals, which were plastered on government buildings and revealed in the Declaration of the Rights of Man, were seen as universal, applying to the downtrodden everywhere. The French freed the slaves in Santo Domingo (Haiti) in 1791 for a brief time. Although not seen at the Paris Opéra, *La Constitution à Constantinople* (1793) and *La Liberté des Nègres ou Sélico* (1793) professed the importance of freeing the enslaved everywhere. Turkish and Muslim/African costumes brought the proper atmosphere to their situations. In London, Dauberval created *La Foire de Smirne* in 1792, in which the leading character was a villainous slave trader. Harems, slave markets, and fairs served as exotic sites for the long and complex story. Luxury and opulence characterized the costumes, with satins, sequins, and trimmings of gold and fur. Such fabrics hardly seemed to make a liberal political statement.[35]

The politics of costumes on stage took on new meanings when women assumed male roles in important ballets. During the revolutionary 1790s, quite a number of ballerinas played Cupid and other travesty characters. There was a fascination for the female as a male dancing body. She/he titillated the audience almost as much as she/she. Women have appeared in

Fig. 24 Mademoiselle Hilligsberg enhanced her reputation as a fascinating dancer by wearing a man's costume in *le Jaloux Puni* in 1793. Stipple engraving by Jean Condé after H. de Janvry. Courtesy of the Theatre Museum, London.

travesty for centuries, and it is well known that many dancers, actresses, and singers played men's roles in the late eighteenth century through the nineteenth century. As was mentioned before, it was also common, to some extent as a result of Anglomania, for upper-class French women to dress in a riding outfit called *Le Redingote* that imitated quite closely the male riding habit. The tradition of travesty steadily grew. In "The Nineteenth Century Travesty Dancer," Lynn Garafola explores the oddity and significance of the woman dressed as male while partnering another woman on stage. Garafola remarks that the charming buttocks of the female dressed as male became a major focus and represented a "heightened erotic vision for the spectator."[36] The stage became a privileged site of transgression, where audiences happily witnessed and enjoyed displays of gender swapping.[37]

The dancer Parisot pleased and astounded her audiences when she played the male role of Lindor in the *Agreeable Surprise* (1799). Women dressed in men's costume with a jaunty air. Other travesty dancers at this time were Mademoiselle Hilligsberg in *Le Jaloux Puni* (1793), as well as Madames Laborie and Leonora Simonet, who both played Henry in *Le Déserteur* as early as 1785. Hilligsberg's popularity was enhanced by her custom of dancing in men's trousers. At her benefit on March 26, 1795, she and her younger sister performed a Russian dance in men's clothes. The audience interrupted a performance at the King's Theatre asking that Madame Hilligsberg perform the ballet she had danced at her benefit. The manager said she would perform the role of Paul the following week.[38]

In 1795 the government of France elected the Directorate or the Council of 500 "Ancients," which replaced the Jacobin radicals. The legislature commissioned designs for an appropriate outfit. In this case, David was not hired to carry out the symbolic effort, as he was in disfavor for his association with the Jacobins. Designer Grasset de Saint Sauveur mixed classical with historical touches but with an emphasis on luxury, perhaps to distance this government from the intractable Jacobins. They wore long white robes, open-sided, with red cloaks and velvet toques, or hats. The more prestigious five wore embroidered gold trimming. In 1797 the clothing changed to a blue coat, a tricolored sash with gold fringes, a red mantle fastened at the shoulder, and a toque with tricolored feathers.

During the Directorate (1795–1799), fashions in general leaned toward the quiet, sober, and discreet, as property and privilege were reflected in dress. Laces, silks, and embroideries were a thing of the past, while waistcoats, large lapels, starched white cravats, and linen shirt ruffles distinguished the middle classes. During the day, women covered up their breasts with a shawl, which they removed for the evening. In general, the middle classes began to feel safe as they stepped out at night in various styles of evening clothes. The men's cloak added to male fashions; often associated with the later Romantic hero, there was a certain bravura and flair to the Renaissance cape that served as a warm garment.

One of the significant consequences of the violence and terror of the Revolution was a newfound interest in social dance. Fashion played a role in facilitating the way people danced in couples and large groups. During the Directorate, hundreds of dance halls opened across the city and Parisians twirled and swirled to the changing tastes for dance forms that drew couples together and helped them to release the tensions of the Revolution.

Fig. 25 Social dancing and popular fashions went hand in hand. In the ballroom, couple dancing and complicated partnering made dancing lessons more necessary than ever to those wishing to climb the social ladder (1791). Courtesy of the Cabinet des Estampes.

Dancing became the rage of Paris that also represented a rebellion against the excesses of the Republicans' passion for virtue. In a history of French society during the Directorate, Goncourt exclaimed, "France dances; she has been dancing since Thermidor, just as she used to sing before the Revolution. She dances to avenge herself and to forget."[39]

People began to let loose and enjoy dancing as never before; they danced the waltz for the first time facing and holding one another, and they whirled away the time in dizzying spins. An Englishman, Sir John Dean Paul, offered a description in August 1802, visiting Paris and the new dance hall, Tivoli:

> On a vast stage, two hundred couples take part, accompanied by slow music, turning together around the stage. The women's movements are attractive and pleasing, but, for the spectators, and without any doubt for those who do it, this dancing would never be popular in England.[40]

Although the waltz may not have had the same popularity in London as in Paris, as early as 1787, the waltz was being danced in the London theater. For the French, the waltz at that time seemed more of a contradance, with the men and women holding hands or holding each other's waists. During the late eighteenth century, the waltz, with its free moving spatial directions and its new hand hold, had its beginnings with the *allemande* figures in *contredanses allemandes*.

> There seems no question that the position and notion of couples while utilizing various arm positions, was introduced into France through the conventions of the contra dance allemande and, by the 1790s, numerous publications began to appear with independent compositions labeled 'waltz.' All in 3/8 meter and similar in compositional technique to those composed in Germany.[41]

The waltz repudiated centuries of previous social dances. "It was denounced, deplored and banned at times for its 'immorality' but was irresistible to the independent-minded and the newly powerful middle classes."[42] Along with other new social dances, it caused contradictions in attitudes toward women's behavior. Even though women were cautioned not to sweat or to lose their composure, some of the dances at the turn of the century used a considerable number of energetic steps and twirling.

The famed romantic poet and adventurer Lord Byron wrote a disquisition on the Waltz; it remains one of the most tuned descriptions of the dance craze of the period. "The fashion hails from countesses to queens, And maids and valets waltz behind the scenes; Wide and more wide thy witching circle spreads, And turns—if nothing else—at least our heads."

Byron spoke of styles: "Hoops are no more, and petticoats not much; Morals and minuets, virtue and her stays, and tell-tale powder—all have had their days." He prudishly referred to the body positions: "One hand reposing on the royal hip; The other to the shoulder no less royal . . . Thus front to front the partners move or stand, The foot may rest, but none withdraw the hand." He criticized this lubricious stance: "Where were the rapture then to clasp the form From this lewd grasp and lawless contact warm?" and concluded with, "Voluptuous Waltz! and dare I thus blaspheme? Thy bard forgot thy praises were his theme."[43]

The emotional and sensitive Byron was upset by the waltz's sensuality and breathless qualities, perhaps because his disabling limp prevented him from enjoying the experience. But aside from this strange critique, Byron's personal dress and sensibility influenced the chic-driven intelligentsia of Paris. He became famous during the late eighteenth century for wearing cloaks and also for carefully arranging his hair so that his coiffure had a wild look to it. These stylish qualities quickly caught on in France, especially at public balls. Women returned to wigs, especially if they had dark hair, and surprised everyone by wearing blond wigs, which became extremely popular. In addition, jewelry came back into fashion, permitting women the opportunity once again to glisten, glow, and show their wealth in a more muted way, as they did before the Revolution.

The writer Louis-Sébastien Mercier spent time at public balls, where the crème de la crème assembled. He noted that ravishing beauties in Greek attire congregated alongside washerwomen in sabots. He spoke of models' bare arms, naked breasts, and charming hairdos, with curls shaped close to the head. Mercier formed the opinion that women did not carry handbags for their money and cosmetics because they were living statues with no need for real necessities. He also gazed at their gorgeous bodies that were there to reveal all their secret charms. What a moment in time! It was not long before stage dancers also wore little material on their bodies, ready to display their exquisite moving arms and legs.

In theaters at the end of the Revolution in 1798 and 1799, few actors and actresses followed any particular standards for dress, either historical or geographic. Talma's popularity suffered, as did his interest in historically accurate costumes. The theater imitated the modes of the street, which were becoming increasingly absurd and pretentious. Display was the rule for the young turks. Extremely ornate designs and shapes common to prerevolutionary France began once again to grace the stages; e.g., a cavalier would wear a hat with tall plumed feathers. Actresses tended to imitate Greek styles but with inappropriate ornamentation. Costumes from different historical eras created odd mixtures. In the opera Anacréon, "the princesses wore costumes out of paintings by Gainsborough or Lawrence, while their confidantes wore Greek tunics and the soldiers wore Arlequin costumes, with pigtailed wigs under their helmuts."[44]

By the end of the eighteenth century, a chaotic aesthetic guided the people and even the best of performers. There were numerous ways in which dress could be expressed after the Reign of Terror. After the death of Robespierre on July 27, 1794, people lashed out against the violence and indignities of his harsh administration, and those who had survived the guillotine began once more to dress as they pleased. Certain aristocrats chose to wear a fantastic version of English country clothes and their unpowdered hair was worn in a wild mop sometimes brushed forward over the forehead.[45] The 1799 *Journal des Modes et Nouveautés* touted the fact that "The fashion now is to follow none. In a circle of thirty women, you will not see two hairstyles, two dresses, two get-ups that resemble each other."[46]

CHAPTER **4**

Neoclassicism
1780–1820

Poem read on stage by Jean-Etienne Dépréaux (husband of Marie-Madeleine de la Guimard):

On Fashion or Without Cares

Thanks to the fashion way
we have no more stays
Ah! how happy this day
as we have no more stays
We take it in stride
Thanks to the fashion way
we have nothing to hide
Ah! how happy this day.

We have nothing to hide:

How unfortunate that I must abide!

De la mode ou Sans Gêne:

Grâce à la mode
on n'a plus de corset
Ah! Qu' c'est commode
on n'a plus de corset:
C'est plus tôt fait!

Grâce à la mode
on n'a rien d'caché.
Ah! qu' c'est commode,
On n'a rien de caché:
J'en suis fâché[1]

Fig. 26 Statues of Elgin Marbles at The British Museum. Photo by author.

Neoclassicism, or looking back to Greek and Roman times for inspiration, bridged the period of the Revolution and the Empire between the end of the eighteenth century and the beginning of the nineteenth. During this time period, in November 1799, the coup d'état of 18 Brumaire in the revolutionary calendar brought Napoléon Bonaparte to power and, in December, the Constitution of year VIII gave him authority as First Consul of France.

Fig. 27 Statues of Elgin Marbles at The British Museum. Photo by author.

With the coronation of Napoléon as Emperor in 1804, the fascination for things antique reached its apogée. Although Napoleon is discussed fully in the next chapter, it is important to note his presence in the Neoclassic Period.

> The late eighteenth-century's fascination with classical dress paralleled its intriguing new discourse with the body and the classical body. Dressed in soft, slender drapery, women returned to an idealized, ritualized experience of democracy, of equality, and of the recognition that clothing had transformative values. The revealed body became the means through which the evolving meanings of political and social life in Greece and Rome were reinvented as circumstances changed.[2]

The Neoclassic Period was the first time in the history of fashion when there had been a revival of such a bygone mode. A variety of reasons was responsible for its influence on clothing and costume—discoveries in archeology, the shift to historical accuracy in costumes for mythological plots, enlightened attitudes toward clothing and pleasure in the revelation of the female body, and, of course, politics. Neoclassicism was the movement that freed the body from the recent past and was pivotal to the history of ballet fashion.

Archeological revelations and writings by Johann Joachim Winckelmann (1717–1768) threw light on Greek influences in Roman art and architecture. The 1738 discovery of art and artifacts in Italy's Pompeii and Herculaneum brought a new and lively awareness of the ancient world. In 1750, books of engravings and other pictures helped to publicize and popularize the draped gods of Pompeii and Herculaneum. Excavations of ancient amphora and Greek artifacts were unearthed and sent to the British Museum by Sir William Hamilton, who published his *Illustrations of Greek Vases* in 1770.

Political relations between England and France at the time of the war (1803) were also responsible for the emergence of neoclassic fashion. When war led to the British Blockade, ports of entry that provided particular products such as silks or feathers were closed and fashions were forced to change. Cotton, which was more readily available, was particularly suited to the tunic line of Greek statuary.[3] "Newly fashionable fabrics such as printed cotton and fine muslin were widely worn; when silk was worn it was often silk gauze, to provide the fluttering, floating look popular in the 1780s, or painted silk from the East."[4]

Implicit in the neoclassic costume revival was the fact that Greek vases and sculpture, as well as Roman imitations, were not just archeology or ethnographic proof of other cultures' artifacts but forms of art with clear aesthetic and ideological intentions. Art informed the stage, as it should, and the audience liked it because the vision it held spoke the truth to them.

The moving sculptures of the Elgin Marbles recalled a past in which the principles of democracy were born and ideals of philosophy and behavior were pronounced. One particular book, *Travels of Anarcharsis* by the Abbé Barthélémy, encouraged many people to return to the past. The beauty of the Greek past helped to restore brotherhood and "invited people to identify with it."[5] Costumes for the stage and clothing on the street became "expressive" of the new French citizen, one who believed in freedom and the more personal self.

For centuries classical stories had been routinely presented at court, especially in the form of tragedies. During the years preceding the late eighteenth century, rather than recounting the problems of humanity in a larger sense, the myths became trivialized and, in operas and ballets, were more like subplots of little import to the larger questions of mythic tragedies. As flouncey, hooped creations were replaced by Greek tunics and chitons, "a new kind of middle-class moral illustration became an artistic mode and seems to have cut across other forms of art."[6] The emerging middle-class audiences held to different standards than the aristocracy they had replaced. The trend to authenticity in mythological tales led to a need for truth in all performance, including paintings, as we have seen with Diderot's writings. Theater owners acceded to the middle classes as ticket sales dictated the style and presentation of art. When audiences sensed that their understanding of reality was acknowledged and confirmed, they felt respected. "Realistic conviction became a dramatic necessity, perhaps because rigid conventions began to look suspiciously like tyranny.[7]

Several philosophical ideas revolved around the notion of classical dress. One was that this clothing represented the simple truths that the great Greek tragedies instilled in Western European education since the Renaissance. During Napoléon's reign two theories in the fine arts divided people into two camps fueled by the interest in neoclassicism—the ideal and the natural schools. Quatremère de Quincy, whose *Essay on the Ideal* appeared in 1805, maintained a doctrine of ideal aesthetics. According to him, there existed an ideal beauty, absolute, heroic, and final. It was the duty of the moderns to rediscover the beauty the ancients had succeeded in expressing. The artist was bound to study things as they were, but only in the spirit of idealism, or in the light of an aesthetic law to which he must subordinate his own individual tastes and temperament.

Éméric David, whose *Disquisition on the Art of Sculpture* appeared in 1805, was a leader of the naturalistic, or liberal, school. It aimed at reconciling the realization of classic beauty with personal inspiration, with truth of expression and with sincerity of observation. The public became interested in the controversy, but it was not converted to the ideal. Indeed, the tendency

TOO MUCH   and   TOO LITTLE
or Summer Cloathing for 1556 & 1796

Fig. 28 "Too Much and Too Little, or Summer Clothing for 1556 and 1796." Satire by Isaac Cruikshank on the contemporary fashion for antique draperies. Courtesy of the British Museum Print Collection.

of neoclassic dress reflected both the classic beauty of the time as well as personal and individual expression.

Napoléon was indifferent to these artistic concepts, but he thought it advisable to encourage the arts, in order to add splendor to his reign. Out of the conflict of doctrines, the tastes of the public, and the influence of the government, there was born an artistic style sufficiently original and definite to give Napoléon a certain distinction. His interest in the power of the stage grew with his own power. Social behavior had loosened, and people sought amusement after the strain of the revolutionary years. Napoleon used the theater to present an image, a role model for society to adulate and imitate.

Neoclassicism engendered a remarkable shift in the aesthetics of clothing. The female body lost its extremely defined waist in the 1780s and gained a soft, long skirt line with indented material, typical of the chiton, to permit free movement of the legs.[8] The look for the breasts became round and full, or "two well-defined hemispheres," rather than the eighteenth-century pushed-up and high-breasted look. Flowing, transparent tunics revealed and idealized the female body and added sexual attractiveness to the new attire.

Neoclassic dresses, however, were more suited to the climate of Greece, which was warmer. Sometimes the muslin was dampened so that it clung to the body in imitation of the folds of the Greek dresses.[9] The new fashion greatly enhanced a young girl's figure, which also accounted for its great popularity. This was the first time that a fashion had been introduced that was especially attuned to the young. Children's fashions, simple and easy to wear, began to influence adult clothing.

One consequence of the new style was that women could now pack all of their wardrobe in one bag. Certainly, this was a great advantage to the dancers on stage who previously had to carry the more weighty costumes. Hairdos also weighed less and were reduced in size to fit a more natural and sculpturally smaller head: light curls on the forehead and the fullness behind the head or short hair with ringlets or curls. On the other hand, the simple white neoclassic tunics did not display ornamentation or heavy jewelry very well. During the Revolution, painter Jacques-Louis David's wife and wives and daughters of other leading artists "dressed in white with tricolor cockades in their hair when they went to publicly donate their jewelry to the National Assembly."[10]

Discussion of this central moment in fashion history must focus on the newly discovered female body. Changes in clothing were startling and radical. One reason for the popularity of the soft material and lines without corsets was that breast feeding was slowly gaining in popularity with the influence of Locke and Rousseau.[11] A mother could more comfortably nurse a baby with that kind of clothing. "Breastfeeding became fashionable! To call attention to this change in attitude about women's bodies, women also walked around with breasts showing."[12] No longer would the aristocratic lady send her newborn to a wet nurse in the country.

Fig. 29 "Two Sisters," by Adam Buck (1796). Dancing *à la Grecque*. The lyricism of the flowing costumes inspires the sisters to dance. Courtesy of the Theatre Museum, London.

The GRACES of 1794.

Fig. 30 The Graces of 1794. Isaac Cruikshank. "It's the watch fob that grabs the eye. Feminine dress of the present fashion is perhaps the most indecent ever worn within this country. The breast is altogether displayed, the whole drapery is made to cling to the figure. Well may it be necessary to veil the face." Courtesy of the British Museum Print Collection.

Louis-Sebastien Mercier offered this vivid description of women dancing at a public ball dressed in neoclassic attire:

I know not whether the first of these dancers have any great affection for the republican forms of the Grecian governments, but they have modelled the form of their dress after that of Aspasia (fifth century BC Greek courtesan and mistress of Pericles); bare arms, naked breasts, feet shod with sandals, hair turned in tresses around their heads by modish hairdressers, who study the antique busts . . . The shifts (underslips) have long since been banished, as it seemed only to spoil the contours of nature; and besides, it was an inconvenient part of dress . . . The flesh-colored knit-work silk stays, which stuck close to the body did not leave the beholder to divine, but perceive every secret charm. This was what was called being dressed *à la sauvage*, and the women dressed in this manner during a rigorous winter, in spite of frost and snow.[13]

Despite rumors to the contrary, women did wear some form of underwear. They wore tights to keep warm or a body-stocking (also called a *maillot*) under these extremely suggestive styles, but somehow the bosom became more exposed. From 1800 to 1811, short or long corsets became more common. With the slim sheath, bust improvers or falsies were worn.[14] A notice in the *London Times* in 1799 stated "The fashion for false bosoms has at least this utility, that it compels our fashionable fair to wear something." The falsies were called "bosom friends."[15] Extreme devotees of neoclassic fashion discarded the corset or wore a narrow band of leather or other material over the breasts like the Greek zone (a bra-like sheath). Others wore short linen stays, beginning in 1790. The gauzy frocks called even more attention to the breasts, which later became the center of attention, emphasized by the high waistline of the Empire style.[16]

For those who continued to wear fuller skirts, drawers appeared. Little girls first wore "trowsers" which could be seen hanging below the dress. The drawers, which were open at the crotch, were not visible, and served the purpose of underwear. Hundreds of years before, Catherine de Medici (when she married Henri II) may have worn drawers for riding horses.[17]

The fashion in the street dictated that a new shoe shape be worn with the tunic style of dress. Neoclassic fashions called for sandal-like small heels or heelless slippers tied about the ankles with satin ribbons. The ribbons secured the shoe on the foot and created the impression of a Greek sandal. This petite slipper began to grace the ballet studio, as well. The discomfort of wearing a shoe smaller than one's natural size could be endured, as the young girl was trained from an early age to bear pain.[18]

The developing fashionable ideal had evolved a very narrow, light, flexible heelless slipper, constructed with a sole slightly too small for the wearer. The fabric of the upper, wrapping closely around the foot, compressed the bones together and encouraged them into a slender, elongated elegance demanded by the mode.[19]

In "Sensible Shoes," fashion historian Anne Bryden refers to shoes as artifacts that express identities and transact gender and class relations. "They

No Flower that Blows, is like this Rose.. "

Fig. 31 "No Flower that Blows is Like this Rose." Picture of the ballerina Rose Didelot, wife of the choreographer Charles Didelot, in a costume of "transparent simplicity." Courtesy of the Theatre Museum, London.

are commodities that in their deployment also distribute knowledge."[20] Like a number of other fashion writers, she theorizes about the sexual side of footwear. "Small feet on a woman suggest a slender, virginal opening, and in order to achieve the appearance of such, women have been known to wear shoes too small."[21] The slimmer shoe connects to fetishist instincts and what lies below the surface of the unconscious. Just remember Cinderella and her tiny glass slipper.

The costume of the day became the preferred look of the evening ballet performance. A number of interesting articles on the sexuality of the ballerina's body and attendant questions have emerged recently.[22] This curious focus begins when the female dancer's body is viewed as a charismatic performing object. What may have contributed more than any other factor to the fascination with the dancing female body were changes in attitude toward clothing on the street and, therefore, costuming on stage.

In the myth ballets the short, light, transparent tunic for dance became common with the radical tendency to reveal the woman's body on stage. This is attested by a review in the November 26, 1791, *Mercure de France* of the opera *Diane et Endymion*, in which Mademoiselle Saulnier "wore a costume of almost transparent simplicity. . . . She appeared almost naked yet her bearing banishes any licentious thought. She brings to mind those beautiful Spartan women on the banks of the Eurotas, who, to borrow a phrase from Rousseau, were clothed only in public respect."[23] In an earlier article on November 20, 1791, in the *Chronique de Paris*, Victoire Saulnier is praised for her performance in the same opera: "We must give her credit for being almost the only dancer at the Opéra to have adopted an authentic costume."[24]

At the Archives Nationales, in the cluttered boxes that hold the folders of the Opéra's accounts and spending, a document lists the *tunique blanche* as the favored costume for dancers, probably the corps, from 1800 onward. Accessories were maillots or tights, flower or laurel crowns, tambours for Terpsichore, and so forth. This confirmed the shift to a more uniform, simplified profile for the corps de ballet and recognized that ballet technique could more easily be explored if the dancer wore less cumbersome attire.

Important changes in shoe wear affected the way in which both the social and the professional dancer moved. The dancing shoe of minuets, waltzes, and quadrilles rapidly became the ballet slipper, standard apparel for preparatory classes. Some dance historians, for example, Marion Hannah Winter and Ivor Guest, alluded to the fact that rope dancers wore soft shoes for balancing and that the ballet dancers of the late eighteenth century imitated this practice. The gradual change from high heel to lower heel to sandal to slipper and finally to pointe shoe seemed completely within the concept of how women's feet looked to society, regardless of their natural shape.[25]

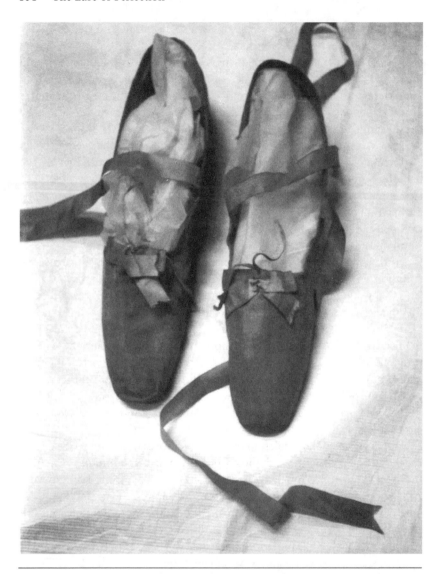

Fig. 32 Early nineteenth-century dress shoe. Light, flexible, and narrow, the evening slipper had no heel and a sole that was slightly too small for the foot, thereby pressing the bones together and creating a slender, elegant appearance. Courtesy of the Victoria and Albert Dress Collection.

Despite discomforts, satin or silk slippers provided dancers flexibility for the foot and enhanced the possibilities for jumping, balancing, and turning. For example, when making a *demi-coupé* and stepping onto a *demi-pointe*, the foot takes a shape where, with an enforced arch or instep, the toes are extended, as well, making the foot arch and point so that the line of

SMART SHOES MADE TO FIT—WITHOUT A LAST.

Yes my Lady They sit neat about the Quarters, they only want a little Bobbing.

Published 15ᵗ Janʳ 1794 by Robᵗ Sayer & Cᵒ Fleet Street London.

Fig. 33 "Smart Shoes Made to Fit—Without a Last." Isaac Cruikshank satirizes the pain women will endure in order to be fashionably shod (1794). Courtesy of the British Museum Print Collection.

the leg becomes much longer and vertical. These are directives about which Magri wrote in his Treatise (1774). Gradually, the foot became more than a balancing device to help shift the weight; it became a mechanical tool or organ that could be strengthened and exercised and expanded in its own right. And this is exactly what began to happen in the latter part of the eighteenth century, but it could not really evolve until the foot was freed from the high heel.

A major contribution to stage costumes in 1791 was made by Charles Didelot in *Bacchus et Ariadne*; he appeared in flesh-colored tights with a Dionysian tiger's skin thrown over his shoulder, grape leaves in his hair, and a staff of Bacchus in his hand.[26] During the same year, another costume innovation occurred in the opera *Corisandre*, when, in one of the dances, Didelot as Zephyr appeared in a transparent tunic.[27] The value of this filmy *tissu* was that "The shortening of the dress and the use of transparent material in its construction led to the introduction of maillot or tights, a combination of long stockings with skin-tight knickers. The invention of this

Fig. 34 Madame Récamier. As one of the lioness *Merveilleuses,* Madame Récamier sought inspiration in Greek attire in order to reconstitute the glory of Ancient Greece in Paris. Courtesy of the Chateau de Coppet, Geneva.

garment is generally attributed to Maillot—a costumier at the Opéra at the beginning of the nineteenth century who died in 1838. But the use of tights, which occurred as early as the 1400s, was certainly known to Guimard, who retired in 1790; moreover, the transparent dresses associated with the *Merveilleuses* must have necessitated the wearing of a similar garment."[27] Both Aileen Ribeiro and Susan North, English fashion historians, acknowledge that ballroom dresses of the early 1800s and 1820s contained many layers of thin, transparent fabric, probably fine muslin or tulle, and, almost certainly, women had to have covering for the legs.

Many intellectuals and artists cultivated an interest in the Neoclassic Period by reconstructing a more glorious past. Like Vigée-Lebrun, Emma Hamilton and the *merveilleuses* (who could be likened to the female counterparts to the *Incroyables*), Madame de Genlis, and the painter Jacques-Louis David used to organize *tableaux vivants,* or improvisations like paintings at the house of the Duc d'Orléans. Madame Tallien and Madame Récamier, the *merveilleuses* of the Directorate, took refuge in dinners constructed to look entirely like an antique banquet, reclining on sofas, eating grapes, wearing chitons and various draperies, with flowing hair and sandals. They led the way to philosophical changes in fashion and a way of life. Madames Récamier and Tallien represented this liberal thinking. "They were returning to the antique, to Greek sculpture, to drawings on classical vases . . . They wanted to bring art back under the authority of thought. They appealed to nature to restore simplicity and strength to art, to free it from excessive finery, superficial joys."[28]

Elizabeth Vigée-Lebrun narrated a story of one of their archeological feasts in her *Souvenirs*:

> One day in 1788 I had invited a dozen or fifteen people to come that evening and hear a reading by the poet Lebrun, my brother and, during my rest, he read me a few pages from the *Travels of Anarcharsis.* When he came to the passage which describes a Greek dinner and explains how to make some of the sauces, he said, 'We ought to serve this to our guests tonight.' As I was expecting some very pretty women, I thought we would all dress up in Greek costume so as to give a surprise to M. de Vaudreuil and M. Boutin . . . I could get all the clothes I needed from my studio, which was full of stuff I used to drape my models, and the Comte de Parois, who lived in my house in the rue de Clery, had a superb collection of Etruscan vases.[29]

Vigée-Lebrun set the scene as if for an improvised, inexpensive whim:

> At half-past nine the preparations were complete, and when we all took our places, the effect of the table was so novel and picturesque that each of us stood up in turn to look at the others sitting around. At ten we heard the carriage of the comte de Vaudreuil and M. Boutin drive in, and when they got to the dining-room door, which I had had set wide open, they found us singing Gluck's chorus "Le Dieu de Paphos."[30]

Private gatherings were also the sites of dance improvisations in neoclassic garb. In the last two decades of the eighteenth century, the notorious

Emma Hamilton (wife of Sir William and lover of Lord Nelson) created a performance art improvisational *tableaux vivants* entitled "Attitudes." Inspired by her husband's revelatory book on Greek statues, she performed different pictorial moments while draped in soft materials. In such poses she was a living embodiment of the past. She became known as Sir William's "Gallery of Statues" and was described as being "Fluid, graceful, sublime and heroic."[31] For example, she played Sophonisbe, the Carthaginian Queen, taking the cup of poison, changing her countenance at a stroke. During her enactments, she fled like the Virgilian Galatea or she'd throw herself down like a drunken Bacchante, extending an arm to a lewd satyr; she cleverly manipulated a long shawl that changed her from a figure of tragedy to a demure supplicant. Pietro Antonio Novelli painted pictures of her in 1791 as these charismatic figures. "In a marvelous way, according to her contemporaries, she could thus give new life to ancient figurations . . . one has to emphasize their broad resonance in the fashion and taste of society that neoclassical aestheticians believed, somewhat ingenuously, could be modified simply by appealing to the classical ideals of simplicity and purity."[32]

Attending the Opéra in the presence of Bonaparte, Madame Tallien and two of her friends dressed as nymph huntresses in tunics that came to the knee. Their feet were nude and adorned with rings in sandals with purple ties. Napoléon's wife, Joséphine contemptuously told the three "nymphs"

Fig. 35 Jean-Simon Berthélémy, costume sketch, *Proserpine* (1803). Costume designer and painter, Berthélémy was a distinguished artist. His designs have a lively and dramatic action. Courtesy of the Bibliothèque de l'Opéra.

on the part of the *Premier Consul* "that the era of Fable was passed and that now is the beginning of the reign of history."[33] Despite this jab, Joséphine spent many evenings entertaining herself with the *merveilleuses*. For her fashion statement, Joséphine created the style of wearing shawls and mantles over her tunics. Often they were woven of cashmere and the most expensive materials. "Along with Mesdames Tallien and Récamier, she was one of the leaders of Directory society—they were inevitably called the three graces when seen together dressed 'à l'antique.'"[34]

Although David institutionalized the "cult of the antique," it is believed that the artist/costumer Jean-Simon Berthélémy initiated the antique style at the ballet when Pierre Gardel was dancing master. Berthélémy was brought in as costumier in 1787 at the Paris Opéra by François-Guillaume Menagéot, who was originally appointed to the position but took a more prestigious job and gave his to Berthélémy. Berthélémy succeeded Boquet as "dessinateur en titre des costumes de l'Opéra" and remained until 1807, when Ménagéot recovered his original position. Boquet's tenure lasted the middle years of the eighteenth century. He was a decorative artist, greatly skilled in creating delicate Rococo confections that were firmly based on the stiff and standardized costume shape, and seemed to be out of touch with trends in the artistic community. His sketches of Persians, Indians, classical gods, furies—

Fig. 36 Jean-Simon Berthélémy, costume sketch, *Achille à Scyros* (1804). Courtesy of the Bibliothèque de l'Opéra.

PIERRE GARDEL

Maître des Ballets de S. M. I. et R.

de son Académie Impériale de Musique,

et Membre de la Société Philotechnique

Fig. 37 Pierre Gardel (1809), member of the philotechnical society (or follower of enlightened ideas of philosophy), ran the Paris Opéra from 1787 to 1820, one of the longest-reigning ballet masters in the history of the Paris Opéra. Courtesy of the Bibliothèque de l'Opéra.

the whole theatrical stable—looked sprightly, delicate, and as formal as Bérain's a century earlier. But following him, a serious change was afoot. Both Berthélémy and Ménagéot were serious painters who had studied in Rome and learned the standard rules of painting techniques that brought neoclassicism and draperies onto the opera stage. Berthélémy's talents as a ceiling painter and designer of historical pictures demonstrated that he understood beautifully the value of a dramatic setting. His designs depicted the perfect moment to display his costumes, showing the characters during an expressively vivid scene. Another important contribution was his insistence on rules to protect the design of the costumes and scenery, a kind of early copyright. He also wished that the costumes be properly maintained and catalogued by the chief tailor. No doubt, one of the reasons for the great success of Gardel's myth-based ballets during revolutionary times was the work of Berthélémy.[35]

Ballets in Antiquity

Ballets based on Greek and Roman mythology were common to the world of dance long before the French Revolution. Literary and artistic currents affected ballet, and myth—perhaps more than any other source—informed the realm of dance. Irritating Cupids, indignant Venuses, and diffident Psyches abounded on the stages of eighteenth-century France. Everyone knew these stories, which told of human vices with a certain doleful tolerance. Love was their theme, and the threatened love affairs almost always ended happily.

Mythology had been taught methodically in school; manuals detailed who the gods and goddesses were and listed their accoutrements. Handbooks describing the adventures of Olympian gods provided pretexts for French ballets and operas, and in the hands of court poets, Greco-Roman mythology was a veritable mine of ideas for livrets.

The *Maître de Ballet* of the Opéra, Pierre Gardel had discovered during the Reign of Terror that he could keep his head and satisfy the early revolutionaries as well as audiences if he ascribed to the popular mythological themes. They had played a vital role in court performances from the sixteenth through the eighteenth centuries. Under the prophetic influence of Noverre and Angiolini, Gardel produced the romanticized myths as ballet-pantomimes with dancers who could act and who gave their movements and gestures an expression of feelings that we associate with romantic literature. *Télémaque dans l'Isle de Calypso* and *Psyché* in 1790, and in 1793 *Le Jugement de Paris*, succeeded beyond all expectations. Later during the Empire, it was natural for Gardel and other choreographers at the Opéra to appeal to Napoléon's conservative taste for antiquity. Each of Gardel's

Fig. 38 Mademoiselle Clothide as Calypso in the ballet *Télémaque dans l'Isle de Calypso* (1790). Her beauty is enhanced by the short Grecian dress and sandals. Courtesy of the Bibliothèque de l'Opéra.

myth-based ballets became so popular that they still remain on the lists of the most well-attended performances at the Opéra. Certainly their touching stories and the more dramatic and emotive manner of presentation gave them tremendous impact. The transformations enhanced their visual splendor. Since Gardel's teacher was the distinguished choreographer Jean-Georges Noverre, he emphasized carefully structured scenarios and dancing with gestural power and realized in his ballets the a esthetic principles of *ballet d' action* with great success.

Like the contemporary paintings of Constable and Turner in which sudden winds and tumultuous seas disturbed a once peaceful environment, the setting for *Télémaque dans l'Isle de Calypso* (February 23, 1790) contained some early signs of Romantic ballet. It tells the story of Ulysses' son who returns to Calypso's island, where he discovers true love. Storm scenes, shipwrecks, a clever Cupid, played *en travesti* by the stunning Mademoiselle Chameroy, Calypso (an evil princess with magical powers), and great romance helped to contribute to this ballet's startling success. Jean Berthélémy's costumes for the ballet adhered to the principles of historical accuracy. Télémaque's tunic and mantle displayed the gentleness of a draped dress to the knee with decorated hem and neckline. Calypso's revealing skirt fell above the knee. A rope-like belt defined a high waistline over a sleeveless bodice that hung over the skirt (as seen in pictures of Greek women). Sandals were the preferred shoe. In a later 1801 recreation of the *Télémaque*, the British observer Mary Berry described the dancers in the corps as wearing "one petticoat of white muslin, or something as thin, with another drapery of the same stuff arranged in various ways about half as long as the first, but both allowing the whole form to be fully perceived up to the waist, covered with flesh-coloured tricot."[36] The ballet remained in the repertoire for thirty-six years and played 408 times.

The ballet *Psyché* (December 14, 1790) depicted the tale of the young goddess upstart who attempted to compete with Venus while falling madly in love with Cupid, Venus's son. Psyché endured classic suffering for her sins while the stage was filled with dazzling scenic spectacles. Psyche was an important symbol of the times; she had to endure demons, cures, physical harm, and even death in order to reach her lover. Perhaps she symbolized France in her effort as an adventurer to brave impossible feats and survive. Through her essential courage, she, like the French women of the Revolution, no longer succumbed as a victim.

What contributed to the fortune of this ballet was Psyche's costume. The *robe à la Psyché* became one of the most touted fashions of the time. *Le Journal de la Mode et du Goût* of December 25, 1790, mentioned that this costume was tastefully designed to suggest one breast exposed. The dressmaker,

Fig. 39 The *Robe à la Psyché* became one of the most touted fashions of the time. Courtesy of the Cabinet des Estampes.

Madame Teillard, offered the *robe à la Psyché* for sale at her shop.[37] However, it is doubtful that women actually wore one breast exposed on stage; sources of the time do not confirm this practice. For a brief period in the early nineteenth century, dancers wore as little as possible, although there is no mention that their breasts actually were nude. A few society women did indeed expose one breast in social situations. It was a sensational as well as suggestive gesture. When Psyché was reproduced in 1801, Miss Berry sought out her favorite dancer at the Opéra, Monsieur Vestris. However, she was shocked by his hairdo. "His coiffure was one of those bustling, frizzed and powdered heads which were worn about twenty years ago, and in dancing, showers of powder came out of it, and it flapped up and down in the most ridiculous manner."[38]

In *Le Jugement de Paris* (March 6, 1793), gods and shepherds danced together while Paris took his time falling in love with Oenone. First, Paris had to judge "the most beautiful," a contest between Venus, Minerva, and Juno, and, of course, decided that Venus merited the title of most beautiful woman in the world. Ultimately, he chose the lovely young Oenone for himself. In *Le Jugement de Paris*, historical accuracy gave way to convenience,

Fig. 40 The dancer says, "Wat, you see enof?" to the Bishop of Durham, who, in 1798, made an example of Parisot's immoral dancing and denounced her to The House of Lords. Courtesy of the Theatre Museum, London.

as the dancers no longer wore the traditional Greek cothurnes but lightly sported the Phrygian sandal in which one moved much more easily.[39]

A capable designer of Italian origin, Vincenzio Sestini, the King's Theatre costumier, was initially a singer married to the well-known soprano Giovanna Sestini. He first became a tailor, then a costumier, renowned for his neoclassic opera and ballet designs. He created dresses for the ballets *Venus and Adonis* (1793), *Iphigenia in Aulide* (1793), Madame Hilligsberg's benefit (1794), *L'Amour et Psiche* (1796), *Sappho and Phaon* (1797), and *Alessandro e Timotes* (1800). He also designed a costume parody for the caricature engraving by Thomas Rowlandson in 1791, "The Prospect Before Us," which depicted members of the King's Theatre company begging in the streets. Among those in the picture are Madame Hilligsberg and "Poor Old Servini," a nickname or a mistake for Sestini, since no one by the name of Servini is known to have been with the King's company at that time.

Neoclassic costume contributed to the renown of famous female ballet soloists throughout the large cities of Western Europe and brought increasing attention to the development of their virtuosic and dramatic capabilities, one outdoing the other. Mademoiselle Parisot shocked London audiences in 1796 with her long legs flying in the ballet *le Triomphe de l'Amour* performed in London. The *Monthly Mirror* (October 1796) cited Parisot's flexibility that "created a stir by raising her legs far higher than was customary for dancers." In 1798, the Bishop of Durham made an example of her immoral moves and denounced her in an intemperate speech before the House of Lords. The opera administration changed the colors of dancers' maillots from flesh-colored to white.

In time, interest in the antique myths of the Neoclassic Period began to fade and was replaced with the desire for romantic scenarios. People began looking for more realism, and female heroines became more popular than the goddesses. Newly found freedoms exposed their limitations: "Rather quickly the antique style imposed new conventions that were as unrealistic as those that came before: the required flesh colored tights, the filmy tunic, the supple ballet slipper necessary to execute the pirouettes, which predicted the next design of the point shoe."[40] Several writers of the late eighteenth century saw the fascination for the antique as regressive and stultifying rather than exciting and appealing because it called back what they felt were conservative ideas about art and décor rather than an appeal to fantasy and to the artist's imagination. Again, it was time to move forward.

CHAPTER 5

The Consulate (1799–1804) and the Empire (1804–1815) of Napoléon

Imperial Designs Pervade Street and Stage Fashion

From the moment Napoléon took office, Europe became his playing field. Napoléon established himself as a powerful warrior, and he was voted into the government by the people. During the Consulate, Napoléon consolidated his power and prepared for his heart's dream, which was to found a dynasty. "For fifteen years, France and Europe were to be at the mercy of a gambler to whom fate and his own genius gave for a time all the aces."[1] He created a system of administrative law that exercised an unlimited supervision over local administration and all public establishments.[2]

Italy's Austrian colonizers were defeated by Napoléon's army in 1803 at the battle of Marengo in the north of Italy. When the Empire was established in France, Italy became completely subjugated to it. By 1803, France's relations to the major European powers had deteriorated so much that a state of war ensued. France threatened England by installing large numbers of troops in Boulogne. French royalists hoped that defeat of Napoléon in a war with England would install Louis XVIII, the brother of Louis XVI, on the throne. In return, the English sent vast numbers of people to France to create an insurrection in 1804, with the hope of bringing a Prince, the Duc d'Enghien, to the throne. The Duc never conspired against Napoléon and did not go to Paris nevertheless, he was shot and killed on March 21, 1804. Napoléon overwhelmed the royalist cabal.

Despite internal politics, England remained king of the seas and proved to be an invincible power as France was defeated in 1805 at Trafalgar by Admiral Nelson. Napoléon then deployed his army all over Europe. In 1806 the Confederation of the Rhine was formed with Napoléon's defeat over Maida, Jena, and Auerstadt; Portugal and Spain were invaded in 1807 and in 1808, respectively. In September 1812, the battle of Borodino ensued, which was followed by an ill-conceived invasion of Moscow in September.

In January 1814 the Allies (Russia, England, Prussia, and Austria) invaded France and, in February, Paris capitulated. On April 11, 1814, Napoléon abdicated and by March 31, 1814, the people of Paris cried, "Vive le roi! vive Louis XVIII!" The glory of the Bourbons rose from its ashes; that of the Empire seemed forever departed. A Treaty of Peace was issued between France and Europe on June 4, 1814. That peace was costly and the French people did not like wearing a white cockade.

The vast body of the middle class, the manufacturers, the merchants, and the indifferents, were heartily glad of peace and willing to support the new régime. But, overall, people were upset because royalists were forgiven everywhere and returned to power, or so it seemed; the wings of the Imperial Eagle were not yet finally clipped.

Napoléon triumphantly returned from Elba in the spring of 1815 to retake France; this abortive attempt lasted one hundred days, until his major defeat by Wellington at Waterloo, whereupon, in July 1815, Louis XVIII was brought back from exile in Brussels to reimpose a Bourbon reign on France.

For the short time that Napoléon ruled, he gained tremendous influence over European politics. One might say that he made possible the national movements of the nineteenth century—he was the herald of Italian unity; he was one of the makers of modern Germany; he helped to create the modern kingdom of Holland and several countries of South America; and he enhanced the prestige of the Spanish and Portuguese monarchies. Finally, he dared England to create the greatest sea power in the world.

Napoléon's Reign

Spouting the rhetoric of the Revolution, Napoléon's forces continued the policy of the Revolution by invading countries and encouraging a surge of nationalism that thrived and signaled each nation's hunger for identity. Feeling the fresh winds of revolutionary accomplishments, early symbols of the Romantic movement swept across western Europe, just as Napoléon's forces swept across Italy and Spain, eventually to meet his downfall in Russia.

Romantic sylphs and dreams of an idealized society mirrored philosophical concepts of the period. Parallel tendencies in ballet scenarios of the expressively emotional and exotic, as well as the realistic, reflected other ideas, such as certain of the philosophical underpinnings of Napoléon's reign. Sensation theorists and ideologues dominated intellectual circles. The ideologues were freethinkers in religion and liberal in politics. Deeply influencing

Robe de Cour, en Satin; Le Manteau, en Velours.

Fig. 41 *Robe de Cour* (1809). Napoleon's court dress which, in spite of the relatively long and simple lines, displays rich materials of satin, velvet, and jewels. Courtesy of the Cabinet des Estampes.

the advent of Romanticism in France, the philosophy of the sensualist school of the eighteenth century claimed to explain everything by sensation. Napoléon detested their way of thinking, threatened by their interest in a free press and their belief in the power of public opinion.

During Napoléon's reign, changes in fashion were initiated and mandated by the dominant political forces. The culture of war governed the nation. Whenever a new office was created, a minute description was given of the uniform of the new officials. Napoléon's persona as the soldier, warrior, and power player ruled France from 1799 until 1815. During his reign, he drafted one and a half million men. Many men were already in uniform. His dress as uniform suited his authoritarian representation. One might say that "fashion exists perilously between freedom and oppression."[3] Using the uniform as a symbol of power, freedom, and nationalism, Napoléon transformed the meaning of the way men dressed and their former interest in beauty of attire. Clothing reinforced a person's role and responsibility in society; dress performed the function of an "identity kit."[4]

Like most ambitious political geniuses, Napoléon was painfully conscious of outward symbols, those indications of wealth and prominence that acknowledge strength and power. He knew well that Paris fashions were copied by all European nations, England, and the Americas and that people paid attention to the smallest details of his entourage, noticing any indignity or slight.

After Napoléon's success at the Battle of the Nile in 1798, he took on the illusion of a grand Egyptian leader and wore *bonnets en crocodiles* as well as clothing *à la mameluke*, calling attention to his conquests through fashion. He wore dashing red boots, balooning white trousers, and a red velvet jacket. One of Napoléon's first decrees in December 1799 was to decide what he and his two Consuls should wear, and he chose the colors of the Revolution, as did the Directory before him. The everyday suit consisted of a blue coat cinched by a fringed gold sash and white, close-fitting pants. His taste for red extended to the state room, where his formal attire consisted of a formal red velvet coat with lace and ruffles, embroidered in gold, and a sword. But inevitably Napoléon, the dominating ruler, chose not to decorate his court room with frilly clothing. He preferred his image as conquering hero and military mastermind. Thus, with a black cravat and white pantaloons, the gold embroidery and lace were toned down and the military uniform became the uniform of political power. We learn in *The Book of Costume or Annals of Fashion* that Napoléon regulated what women wore at court. The French court during the Empire was the most sumptuous, the most brilliant, and the most elegant ever witnessed in Europe. Bonaparte passed a sumptuary law to regulate the dress of the ladies of the court, of which Madame Junot gives the following description:

This costume was then almost as it still is today; the gothic ruffle with long u-shaped scallops made of tulle, edged with gold or silver like the outfit (. . .) which was promptly shortened, fitted the part quite nicely; the coat and the skirt were as we wear them today, save that originally the edge of the coat could not exceed four inches; only princesses had the privilege to wear coats that were totally embroidered. Such were the orders of the emperor at first. We should be the ones, he said to Junot, to show moderation, and not to be overbearing through ridiculous splendor.[5]

These were opulent designs of the women's court dress, despite the fact that Napoléon believed in the shibboleths of the French Revolution. The Napoléonic Wars created miserable political and economic conditions that left the poor and middle classes much less affluent and unable to imitate court fashions.

Napoléon also attempted to control fashion by ordering his court painters, Jacques-Louis David and Jean-Baptiste Isabey, to create ceremonial dress, especially for himself and Joséphine, his empress. For the 1804 coronation, Isabey designed an extraordinary confection for Joséphine. Her short-sleeved gown had an "empire" waist, and a square décolletage framed by pleated flounces raised like a fan over her shoulders. The gown and the train were embroidered with gold thread around the hem with vertical bans and palmate patterns. There were yards and yards of trailing and lustrous material.[6]

There were but a few women *couturiers* of the period, and their creations cost somewhat less than those of their famed male counterparts. Several of their names have survived: Madame Despaux, Mademoiselle Annette, Madame Germont, Madame Lasnier, Mademoiselle Louvet, and Madame Sandoz.[7] However, Joséphine's preferred couturier was Louis-Hippolyte Leroy, who, interestingly enough, was forbidden by Napoléon to make cotton or muslin fashions. It was unpatriotic to create fashions that depended on the cotton manufacturing of nations far away. Those who crossed Leroy's threshold might spend twelve to fifteen thousand francs a year for their toilette. His hats were inimitable. Leroy's designs were meant to exaggerate Napoléon's greatness and to create a unified vision of himself and his entourage as rulers of the world.

In addition to extravagant court clothing, dress styles during the Empire continued to reflect neoclassicism with ankle-length skirts, medium-high waists, short sleeves and low V-shaped, round, or square necks. The softer pseudo-antique line with high waists and skirts above the ankle gave the impression of little girl's dress. Gathered at the waist with puffed sleeves, the dress was accompanied by flat shoes and a large bonnet; all made a becoming fashion for the very young.[8] Fancy dresses often had trains that were difficult to maneuver while dancing. The hair was kept much closer to the head, with some antique styles based on the Egyptian, Greek, and Roman styles. Ornaments such as jewelry, turbans, and bandeaux were common. After 1810, shortened skirts became A-shaped and sleeves were short and puffed, while the skirts were busy with pleats, ribbon, ruffles, and flounces. Layers of lace and net were added over the basic outline of the dress. Dress shoes continued to be flat, often of soft satin, though the soles might have a firmer leather quality.[9]

The rising bourgeoisie in France "worked out an elaborate system of appearance, which reveals the importance it attached to clothing's signifying role as opposed to its functional role."[10] As prosperity grew along with social mobility, clothing presented each class with peculiar and particular status symbols. As was typical of the upper classes, attire signified certain qualities; it did not necessarily serve usefully as covering. Aristocratic dress of the *ancien régime* symbolized lineage when it presented magnificence. In the same manner, the male bourgoisie, free from sumptuary laws, put forth its clothing presence in the black suit, telling everyone that it was a hard working, puritanical, highly motivated, and practical group. The clothing of women once again became decorative, suggestive, and advertising a life of ornamentation. "Women's dress carried all the messages of social distinction, while men's dress began to shun them."[11] At the same time, the working-class woman wore most practical clothing that did not impede her from working long hours, bending, and walking.

Recognizing "the exotic" in fashions of the time was limited to fairly superficial and temporary fads: turbans and ornamental jewelry from "the Orient." However, after the Revolution in the 1790s, there were crazy outbursts: of the Incroyables and Merveilleuses—children of aristocrats killed during the Revolution—as people breathed a sigh of relief and went into the streets for promenades. The period of the Empire, from 1804–1815, presented a more conservative perception of fashion by calling the free tastes of the Directorate and the Consulate loose and unpatriotic. It was said that their clothing was too scanty and unsuitable for either the physical or political climate in Paris. Since Napoléon prohibited the importation of Indian muslin, the old silk industries of Lyon flourished again. Weightier fabrics such as taffeta, velvet, and brocade returned, and long gloves covered the arms of daytime short-sleeved dresses, adding a modest allure to the costume.

Flax and hemp were cultivated in France, and Napoléon offered a prize in 1810 of a million francs to the inventor of the best flax-spinning machine. The manufacture of woolen goods was greatly improved. Jacquard invented the loom that executed by mechanical means even the most intricate designs in the richest materials. In 1811, a fabric, *le pékin*, with vertical stripes, alternately mat or shiny, attracted upholsterers more than dress designers. Tulle had to be imported from England until 1817 when the city of Cambrai began to manufacture the filmy, light material. Despite Napoléon's ban on Indian muslin, the progress of the cotton industry in France was astonishing when one thinks of the difficulty of obtaining the raw material from America, of bringing the Levantine cotton overland, of the inadequacy of the supply from Naples and Sicily, and of the apparent failure of the attempt to cultivate cotton in Corsica. Nevertheless, Lenoir-Dufresne and others succeeded in establishing important cotton-spinning factories with the machinery of the English Spinning-jenny. By 1810, Lenoir had six cotton-spinning mills with 3,600 workers in Normandy. Ternaux, a wool manufacturer of Sedan, employed 24,000 workers. Between 1788 and 1812 the number of looms increased from some 7,000 to 17,000 and the workers increased from 76,000 to 131,000.[12] In England, by 1812, the cotton industry "outstripped the woolen industry in national importance. At this stage there were about 100,000 workers in cotton-spinning factories

Fig. 42 La Walse (1801). Illustration from *Le Bon Genre*. "La Valse is a German dance adored by the French as the arms are interlaced in the middle of the body, while 15, 20 sometimes 30 groups of dancers turn following a circular direction. The cavalier is like the pivot of the group that's moving." Courtesy of the Irene Lewisohn Costume Reference Library, the Costume Institute at the Metropolitan Museum of Art.

Fig. 43 Le Trénis (1805). Illustration from *Le Bon Genre*. "The title of a contra dance named after the inventor, a sad celebrity whose mania for pirouettes drove him to distraction, dying at Charenton." Courtesy of the Irene Lewisohn Costume Reference Library, the Costume Institute at the Metropolitan Museum of Art.

and probably another quarter of a million weavers and their auxiliaries working on cotton goods."[13] The Revolution and the Empire in France promoted progress, but it did not occur quickly. By 1815, French industry was at the level of mechanization (in general) reached by Great Britain in 1780.[14]

Fashions were fed by this increased industrialization, and Paris remained the center of the fashion industry. Before the Revolution, fashion came from Versailles, and members of the court were the masters of the elegant. That tyranny was swept away in 1789. Fashion was now dictated by people of the city and was therefore in the *domaine commun*.

Well-illustrated journals and magazines helped to promote the material values of Napoléon's regime. Vernet's composed and thoughtful pictures of elite society were inspired by the beautiful publication *Le Bon Genre* that presented a life like series of costume plates illustrating moments in the life of society people.[15]

Fig. 44 La Poule (1810). Illustration from *Le Bon Genre*. "The Hen or Lady Bird is a gay and animated dance in which one amuses oneself with decency and sparkles without pretentions." Courtesy of the Irene Lewisohn Costume Reference Library, the Costume Institute at the Metropolitan Museum of Art.

Balls were a featured topic in columns of the *Le Bon Genre* depicting women wearing national costumes from Switzerland and Normandy (1801), or at the ball observing exotic dresses of their neighbors, or at a masked ball where "one must beware of the old husbands of young women."[16]

According to *Le Bon Genre*, dance was an important pastime, and Vernet offered an explanation of the Quadrille's La Trénise—named for the person who invented the dance. He had a mania for pirouettes and he died in the Charenton asylum, it was said, because the excessive spinning went to his head. Another plate of the dance, "La Sauteuse," explained that "The feet graze the floor without leaving it; one hand grabs another as it is being held." Vernet also featured the popular rope dancers reaching dangerous heights. In a later illustration, the corset is also presented as a major fashion accoutrement in an illustration showing a Mademoiselle Busc and a Monsieur Corset (1819) with an inscription, "In order to have a slim waist, there are young men who, like young women, wear corsets today." This was particularly true of military men, whose stand-up-straight dictates guided the practice of wearing corsets for their posture.

Fashion magazines and journals of etiquette described the values that drove taste in body shapes and behavior. *The Mirror of Graces,* published in London in 1811, pontificated on many subjects. It was especially French women during the Napoléonic period who led the world in beauty of gait and ease of movement. Extolling the loveliness of French dances and dancing, *The Mirror of Graces* stated:

> French dances, which include minuets, cotillions, and all the round of ballet figures, admit of every new refinement and dexterity in the agile art; and while exhibiting in them, there is no step, no turn, no attitude within the verge of maiden delicacy that the dancer may not adopt and practise.[17]

Once again praising the French for their charm and delicacy of carriage, *The Mirror of Graces* (1811) mentions:

> In the details of carriage, we must not omit due attention to gait and its accompanying air . . . In this particular, the French women far exceed us. Pope observes that "they move easiest who have learnt to dance." And it is the step of the highly-accomplished dancer that we see in the generality of well-bred French women.[18]

The popularity of corsets returned, although the young and very thin enjoyed the freedom of wearing the tunic style without heavy stays. Most women preferred some support for these lines; the more relaxed stays were called the "Ninon." Unlike earlier "corps," the "Ninon" corset that appeared around 1810 was only slightly stiffened and considerably shortened; its purpose was to separate the breasts, as fashion then required. It is ironic that during the highlyregulated and uniformed regime of Napoléon, tight lacing had a brief respite until Napoléon's demise. Indignant at the confining qualities of the corset, Napoléon stated that the corset basically remodeled and imprisoned the breasts; he called it a poetic prison for the lazy woman where the breasts were always held.[19] Oddly enough, Napoléon found the corset to be a stupid accessory. He wrote to his friend le Corvisart that "the corset is the assassin of the human race. This piece of coquettish clothing and bad taste tortures and murders women and destroys their future offspring. The corset is a product of frivolity and terrible decadence."[20]

Above all, this period fostered a reversion to older fashion notions, putting the woman further back in her wasp-waist place. Questionable medical treatments offered corsets for therapeutic value, as they were used to correct curvatures of the spine from a very early age. In the late eighteenth

Fig. 45 Marie-Louise of Austria marries Napoléon after he divorces Joséphine. Marie-Louise holds the future King of Rome in 1813. Courtesy of the Cabinet des Estampes.

century, English doctors heeded Rousseau's and Locke's precautionary remarks about the long corset. "Most discussion of the evil effects of stays occurs at the end of the century, after they had become less restrictive."[21] Occasionally, to correct their backs, girls at boarding schools spent time suspended by their chins to straighten their necks, or strapped to backboards.[22]

In a sense, the corset framed the picture of the ideal woman of the period. What kind of life could a woman of means be disposed or indisposed to lead? In England (despite the social class) the female body suffered even more deprivation than it did in France. Manuals for a young girl's education and treatises on the conduct of a perfect lady cautioned young women not to eat excessively. The warnings against eating too much were partly based on general principles, and partly on the idea that it was unattractive for women to be too strong and healthy. Heroines of English novels became more fragile as the century moved along, while educational writers argued about how much exercise was appropriate for girls. John Gregory alleged that girls needed to retain a "female softness and delicacy with a corresponding delicacy of constitution . . . when a woman speaks of her great strength, her extraordinary appetite, her ability to bear fatigue, we recoil at the description in a way she is little aware of."[23] Dance was probably the only really energetic, physical pastime permitted to women (other than horseback riding), as it allowed for training in posture and aplomb. One wonders how the soft, delicate "china doll" could maneuver in the steel or bone structures that enclosed their small figures. These regressive attitudes toward young women seeped into Parisian society, as well.

Wanting an heir to inherit his crown, Napoléon cruelly divorced Joséphine in 1810 and married Marie-Louise of Austria, who was able to conceive him a son, the future King of Rome. At the height of Napoléon's brilliant reign in 1811, with a son to inherit the Empire as he built it, Napoléon thought it essential to present himself at court with total aplomb. For this reason he hired the dancer, writer, and husband of La Guimard, Jean-Etienne Despréaux, to give dancing lessons to his new wife Marie-Louise and himself. In his *Souvenirs*, Despréaux wrote of a fascinating encounter with Napoléon and Marie-Louise. It demonstrated Napoléon's desperate need to know the rules of etiquette, social graces and to be in control at all times. Despréaux entered a palace room where Marie-Louise greeted Despréaux. Napoléon warned her. "You must do everything that M. Despréaux bids you, because I shall not take you to Paris until you are able to walk, to hold yourself correctly, and to dance."[24] In a lesson worthy of *My Fair Lady*, the dancing master cautioned Marie-Louise to lift her head and keep her chin from resting on her chest, while Napoléon reminded her to bear herself like an Empress. Napoléon demonstrated his bow, whereupon Despréaux added that in his position, he need not worry about bowing slowly. "Your majesty, respect is shown in the quickness with which one sinks to the ground and the slowness with which one rises . . . The bow of an inferior consists in sinking quickly and rising slowly." The waltz was next. Napoléon placed his arm on the master's shoulder and began. "As soon as I felt that the pressure he exerted would bring us both to the ground, I begged him to stop."[25] He ran to Marie-Louise and asked her to dance with him. Eventually Despréaux danced again with Napoléon, watching him leap like a goat and, at the same time, defend his bent knees on the advice of an old teacher. Napoléon was an avid listener and attempted to copy everything the master did, perspiring and working hard. Despréaux tried to reassure Napoléon that he thought he was dancing and holding court at Versailles, but, in truth, the new leader was like a duck out of water.

It is doubtful whether music interested Napoléon, but unsurprisingly Napoléon's tastes were in the direction of Italian music. He favored composers like Spontini, Cherubini, Salieri, Paër, Paisiello, and Della-Maria. The French School developed rapidly after the Revolution, and the works of Catel, Berton, Lesueur, and particularly Méhul, with the comic operas of Dalayrac, Gaveau, Nicolo (whose real name was Isoard), and Boïeldieu, illustrated the best qualities in French music.

In painting, the famed Jacques Louis-David (1748–1825) stood high above his contemporaries by right of genius, knowledge, and personal influence. He was one of the protagonists of the idealistic school, but whether he willed it or not, in his hands the orthodox doctrine was unable to shed its attitude of uncompromising rigidity. Diderot's preferred Jean-Baptiste Greuze and Jean-Honoré Fragonard, who lived till 1805 and 1809, respectively, were the survivors of a bygone age: the day of that charming, iridescent, dainty, eighteenth-century art was over.

Among the younger painters, Dominique Ingres (b. 1780) and Horace Vernet (b. 1789) were already at the height of their powers. In the Salons of 1812, Géricault (b. 1790) exhibited epoch-making pictures: all Romantic art was in them—thrilling, passionate, already triumphant. In painting, as in literature, the First Empire saw the dawn of Romanticism but with the difference that in literature, the classical school was definitely moribund and sterile even before the Revolution, while in art, its glorious period was that of Napoléon.

The art work of Horace Vernet was extremely sensitive to clothing styles and, as we have seen, provides marvelous depictions of life during the height of the Empire. Vernet painted and then published his description of fashion of the period. As a young man, he worked for the owner of the *Journal des Dames et des Modes* (a publication that began in 1797), learning quickly the importance of beautifully drawn fashion plates. The *Mercure de France* wrote about Vernet's presentation book of Parisian style entitled *Incroyables et Merveilleuses: Costumes et Modes D'autrefois, Paris 1810–1818,* demonstrating his talent for an "extreme fidelity to fashion with its gracefulness and the variety of details." Vernet looked at the Napoléonic period wistfully, celebrating through his illustrations both the austerity and the new energy of Napoléon's regime. The models for this book are not commoners, nor are they the old or new "nobility." In contrast to his painter father Carl Vernet's *Incroyables et Merveilleuses,* whose dress reflected a kind of distorted madness after the Revolution, the younger Vernet examines the inhabitants of the new rich, the Chaussée d'Antin and the rue de Mont Blanc financiers, speculators enriched by national funds and by army suppliers. The new rich, or "bon genre," are the direct ancestors of the modern snob. They came to their fortunes too quickly for their tastes in intellectual and artistic manners to develop. Their passion for fashion and style persuaded them of their rank and importance.

It is no mere coincidence that two of the greatest literary personalities at the beginning of the nineteenth century, René de Chateaubriand and Madame de Staël, belonged to a growing and vociferous opposition party to Napoléon's authoritarian regime. Another monumental giant of literature, Stendahl (Henri Beyle) paradoxically sustained his admiration and loyalty for Napoléon. Both Chateaubriand and Madame de Staël created the mood and sensibility that gave impetus to the Romantic Movement in France, and that influenced the creation of Romantic Ballet as an institution in the ballet world.

In 1801 Chateaubriand, a former emigré, published *Atala,* an episode detached from *Le Génie du Christianisme,* which first saw light in 1802, about the time of the promulgation of the Concordat, an alliance that established Roman Catholicism as the state religion in France. Chateaubriand demonstrated the poetic beauty and civilizing power of the Catholic religion; his book appeared at the right psychological moment. *Le Génie du Christianisme* rediscovered the living God of Christianity and substituted him for the Supreme Being of the philosophers and for the obsolete mythologies of the men of letters. His celebrated *Mémoires* evoked his longings; he returned to the Christian faith as if he were thunderstruck. He described his first real confession with a Catholic priest:

> I shall never experience a like moment in the whole of my life. If the weight of a mountain had been lifted from me, I should not have felt more relieved: I sobbed with happiness . . . How divine this religion is which can thus take hold of our best instincts! What moral precepts can ever take the place of these Christian institutions?[26]

He shook himself free from the outworn forms of the classicists. History was to him only the past restored to life; and this past he made others see as he himself saw landscape, color, and sunlight. Whatever he did was steeped in his own personality, his aloofness, his disillusionment. French Romanticism springs from these urges toward sublime nature, personal expression, and mysticism.

A portrait by Girodet shows Chateaubriand as an intense and dashing character in a double-breasted coat, with a windswept and slightly disheveled look. This style reflected the new Byronic spirit of dress and fashion, displaying his inner turmoil and heartfelt emotions (see, Frontispiece of his *Mémoires*). Certainly this picture contributed to his romanticized personality.[27]

In 1791, at the age of twenty-three, Chateaubriand departed for America to take part in a romantic scheme to discover the Northwest passage. The tragic tale of *Atala, or the Loves of Two Savages in the Desert* (1801) takes place in Louisiana and recounts the love story of an Indian woman and Chactas of the Natchez, an imaginary Native American tribe. The book was an immediate sensation. The beauty of his writing, the splendor of his vocabulary, and the harmony of his poetic sentiments invigorated French prose.

Chateaubriand entered the diplomatic service but resigned after the murder of the Duc d'Enghien. He then published *René*, another fragment of *Le Génie*; and, having formed the project of writing *Les Martyrs*, a kind of romantic prose epic depicting the antagonism between the Christian and pagan worlds, he set out for the Holy Land in 1806. Once again in his *Mémoires*, he recalled the beautiful women of his youth, often muses of his heartfelt artistry, specifically exotic Italian women, speaking of the sylphs of his passion:

> Could my sylph be hidden beneath the form of some of these dazzling Italian women? No: my wood-nymph has remained faithful to the willows of the meadows where I used to talk with her on the other side of the grove at Combourg . . . Yet there is a certain intoxication in this enchanted scene which goes to my head . . . Then the petty sights of the earth disappear, and I can find nothing to match the sudden change of scene but the old melancholy of my early days.[28]

Chateaubriand returned to Paris in 1807; he published *les Martyrs* in 1809 and his travelling impressions under the title of *Itinéraire de Paris à Jérusalem* in 1811. His dislike for Napoléon had become invincible; though he took few pains to disguise it, he was not subjected to any persecution. He was in no way a man of action and, therefore, was politically harmless. Moreover, his pride kept him aloof from affairs and all that he wrote reflected his

Fig. 46 Madame Queriau in the ballet *Sauvages de la Floride*, which was the site for a conflict between Napoléon and Chateaubriand. 1810. Courtesy of the Bibliothèque de l'Opéra.

Fig. 47 Portrait of Madame de Staël and her lovely daughter Albertine, by Elisabeth Vigée-Lebrun, Courtesy of the Chateau de Coppet, Geneva.

own personal views. Because he had a marvelous gift for reproducing with the precision of a painter and the sensibility of an artist his impressions of nature and of history, he succeeded in stamping his mode of thought and feeling upon his contemporaries. The Opéra's scenarios quickly responded to his influences, as did other theaters, where, for example, the Théâtre de la Porte Saint-Martin presented *Les Sauvages dans la Floride ou Atala* in 1807. Odd events influenced the performance of "Les Sauvages." The censor delayed its opening since its imagery seemed too reminiscent of the conflict between faith and love in Chateaubriand's writing. Also, the expected happy ending weakened the plot. Finally, the name of the ballet became *Les Sauvages de la Floride* with a renaming of the leading roles so that the ballet lost its close connection to Chateaubriand. He was probably unaware of this retake on his novel since he was traveling in Greece and the Holy Land. The effect of Chateaubriand's work did not reach its height for another generation, but during the Napoléonic era, he stood for reaction against Napoléon's dictatorship and what he called the narrow skepticism of the eighteenth century.

Another of Napoléon's strongest foes had charismatic status in France at the turn of the century. Madame de Staël was a romanticist and one of the first writers to use the word Romantic in its present sense. Banished by Napoléon from Paris after the Consulate (1799–1804), she made her home at Coppet, near Geneva, traveling to Germany, Italy, and France. In a portrait by Gérard that hangs in the Versailles Museum, one sees a woman who has a deep and thoughtful expression, dressed in the white bodice of her time, with soft lines and little puffed sleeves and a note of the foreign in her headress, a lush and colorful turban, showing her free vision of the moment and her interest in lyrical inspiration. She published her treatise, *De la Littérature considérée dans les rapports avec les Constitutions Sociales,* in 1800 and two novels in 1802 and 1807. It is not surprising that Napoléon dealt more severely with de Staël than with Chateaubriand, as her Salons were the focus of intense political and social dialogues and, she was a woman.

De Staël's novel *Corinne: Or Italy* (1807), an undisguised autobiography, became an eloquent protest in favor of women victimized by their social constraints (Corinne had to accede to her father's wishes at all times). De Staël spoke of romantic love in a scene where the peasants dance for the foreign interlopers and leave. Corinne was Italian but had to move to England where her father remarried. There she became sick with boredom. When her father died, she began to live the life of a famous poetess. In *Corinne* resides the contradictions that romantic literature and performance profess—love of abandon and vicissitude in conflict with the conventional and repressed, and love of genius opposed to love of duty. When Corinne danced the shawl dance, she summed up the character of Germaine as well as Juliette Récamier: "de Staël confronts not only the extraordinary woman with the ordinary man; she confronts the North with the South, Romanticism with classicism, reason with passion. *Corinne* is *De la littérature* in fictional form."[29]

In 1810, de Staël traveled to England, where she published *De l'Allemagne*. This most impressive discourse could not be published in Paris until after the fall of Napoléon in 1814. In *De l'Allemagne* she distinguished between the mental attitude of the Latin and that of the Teuton, and she revealed Germany to France and made the Romanticism of the North acceptable to the classical taste of the Latin cultures. Following the philosophers of the eighteenth century, she believed in the boundless progress of humanity; to her the march of European literature was a harmonious concert to which each people contributed its peculiar note. She revived Montesquieu's ideas on "climates"[30] in her treatise on evocations of the Romantic spirit, especially the fascination for what might be considered the dream world or the place where imagination comes into play. She called attention to the extraordinary *sturm und drang* German writers Goëthe, Lessing, and Schiller, those who evoked the *féerie*, the *farfelu*, the unknown, and the somber side of German literature, soon to be realized in various libretti of the Romantic ballet.

Napoléon and the ballet met in an unexpected and diabolic design. Early in Napoléon's career, on December 24, 1800, when he was on his way from the Tuileries to Hayden's oratorio *La Création* at the Opéra, assassins exploded an "infernal machine." Many were killed and injured, but Napoléon went unscathed. Violent indignation ensued and Napoléon, the police who had been taken unawares, and the best instructed royalists in Paris, vied with each other in accusing Jacobins. Fouché, and Napoléon's Minister of Police, who was adept at cooking up royalist conspiracies, drew up a list of suspects, and one hundred thirty anarchists and Jacobins were condemned to deportation. The Jacobin Party was disposed of, and the consitutional Republicans who had supported the Consuls in their policy of terror were reduced to compulsory silence. The real assassin went freely to America and became a Catholic priest. Two others were condemned and executed. In 1800, Napoléon's popularity increased through the general horror excited by the attempt on his life. Feeling rejuvenated, Napoléon installed himself in the Tuileries, the home of the kings of France—it was his symbolic rise to monarch.

Napoléon controlled all aspects of French theater. This was nothing new, as for hundreds of years, the king and the aristocracy strangled (albeit gently) most aspects of public showings. Though the Revolution gave important freedoms to theatrical presentations, Napoléon wanted more control and he began creating a regressive system for the theaters. In Paris there were to be only eight theaters, four "Grand Théâtres" (the Opéra, the Théâtre Français, the Opéra Comique, and the Odéon) and four "Secondary Theatres." It was to be very logical; every theater was to have a special character of its own, defined by the Minister of the Interior. All plays, operas, and ballets had to be supervised by the police before production. In the Departments, five towns were to be entitled to two permanent theatrical companies each, fourteen other towns to one company each. The Empire was divided into twenty-five theatrical areas, twelve of which were to be allowed two strolling companies each, and thirteen one company each. The companies and their repertories were placed under the supervision of the police and the Ministry of the Interior, the prefects, subprefects, and mayors. This highly structured and censored system kept the theatrical arts in a carefully synchronized relationship to the government and the audience.

Dances, Ballets, and Celebrated Artists

As Napoléon's armies marched across Europe and created a new awareness of foreign regions, on stage, recognition of national or folk origins inspired choreographers to simulate or reproduce what they thought was typical of a certain nation or people. Today we often call these dances character dances. The rise of nationalism, an upsurge of nationalistic feeling created by the Wars of Liberation, and the Romantic movement inspired a movement toward national costume in the streets and salons. An awareness of national characteristics that the ballet world reflected gave rise to the integration of

Fig. 48 P. L. Débucourt (1809), *La Dansomanie*. The postrevolutionary dance craze led to the opening of many dance halls and inspired Pierre Gardel's 1800 ballet. Gaston Vuiller, *History of Dancing* (London: Heineman, 1898), p. 189.

national dances and authentic costumes in many of the Romantic ballets; although, for other reasons, the romantic movement touted the inclusion of *couleur locale* where regional folk dances cum ballet choreography became an essential element in the ballets.

National dances, or character dances, represented a new trend in theatrical performance, especially France's love affair with Spain.[31] Along with this taste for the authentic came the reproduction of the costume, a garment that was immediately recognizable as from a specific region. This is not to say that ballet scenarios during the seventeenth and eighteenth centuries ignored the exotic costuming of particular places and nations. However, during the Romantic era, it became a narrative that represented a political and social awareness, a local knowledge, bringing to light the style and traditions of other people's dance forms.

The very first ballet of the nineteenth century performed at the Opéra, *La Dansomanie* (1800), turned out to be extremely providential—it parodied the old noble forms and dressed the dancers playing middle-class roles in what was worn daily on the streets of Paris. It also stressed the joy and delight in dancing for its own sake, reflecting the new dancing halls that had spread throughout the Empire.

La Dansomanie, a folie pantomime to music by Etienne Méhul, was presented on the 25th of Prairial of the year VIII of the Republic (14 June 1800). It was a lyrical, comical, and light-hearted work which expressed the laissez faire and loosen-up attitudes common to *fin de siècle* social life. In the programs, both men and women were still addressed as *citoyens* and *citoyennes*. Few ballets achieved as much success as *La Dansomanie*, with 245 presentations. In *La Dansomanie*, Gardel makes fun of the *genre noble* or the ballet dancing seen in the mythological constructs, just as we make fun of classical ballet today. The characters on stage looked like those whom one met in a Paris home or salon, with a flourish here or there. They were purposely familiar and comfortable to observe so that the new, growing middle-class audiences were able to identify with them.

The ballet *La Dansomanie* attempted to resolve arguments about technique and the love of dance. The scenario found its protagonist, Monsieur Duléger, in a desperate situation of sorts; he wants his daughter to marry an expert dancer, as he is madly, furiously in love with dancing. A number of dance variations were featured in this ballet as an excuse to show off the *Savoyard*, the *Basque* (a new invention), the *Gavotte de Vestris*, *la Tarentule*, as well as the dance of the Turks and the Chinese.

Duléger, or Mr. Light Step, listens to his dancing master with the same concentration as Monsieur Jourdain, the Bourgeois Gentilhomme of Molière, and practices all day long. A number of farcical moments dot the scenario, when for example, the valet Pas-Moucheté or Mr. Speckled Foot tries to imitate his master but, unfortunately, occasionally trips him.

Vestris

It was the star Auguste Vestris who distinguished the ballet. For some time, the public that visited Boulevard theaters longed for direct energy and excitement at the Opéra. Tired of allegorical and mythological constructs, they welcomed this light and buoyant story of a man who loved to dance. Following the lead from the great Vestris family represented at the time by Auguste Vestris, all the young men in this scenario rivaled one another in their foot competitions, called "les petits Vestris." The taste for dance increased dramatically, allowing a special expansion of the technique.

Auguste Vestris (his father Gaëtan assumed the title "God of the Dance") profited from internal troubles at the Opéra by breaking with traditional categories set up in the time of Pierre Beauchamps (1634–1705). The younger Vestris began to creatively combine the noble dance with character dancing, and even comic dancing, inventing a hybrid genre in which he exaggerated virtuosity for its own sake. The *entrechat*, the *cabriole-battue*, the *pirouette* in second position, and *attitude* and *arabesque* became his specialties. Ten years earlier he was a superstar and able to command a salary worthy of princes. An English newspaper, the *Public Advertiser*, pronounced that "Vestris will clear Ten Thousand Pounds by his condescension to take a Trip to this Country."[32] Vestris was noted for the *sissonne* or *pas de Zéphir,* a kind of rising from the floor with a lifted leg which gave the impression of flying. He was soon imitated by Louis Duport, a young rival who was even more given to lightness and aerial moves. While the public applauded, the critic Mr. Geoffrey was greatly distressed. He demanded to know:

> Where will dance go from here? Maybe one will be able to stop in mid air. . . . I do not know if we should thank this century for it, but the dance is one of the arts that has gone the farthest, and the one where the modern surpasses the old without contradiction. Who can count the *entrechats*, the *pirouettes*, the *tours en l'air*, the beats in front, to the side and I don't know how many ways to move the legs, the difficult combinations of unknown steps, until now a vocabulary way beyond my faculties. Never have the works of Racine or Corneille brought as much enthusiasm as today's ballets. A whole youth prefers the dance, the most physical of all the arts.[33]

Conservative elements in the audience found the unfamiliar and explosive changes in technique discomforting. Criticisms of Vestris, and especially of Gardel, abounded. Gardel's desire to "modernize" the Opéra caused some consternation when he filled his ballets with highly virtuosic movements. In a letter written in 1804 by a professor of dance at Versailles, Monsieur Papillon spoke glowingly of the great dancers at the Paris Opéra and of the ballet master Pierre Gardel.[34] Nonetheless, Papillon found fault with the "prevailing mania for pirouettes,"[35] reminding us that since the Revolution the audiences were unfamiliar with the traditional elegance of ballet; rather, they looked for flamboyant virtuosity and multiple turns. He called it an insidious disease that also infected the ballroom.

Taking to the air became a common theme in ballets, and the *Les Deux Silphes* (1801) pantomime at the Boulevard theater, L'Ambigu-Comique, was no exception. The presence of the sylph existed many years before the writings of Rousseau, Chateaubriand, and other Romantic poets who invoked the mysterious génie or sylph, such as the later 1832 *La Sylphide*. A common literary creature, the sylph, defined as an elemental spirit of air, was named in the Middle Ages by the Rosicrucians and Cabalists from the Greek Silphe, a kind of beetle or grub that turns into a butterfly. Mortals who preserved their chastity enjoyed familiarity with these gentle spirits, and deceased coquettes were said to become sylphs "and spirit and flutter in the fields of air."[36] J. G. A. Cuvelier's script for *les Deux Silphes* (1801) depicted a conflict between Indians from the New World against the malicious English, recollecting memories of the English colonial period in America. There was also a grand shipwreck, characters in beautiful beaded costumes, and a philosophical debate about the corruption of people who live in society.[37]

A sad event occurred at the Opéra in 1802, when the star ballerina, Mademoiselle Chameroy, succumbed rapidly to consumption. Friends, learning she was ill, "were convinced she was victim to fashion, remembering how after a performance during which she had been profusely perspiring, she would put on a light muslin dress that left her neck and shoulders bare, and go out into the chilly evening air without a shawl. She was also pregnant, and gave birth to a child shortly before her death."[38]

An extremely interesting, rather odd libretto, *Achille à Scyros*, about the Greek warrior Achilles, stood out both as an example of neoclassic material and as an illustration of blurred male/female personification. The powerful Achilles symbolized Napoléon's claim to power over all areas of French society, as the intellectual and artistic tenor of the Empire was entirely mediated by the government. Costume played an important role in the ballet as Achilles was dressed *en travesti* as a woman for much of the ballet. Achilles was choreographed by Gardel for performance at the Opéra December 18, 1804, with music by Cherubini, one of Napoléon's favorite composers. This was a time in Paris when the women, more than the men, wore the relaxed seductive tunic materials of the Mediterranean. Men preferred the military uniform or the black suit. The ballet offered a new twist for Imperial France's audiences; it upended traditional thinking, especially as Napoléon was crowned Emperor two weeks before this performance.

The usual and very charming stars appeared (Mesdames Coulon, Clotilde, and Gardel), with the famous heart throb, Duport, playing the travesty role of Achilles. In his preface to the scenario, Gardel mentioned that he had a difficult time finding someone whose looks and talent would satisfy the role of Achilles, but Duport surmounted the "dangers" of this role. "If some success this work that I made to please the public, I owe it to the artists in whom I confided these roles." Though it was not unusual for dancing women to play male roles, men at the Paris Opéra were not in the habit of wearing delicate dresses and impersonating young, delicate women. We witness this hesitancy in a letter that Duport wrote the day after the ballet's premiere. He confessed that he refused the role of Achilles "for a long time. I did not conceal the risk to which I would be exposed by the cross-dressing that he [Gardel] insisted upon. But the management was anxious to give this ballet during the Coronation festivities, pressed me and in the circumstances, I was honestly delighted to sacrifice my own interests."[39] Several years later, Gardel remade the role of Achilles for a woman, Mademoiselle Clothilde. However, it was a great mistake, as it caused tremendous consternation among reviewers. After three performances, she was replaced by a male. The critic described her efforts as "awkward and forced." "Her love scenes with Deidamia appeared cold, and the kiss that signals the victory over that beautiful princess was almost repellent. Nothing is more insipid on the stage than passion between one woman and another."[40] This critic's opinion had little effect later in the century when many travesty roles proliferated in opera houses across Europe.

Gardel

Pierre Gardel, with his sensitivity to political winds, was thankful to have survived the Terror. Through the monarchy, Revolution, Directorate, Empire, and Restoration, Gardel remained unshaken in his position and the works that he produced usually displayed conservative elements in ballet.

It is a paradox, but the Revolution empowered the leadership in the arts while disempowering the artists. Along with the directors of the Opéra and professors of dance, Gardel perpetuated the consolidation of power at the top in the corridors of the Opéra and places of performance. They authorized what happened in the studios and rehearsal areas and mandated the destiny of their underlings. No longer were dancers able to express their anger and dismay in the way Guimard and others did before the Revolution. Female dancers without aggressive mothers or rich patrons were unprotected.

Fig. 49 M. Beaupré in *Paul et Virginie* (1806). Domingo finds himself fascinated by his image in a mirror. Courtesy of the Bibliothèque de l'Opéra.

Despite his ironclad hold on his position as dancing master, Gardel sensed the invaluable primacy of the ballet technique that was rapidly growing and changing. He appointed the great teacher Jean-François Coulon responsible for the first *classe de perfectionnement* in 1806, an advanced exercise class in technical training. Dancers with great ambition who wished to progress quickly flocked to Coulon; it was their ticket to the top. He taught the burgeoning stars Geneviève Gosselin and Louis Duport and, not long afterward, Marie Taglioni.

One of the reasons Gardel held to the old-fashioned myths was that they were sure to pass the censor. Stories of ballets succeeded with the censor if they pleased Napoléon's personal sense of his heroic worth. Ballets of the Empire paid honor to stories such as Figaro that appealed to the rising middle class. He reminded them of themselves—on their way to fortune. The dancer, Louis Duport, created the ballet *Figaro ou La Précaution inutile* (1806) for a performance May 30, 1806, at the Opéra or, as it was known then, Théâtre de L'Académie Impériale.

In the preface, Duport excuses himself for inventing the role of Isabelle, servant to Rosine, in an effort to create more gaiety as well as a respect for the habits of the time. The costumes have a Spanish flavor, as the story takes place in Seville. The leading dancers are Duport and Mademoiselle Colombe. Almaviva (Duport), a young Spanish grandee, tries to woo Rosine (Colombe), Bartholo's ward, by disguising himself as a troubadour. Later in the ballet, he disguises himself as both a drunken soldier and a music teacher in order to have time with Rosine to tell her of his infatuation. Rosine, who is also in love with Almaviva, has little personal freedom because she is kept imprisoned against her will by Bartholo. Bazile, an insidious villain and Rosine's music master, aids Bartholo in his designs. Figaro, the Barber of Seville, plays his clever pranks with the help of Isabelle in order foster the love between Rosine and Almaviva. Almaviva succeeds in marrying Rosine in spite of the jealous precautions of Bartholo and under his very nose. Several character dances are performed—Spanish, French, German, Italian— as well as a light-hearted "valse," performed by Rosine and Almaviva.

In another restaging of a literary piece, Gardel's choreography for *Paul et Virginie* (24 June 1806) with music by Rodolphe Kreutzer reinterpreted Bernardin de Saint Pierre's story of two fatherless children who became lovers. In both the novel and the ballet, they live far from the corrupt society of Paris in Mauritius, where they grow up innocently and happily loving one another. Mauritiusor l'Isle de France is an island to the east of Madagascar that was held by the French from 1715 to 1814 until the English took it over. Virginie is forced to return to France by a harsh and wealthy aunt, but after a short time cannot bear being away from Paul. Unfortunately, there is a shipwreck, and in the novel she perishes due to her modesty in not wanting to save herself by stripping off her restrictive clothing and jumping into the sea where she would have been saved by a naked sailor. ". . . we could see him throw himself at her feet, and even try to pull her dress off; but she, loftily putting him aside, looked away."[41] Gardel's tale changes the ending so that it ends happily with Virginie and Paul uniting. His libretto gives evidence of the mixed colors on Mauritius, with character listings including Nègres, Créoles-Blancs, and Nègres-Marons. In the novel, the sailor's race is not mentioned, but in the ballet the sailor, "a black man kneeling at her feet, begged her to let him save her, but she refuses."[42] The most unusual feature of the ballet resided in its favorable approach to blacks. "In those days black faces were a rare sight in a European city, and the prevailing belief that the coloured races were inferior was somewhat akin to the attitude that a person's station in life was ordained by God."[43] Apparently the black faces shocked Parisians and Gardel decided to change the makeup from black to a shade of brown. Auguste Vestris played the ebullient role of Domingo, one of the black characters. His great moment came in his *pas* with a mirror, in which Domingo finds himself fascinated by his image. The stage in *Paul et Virginie* became a site where racial prejudices were clearly exposed. In other scenes, the issue of liberty and the slaves was openly discussed through the tale of Zobi, who was treated so miserably that he ran away from a villainous slave owner. One might say that skin color became costume here.

And costume clearly became the metaphor for freedom in this ballet. Not permitting the dress to interfere with her desire to reunite with Paul allowed Virginie her future happiness. Other characters in the ballet wore costumes that represented regional island dress. Striped trousers were commonly worn in tropical colonies and also by sailors, although it is unlikely that they were ever quite as short as they are shown (see illustrations). This was an early representation of shorts, worn possibly to give the dancer a juvenile appearance as well as allow him more freedom of action. The shorts were yellow with red stripes, the sash was purple, and the shoes were red— a veritable technicolor hero.

Since Napoléonic times encouraged plots with panache and grandeur, the plot of *Antony and Cleopatra* served the moment very well, with some curious soap-opera-like clues to Napoléon himself. Known for both for its heroic and tragic dimensions involving Antony's tragic love for another woman, it was entitled historic ballet and was choreographed by Jean Aumer to the music of Kreutzer for its debut on March 8, 1808. Aumer created a very complex, action-packed drama in which the imminent battle between the Romans and the Egyptians created the most interest. Antony's love for Cleopatra totally blinded him to important political events. As the love-hero who adored Cleopatra, Antony attempted to seduce her with his physique, even dressing up for her in various costumes in order to excite her interest, offering some odd clues to attitudes about costume and clothing. While Antony and Cleopatra die for their love in the course of the battle, Octavie, the betrayed wife of Antony, heroically rescues the Roman Emperor Octavian, thereby saving the Empire. Aumer courageously gave the ballet a tragic ending. The sad tale of the great Roman warrior Antony foreshadowed the eventual downfall of the Napoléonic era, despite Napoléon's popularity and the grandeur of the French Empire.

In 1810 a curious contretemps occurred that seemed to have political implications. Costumes for *L'Enlèvement des Sabines* were en route on a dark and stormy night. At one of the stops, thieves made off with thirty-two costumes for the Roman and Sabine soldiers. This catastrophe motivated a quick response. "Cynical observers might have found an historical parallel between the incident of the rape of the Sabine women by the early Romans and Napoléon's demand for the hand of Marie-Louise to ensure the continuation of his dynasty."[44] An important source of inspiration for this ballet was David's amazing painting, *An Intervention of the Sabine Women* (1799). A critic of this ballet in 1811 paid close attention to the costumes and their historical truth. They seemed to strike a discordant note, as they offered too great a contrast with the coarse clothing that was worn by the early inhabitants of the Tiber.[45]

A rising star at the Opéra, Mademoiselle Gosselin, attracted a great deal of attention, causing some to dismiss her abilities and others to laud them. "She could rise more often than usual on the point of her feet, presenting an elegant body supported, so to speak, on the big toe, or on a single toe-nail, and suddenly the public cried miracle . . . But from the strength of the toe, one's attention strays to the skill of her feet, and from there to the vivacity of her legs."[46]

One of the most popular comic ballet-pantomimes of the period was choreographed by the very talented and uncelebrated Louis J. Milon, second in command to Pierre Gardel. Unlike Milon, Gardel knew how to use people and sustain his reputation at the same time. With music by M. Persuis, the ballet *Nina ou la Folle par Amour* was presented on November 23, 1813.

The story, which ended happily, demonstrated France's continuing interest in the importance of hierarchy, in the concerns of the upper and middle classes for a well-placed marriage, and in the reality of women experiencing the hapless situation of being unable to influence their marital destinies. Some of the finest dancers of the period appeared in this betrayal and defeat haunted many scenarios of Napoléon's time. They not only made good stories, they reminded the public of Napoléon's inability to brook any disagreement or discontent. The Ballet Pantomime *L'Epreuve villageoise* by Louis Milon was presented on April 4, 1815, and was performed during the

Fig. 50 *L'Enfant Prodigue* (1812). *The Prodigal Son* presented an array of figures from the Bible. Costumes by François-Guillaume Menagéot caught the physical feel and texture of the times. Courtesy of the Bibliothèque de l'Opéra.

brief 100 days when Napoléon managed to rid Paris of Louis XVIII. In this thin plot, there are moments that seem so arbitrary that one wonders if Milon merely sought an excuse to get people dancing on stage. The scenario, a metaphor for lovers of different character traits and their problems, is reminiscent of a square dance. Reminded by Italian tradition of the "grotesque" performer, a comic indulges in all sorts of virtuosic tricks while executing clever *pas*, while an odd device of a monkey savant's portrait is used to intrigue and solve problems. A waltz and a gavotte are also featured in this ballet.

During this period, one of the most innovative and exciting scene designers for the Opéra was the artist Pierre Ciceri. Ciceri's first designs for the Paris Opéra date from 1815, when he decorated Didelot's version of *Flore et Zéphire*. This ballet is in itself a work of theatrical importance since when first staged in London in 1796 at the King's Theatre, it created a sensation due to its flying effects. The dancers traveled on wires, not as the descending deities of the eighteenth-century ballet but as figures in whom flight was yet another aspect of their dancing. It predicted the Romantic aerial dance of the sylphs that was to crystallize in the appearance of Taglioni in *La Sylphide* thirty-six years later.

Biblical references seem to inspire Gardel's *The Prodigal Son*, that loosely told the tale of Reuben, the father of Azaël, the prodigal son. However, rather than basing his ballet on excerpts from the Bible, Gardel explained that he took his ideas for the ballet from a poem by a little-known writer, Campenon. An array of figures from Biblical times inhabited this ballet, from the Israelite Reuben and his family to Lia, a young Moabite, Virgins of Gessen (Goshen), and black slaves. The tragic story line of lost love in this ballet resonated well with Parisians. Since there were numerous costume changes, the number of dressers had to be increased.[47] Set designs by J. B. Isabey and costumes by Ménageot reproduced common artistic renderings of Biblical scenes, recollecting desert costumes that we associate with nomadic peoples in a colorful and realistic manner.

Ironically, France's prodigal son, Napoléon, returned from Elba to retake control just one month before the presentation of *Prodigal Son*. Napoléon, who came to see the third performance, was rapturously received by the audience. Its scenario may or may not have been inspired by this event, but certainly it was influenced by the growing Romantic imagination and a tendency to create a pastiche of exotic styles.

CHAPTER 6

Restoration—One Bourbon Returns!
Louis XVIII and the Restoration (1815–1824)

After Napoléon's demise and exile to St. Helena, the coalition of the Bourbons sought to eliminate reminders of the Revolution and to return to the politics and culture of pre-revolutionary France. Conservatism began to reestablish itself in France, endangering the principles of freedom and liberty. When Louis XVIII, brother of Louis XVI, returned in 1814, the white flag floated again in France. Delegations of young girls dressed simply in immaculate muslin and carried beautiful bouquets of fleur de lys; they attended the new king while white doves were released and flew into the heavens.

Louis XVIII was born at Versailles on November 17, 1755. As a young man, he clearly appreciated the radical writings of Voltaire and the Encyclopedists. An outright enemy of Marie Antoinette, he still fled with the king and queen in their attempted escape to Varennes during the early days of the Revolution. Having avoided the guillotine, he settled in Brussels, which became the headquarters of the emigré French royalty during the Revolution. When his brother was executed, he declared himself regent and when the sons of Louis XVI died, he named himself Louis XVIII. From that time on, he traveled from one city to another while trying to convince the French from abroad of the royalist cause.

After Napoléon's defeats in 1813 and 1814, Louis XVIII's hopes were revived and he proclaimed his loyalty to Revolutionary principles, although these sympathies did not always synchronize with his background. During the one hundred days of Napoléon, Louis XVIII was forced to flee to Ghent. Finally, he returned to Paris, triumphant, but wearied by his exhausting wanderings. His reign was not without its difficulties and internal violence. Napoléon, quoted by Sorel, characterized Louis XVIII: "C'est Louis XVI, avec moins de franchise et plus d'esprit." ("He is Louis XVI with less sincerity and more wit.")[1]

The Restoration was a time when men turned away from flight of fancy and decoration. Men left the home and went to work in offices where seriousness and gravity accompanied their decision-making. Industrialism (a word coined by Saint Simon) ruled their lives as well as their countries and helped them to accumulate the wealth with which their wives' gowns and jewelry dazzled society. The sober black suit became the uniform of choice, just as it has been on Wall Street. These were times when people could afford just so much for their attire; they skimped in order to look like their superiors. The quality of costume sewing, beauty, and craftsmanship were replaced slowly by cheaper, more-mass produced goods. Excess was frowned upon, as middle-class mores became more pronounced.

Uniforms continued to be worn, though with much less pomp and decoration. The middle classes wanted everyone to look alike; thus, a general levelling occurred. Londoners favored fashions that were geared to the rural and outdoors, or they would imitate Paris modes made to look more practical and sober. Parisians were city dwellers and they liked to astonish and excite.

Women's clothes seemed to expand and bloom with the reinstitution of monarchy. Jewelry prescribed royal association, with chains consisting of eighteen links for Louis XVIII in sympathy for his regime. The color white of the Bourbons predominated until 1820, but women also enjoyed colorful evening dresses. Each part of the woman's dress, such as the sleeve, the neckline, the waist, etc., all became larger and more strongly etched. The tight waist and increasing volume of the skirt obscured women's natural lines.

Victorian thinking arrived early in France. The neckline became much higher than the neoclassic's, although during the evening, it might plunge again. Very clear distinctions in dress between night and day began during this time and may explain, perhaps, why the dancer who performed at night was given permission to have a lower neckline.

For street wear, the upper sleeve became much more pronounced. The women's body began to be divided up as it was before the Revolution into pieces that took shapes that were not necessarily natural or flattering to the female figure. Rigid outlines of cones and cylinders lessened the softness of neoclassic lines and distorted and concealed the upper body. Ankles began to show, calling attention to the pronounced trimming on the skirts.

Still there were those who continued to wear the neoclassic fashion. Turning away from Napoléon's pervasive Roman Empire themes, women followed a more Grecian style. They participated in the general return to Greek sources rather than emphasizing a romanticized ideal of the Empire.[2]

Fashion magazines were the major barometers of upper-class taste and proliferated during the Restoration. They continued to inform the rising middle classes of important social and intellectual strategies. Approximately thirty to sixty pages long, published weekly or monthly, they boasted sales in other areas such as Amsterdam, the Rhine, and Germany. Their pages were filled with gossip and advice. *The Journal des Dames et des Modes* of March 26, 1815, a typical example of the period, contained several poems, an article on the English countryside, another on the clothing of Ancient Egyptians, and one on gambling houses and their dangers, with cautionary anecdotes signed by "Guillaume Franc-parleur" (or William Frankly-Speaking). Columns also included rules of etiquette, with references as to how the English observe customs. Births of the wealthy were listed as well as deaths and marriages. Theatrical events were mentioned, as were reviews of extremely successful performances. Sometimes one story threaded its way through a year's publications. For example, June 18, 1815 the story of "Alice ou la Sylphide" became serialized in many issues. Occasionally, an article in French also appeared in German, as there were a number of German readers in Paris.

The most important part of the fashion magazine dealt with what people were wearing and what they should wear. One long article, told in a story-like mode, described the well-dressed woman going for a walk. Another article about the popularity of hats said that they all tended to look alike. In the tradition of Horace Vernet's illustrations, fashion plates were carefully drawn and meticulously described, with specific fabrics, colors, and decorations. Some milliners and modistes advertised themselves.

By 1815, fashion journals were advertising fuller skirts at the bottom, worn just off the ground, which beautifully suited new dance crazes. Waists were beginning their descent and hair was simple and natural. Military fashion favored cords and frogs as trimmings with large, feathered bonnets. Toward the middle of the first decade of the nineteenth century, a gradual trend in the direction of a more decorated costume could be seen in France. Skirt bottoms gained roulettes or gores and flared them out in flounces and pleating. And again, a return to the natural waistline and corset, "the deformity once more drawing the steeled bodice upon the bruised ribs," according to *Mirror of the Graces* (1811).

In order to create more attention for new styles, fashion journalists recounted stories of beautiful women attending the famous bals de *l'Opéra* or major occasions of political and social import. In 1815, many balls celebrated the Restoration, including those associated with the Congress of Vienna, an international conference held after the banishment of Napoléon, aimed at territorial resettlement and restoration to power of the crowned heads of Europe. Social dance and the waltz contributed to the social framework in this time of hope for monarchies. The Congress of Vienna was facetiously called the *congrès dansant,* or the dancing congress, because the participants divided their time between the redistribution of Europe and the dancing floor. Talleyrand is cited as having said, "the congress is dancing but is not making progress." There were two featured waltzes, one during which the couple stood prudently side by side with changes of arms and hand holds, doing intricate steps threaded through a series of complex floor patterns called the *valse mondaine*, and another during which the partners faced each other and turned again and again around one another, spinning in counter clockwise pathways called the *valse populaire* or vernacular waltz.[3]

Continuing to affect fashion was the influence of German literature, thanks to the publications of Madame de Staël. It also gave prominence to Goëthe, whose dramatic works were translated in 1821. His *Faust*, driven by a despairing, satanic energy, proved a fitting companion to the Byronic heroes, as did his *Werther*. Werther, a young student, falls in love with Charlotte, who is betrothed to his friend Albert. He has no wish to betray his friend, but he cannot conquer his passion. He absents himself, returns, and finds Charlotte married to Albert. He fancies that she is not entirely happy, but when one day he makes love to her, she banishes him. Werther's misery driven by his overworked sensibilities was echoed in Goethe's descriptions of nature and storms. Realizing that his passion is hopeless, he commits suicide. Werther was found at the sad ending of the book in the frac coat of his day; he was "fully dressed with his boots on, in blue frock coat, and yellow waistcoat."

The fashion of wearing Werther's unique costume drew attention to a new inscription on the body where those who imitated Werther were bound together in some kind of secret cult. "By dressing alike, young male readers of Werther formed a social identity among themselves."[4] Goethe himself created a sensation by wearing the clothes of his literary figure on a visit to Duke Karl August. "Clothes after all revealed the intentions of the soul: and when worn consistently as a uniform, their signification could be viewed with the same stability as the nose and forehead of J. C. Lavater's studies in personality."[5]

Similarly, the works of Chateaubriand continued to exercise an even more compelling effect on the stage and in life. His call for a religious revival echoed the Restoration's interest in returning religion to the people. "There was now a zealous episcopate and a lower clergy growing in number and in devoutness. Religious houses for women increased from 1,829 in 1815 to 2,875 in 1830."[6] As Romanticism spread, literature became more and more important in the daily lives of the middle classes. Literature was not at first hostile to the Restoration, which "represented emancipation from the straitjacket of the Empire and an age of poetry after prose."[7] The new king took pleasure in reading poetry, especially admiring the early work of Victor Hugo, and offered him a modest pension to help his career along.

The Stage and Impropriety

At the ballet, the Restoration represented a period of important growth and transition until the birth of Romantic ballet; it was a time when variety and entertainment distracted the audiences concerned about their faraway soldiers at war. Comic opera tales amused and took over the Opéra with silly situation comedies, easy laughs, mistaken identities, mismatched lovers—all making fun of people's foibles.

Stage costumes resorted to the same fanciful, nonsensical qualities, defying historical truth and instituting the passion for the troubadour period, as Théophile Gautier entitled it. The fascination for and romanticization of the Troubadour style[8] may have been partially inspired by David's costume drawings for a national dress.[9] The style returned nostalgically to the dash and panache of the cape, sword, and broad-shouldered, corseted, heavy materials that recalled an imaginary time of power, when men were men, and the seduction of women excited a great deal of interest as conquest in other arenas took prominence. One of the outworn traditions that struggled to hold on to its sumptuary importance in ballet was the categorizing effect of the three genres—the noble, the demi-caractère, and the comic. As the century progressed the genres fused, especially with the young Vestris' performances, so that it was practically impossible to tell the difference between them. Provisos of the three genres continued to be described but not taken seriously. Originally, in the seventeenth century, they were a way to channel dancers into roles for which they seemed best suited. The taller figures with great aplomb and noble bearing were given the heroic roles and costumed accordingly. The comic dancers were usually of shorter stature, more rustic with many tricks and humorous qualities—akin to the Italian grotescchi performers. Also, they were likely to do national dances such as the bolero or the pas des Sabotiers. They used such props as tambourines and played furies, while demi-caractère dancers danced the roles of zephyrs, sylphs, troubadours, bergers, Greeks, and Romans. Their technique contained many feats of strength (grand ballon) and tours de force. A majority of the dancers fell into this realm. The Revolution virtually annihilated the importance of noble roles which were mostly danced by men. The result was that gradually the authority of male dancers diminished at the Paris Opéra.

One ballet scenario describing the magic of southern climes recounts an incident during the carnival in Venice when disguises and masks added to the thrill of seduction. For some time tourists and spectators rushed to Italy during Carnaval season in order to share the excitement of masquerades, parades, lively evening activities, and the general free living that occurred during those precious weeks. Goethe even wrote an important journal about the *Carnaval* in Rome. On February 22, 1816, the Opéra presented *le*

Fig. 51 The beauteous Mademoiselle Bigotini in *Le Carnaval de Venise* (1816) wearing a lovely, if skimpy, confection. Imagine what the Bishop of Durham would have said about this costume. Courtesy of the Bibliothèque de l'Opéra.

Carnaval de Venise ou la Constance à l'Epreuve by the clever and resourceful Louis J. Milon. Starring were the crowd-pleasing Bigotinni and Albert as well as an assortment of other dancers. The exquisite Bigottini played a Roman lady of extreme finesse, an elegant waist, and, pretty figure. Her popularity and talent brought her the prestige of *premier sujet* in 1815.

The ballet begins with the Countess and her ladies trying on various fashions for the great Carnival; they mask themselves for the party. Don Carlos demonstrates his love for the Countess as the others prepare. The libretto calls attention to several women with the Countess who are deemed "ugly" and unable to compete with her beauty. Heeding the more common taste, one avid suitor is taken out and beaten so badly for his sincerity that a doctor must be called. In a twist on the typical melodrama, in which the Burgermeister kidnaps a gracious young thing, the Countess abducts Don Carlos in order to force him to prove his love for her. Indeed, he is eventually seduced by the Countess in her gorgeous costume of *la Bohémienne*. Bigottini's costume displayed her shoulders and back as completely nude, the breasts almost nude, with a very light, white tunic dress cut above the knees, with fur trimming and triangular cut-outs garnished with little bells, in other words, a little shift reduced to its simplest expression.[10]

Fig. 52 A Bath Ball or Virtue in Danger (1820). The Assembly Rooms at Bath were the site for many balls of great social importance. The popularity of décolleté dresses caused much conversation. Courtesy of the British Museum Print Collection.

In contrast to the rigid and narrow-minded rules handed down by Napoléon's administrators, costumes at the Opéra now seemed to be free from restrictions still imposed elsewhere. Dancers had little trouble running and dancing across the stage due to the light, even scanty, costumes. Parisians, used to the latest neoclassic ephemera, were not shocked by such a lack of modesty, but foreigners remarked upon it. "The tunics and skirts were, in fact, not only short, but diaphanous, as were the bodices. One was not bored at the Opera!"[11]

The opposite was true of men dancing in the ballet studios. Too much of the leg was covered in their ballet classes due to a new trouser fashion. The trend at the Opéra, even in the studio, was to be in style with the times, sometimes to the detriment of the dancers' technique. Gardel and Milon, the Opéra's ballet masters, stated, "When they recommended that the male pupils should wear breeches instead of trousers, it was to enable the teachers to observe the articulation of the knee."[12]

Two specific works that the Opéra produced brought escape and excitement to its audiences. The scenarios spoke of women at risk and evil gods who needed to be destroyed, scenarios that people found pleasing, as they had recently rid themselves of one god and were on the verge of a new industrial age. *Les Sauvages de la Mer du Sud*, a ballet pantomime also by Louis J. Milon, second Ballet Master, was performed on November 26, 1816, at the Académie Royale de Musique. Costumes for this ballet attempted to defy the imagination with fanciful African and Indian touches. On an island in the South Seas, the king of the sauvages makes offerings to an evil god by performing sun dances. A young woman, Maheine, is courted by the king, who also tries to attack her. Her father saves her. They discuss who should be sacrificed—virgins are brought in—Maheine the heroine finds herself with the virgins to be sacrificed. They all wear collars with red beads. Everyone cries out when they see what seems an omen—a burning ship stranded on a reef. Groups from the ship are led by the Frenchman Dorville and his *nègres*, who flee the flames. They discover Maheine who has returned to consciousness after having fainted. She does her own sun dance while Dorville executes a French dance reflecting a curious interplay between the ruling Europeans and the "other" exotic *bons sauvages*. In an attempt to undermine and scare the Indians, the *nègre* pretends to be an *Idole*. The ship's captain arrives to bring peace between the intruders and the Indians. They throw themselves at the Indian King. The idol of the evil god is destroyed, wherein Indian and European dances take place. Dorville, the Frenchman liberates them. He takes Maheine back with him to Europe. The foreigner invades Europe as Europe conquers the "savages." Could we imagine a more eurocentric and senseless piece? An interesting aside to this ballet is that the dancers made a scene before the premiere, insisting that they

CLARY, grand costume. (Mlle Bigottini)

Dans Clary, Ballet Pantomime en 3 Actes. (Accademie R^{le} de Musique

Fig. 53 Mademoiselle Bigottini elaborately dressed in her costume for *Clari or The Promise of Marriage* (1820). The gold trimming, crown, and elegant line emphasized the wealth of her position. Courtesy of the Bibliothèque de l'Opéra.

did not want to play "savages." It was announced on the posters as *Les Sauvages de la mer du Sud*, a "last minute change from *Les Sauvages*, as it was entitled on the programme."[13] In addition, the site of this South Sea Island ballet could well have been Tahiti. At that time in 1816, Tahiti was struggling to maintain its old religion while missionaries were converting the populations to Christianity. The ballet did not get good reviews.

In 1820, the libretto *Clari, ou la Promesse du Mariage* demonstrated how melodrama and soap opera mingle. Unlike *les Sauvages*, the complex story line had some merit. *Clari*, performed on June 19th, was choreographed by Louis J. Milon, while the music was composed by the *chef d'orchestre*, Monsieur Kreutzer. Some of the most talented and established dancers starred in this ballet—Milon, Coulon, Fanny Bias, Saulnier, and Albert. Costume made this ballet notable.

Auguste Garneray's costume designs for Clari caused a sensation, due to their clinging lines. Garneray, the costume designer best known for his vision of the wispy female, revealed the delicate beauty of the dancer's body. He loved the simply-clad body with delicate, clean lines and preferred angelic white—white silk, white satin, and silver or diamond decorations. He was free to clothe the puerile Clari in a beautiful white dress with silver clusters and gold braid, tight under her breasts and falling to her mid-calf, with little ribbon bows everywhere. Clari's costumes, as with the dresses in the street in 1820, were flared in an almost bell-shaped skirt. Garneray, who preferred to costume "ballerinas," exceeded himself with his materials and colors. The costume historian Fischer commented upon Garneray's fanciful approach in the following manner, "A character on stage who walks always represents a certain kind of reality, whereas a character who jumps frolics in a dream and leads his costume designer along with him. And, in a dream, everything is permitted."[14] Garneray created the perfect illusion with his dancer's costume. *Les Pages du duc de Vendôme* opened on October 18, 1820. In the preface, choreographer Jean Aumer told the public that he hoped they would not find this work frivolous, but the administration wanted this story to be appropriate to the theater of the Salle Favart. That was quite different from the Opéra—it was the main stage for comic opera. Recently engaged by the Opéra as their dancing master, Aumer had to wait until the new Opéra house was constructed on the rue Peletier. Of topical interest because it portrayed the French fighting in Castile, this ballet brought attention to the civil war that had begun in Spain in 1820. The libretto prophesied events that would eventually occur, as when several years later, in 1823, a French army was dispatched to restore the Bourbon King of Spain. Their presence affected a quick solution, and French intervention re-established the king on his throne without difficulty.

VICTOR   (Mlle Bigottini)

Dans les Pages du duc de Vendôme. Ballet, pantomime en 1 acte. (Acad^mie R^le de Musique.)

Fig. 54 Costume for Victor danced by Mademoiselle Bigottini in *les Pages du duc de Vendôme*. The tradition of women in men's roles became very popular and lasted throughout the century (1820). Courtesy of the Bibliothèque de l'Opéra.

MAD.^{me} de St ANGE

Dans les Pages du duc de Vendôme, ballet pantomime en 1 acte. (Académie R.^{le} de Musiq

Lith. de G. Engelmann.

Fig. 55 The costume designer Auguste Garneray dresses Madame de St. Ange of *les Pages du duc de Vendôme* in elaborate materials and ornamentation. Courtesy of the Bibliothèque de l'Opéra.

Une SYLPHIDE. (Mlle Brocard)
Dans la mort du Tasse, Opéra en 3 actes, (Acad R^le de Musique)

Fig. 56 Mademoiselle Brocard in a sky-blue transparent tunic dotted with stars in the opera *La Mort de Tasse* (1821). Garneray flourished in an atmosphere that encouraged his talent and innovation. Courtesy of the Bibliothèque de l'Opéra.

Many commentators remarked upon the continuing trend of the early nineteenth-century taste for scanty ballet costumes. Without the eagle eye of Napoléon's administrators and censors, Garneray was at liberty to indulge his imagination. In the opera *La Mort de Tasse* (1821), a *succès ébouriffant* (a startling success), Mademoiselle Brocard took the role of the Sylphide. Occasionally these sylphides had a certain realistic quality. Brocard wore a sky-blue transparent tunic, dotted with stars. Thirty years later, the critic Castil Blaze was still dreaming about her. One could see the whole body with wings and a crown and a tiny amount of gauze. Garneray's short reign did not limit the influence of his sensitive and imaginative designs, as he demonstrated by placing a fairy in a blue azure dress side by side with a Turkish soldier in red culottes.

The following year, Garneray designed skimpy raiments in the ballet for the opera *Aladin* (1822). Bigottini wore a *bustier* molded in a skin-colored jersey, a kind of very short, transparent and peach-colored loin cloth, along with a white oriental scarf floating along her legs. Aladin's ornamental costume was just as impressive with its feathers, bracelets, necklaces, scarves with pearls, and a medallion with jewels around his neck. Mademoiselle Caroline's costumed role was even more shocking than Bigotinni's. She wore a white muslin, thigh-length tunic. Other dancers who played *bayadères* also wore practically nothing—a little half-skirt, all of it transparent, with a pearl-decorated scarf over the shoulders and the hips. Here, Garneray created an oriental fantasy, the kind of hothouse setting that exploited the public's taste for fantasy and exoticism.

The new opera house provided a training ground for the ingenious decorators, Pierre-Luc-Charles Ciceri and Louis-Jacques Daguerre, the remarkable inventor. Daguerre created the designs and Ciceri executed them. Daguerre was also known as the inventor of the diorama and the daguerreotype. Since their visual talents exceeded all others, they revolutionized stage design by using gas lighting for the opera *Aladin* in 1822. Traditionally, the curtain was not lowered at the Opéra between the acts of a ballet or opera. Scenery had to be constructed so that scenes changed without too much difficulty.[15] In addition, eighteenth-century stage perspectives were still being used until this moment when now, with, the lowering of a drop cloth or curtain between acts, a more elaborate and naturalistic setting could be devised. Daguerre's sumptuously expensive sets in *Aladin* cost 170,000 francs.[16]

Few ballets from the nineteenth century have survived to our time, but *Cinderella* or *Cendrillon* is one such example. Mademoiselle Bigottini as Cendrillon and Ferdinand Albert in the role of Prince Ramir appeared in this highly touted work choreographed by Albert, first produced in London

Fig. 57 Costume design by Garneray for a female soloist in *Aladin: ou La Lampe Merveilleuse* (1822). The jeweled embroidery gives the costume its "oriental" character, although the skirt closely follows street fashions.

LA FÉE MÉLISE. (Mlle Caillet)

Fig. 58 La Fée Mélise in *Cendrillon* (1823). This attractive and romantically exciting ballet still attracts large audiences. Courtesy of the Bibliothèque de l'Opéra.

in 1822 and then put on at the Opéra in 1823. Rossini's well-known opera, *La Cenerentola* was performed originally at the Théâtre Italien in 1822, but the choreographer opted for the musical composition of Ferdinand Sor. Based upon the fairy tale by Charles Perrault, the heroine suffers unconscionable treatment while her stepsisters and stepmother prepare for the ball. A fairy queen transformed from an old beggar lady, magically produces a shimmering dress and carriage for Cendrillon's entrance to the ball. There she meets her Prince, but he loses her when the clock strikes midnight. A glass shoe remains and becomes the precious clue that is needed to prove that she was the person whom the Prince loves. One unusual scene in the ballet contains a variation for twelve attendants to Cendrillon; it was a light contra dance with Spanish and French modes. Another highlight of the ballet takes place when the beggar woman is miraculously transformed into the fairy queen. Apparently, the costumes were designed by Monsieur Albert, the choreographer.[17] In the catalogue of scene and costume designers at the opera, Garneray is listed as the costume designer for Cendrillon. As often in the past, the women's ballet costumes in *Cendrillon* differ very little in shape and embroidery from women's ordinary clothes of the time, except, in this case, for the pseudo-Renaissance hat. A similar hat is worn by the male partner, whose skirted tunic maintains one of the traditions of the eighteenth century while the hose and leg-of-mutton sleeves echo the early Renaissance.

In June 1824, the exhausted and overweight Louis XVIII died and Charles X succeeded him. Fashions paid increasing attention to lowering the waistline and a smaller waist. Skirts became even fuller, puffed out by more and more petticoats. Emphasis below the waistline focused on the skirt's back, with pleating and cotton molds attached to an underskirt. Hair styles, accentuated by ornaments, continued the trend toward more expanded shapes. The toes of shoes gradually became more square as ribbons laced up the ankles and held the shoes in place.

The construction of the bodices of ballroom gowns also changed so there was room for the arms to move more freely. Changing styles accommodated ballroom dances such as the Quadrille and Cotillion, for which fancy stepping drew sighs, such as pirouettes ending in attitude. Not only did the legs and feet have technically difficult movements, but the arms, as well, had to be placed in careful positions. Ballroom-dancing masters, often ballet masters, trained their students in the ballet vocabulary, demanding exceptional amounts of time for learning and perfecting the patterns and steps. In his *Code of Terpsichore*, the famed Carlo Blasis gave detailed instructions about the waltzing steps, including the arms, which "should be kept in a rounded position, which is the most graceful. . . ."[18]

Louis XVIII's relatively peaceful nine years presaged a more tumultuous future. It was a time of transition when the middle classes came into power, displacing the affectations and pretensions of the aristocracy. The Industrial Revolution transposed the economy as well as the decisions of state, and the way men and women wore clothing both on and off the stage.

CHAPTER 7

Pale Goddesses on the Street during the Romantic Movement

Charles X Ruled France from 1824–1830

The Romantic movement grew out of a reaction to the Age of Reason. The sweeping away of religious corruption effected a reevaluation of the meaning of religion. Probing questions were asked about the benefits and adversities of colonial expansion and the Industrial Revolution. These questions were not answered successfully by Charles X, whose reign led to a deeply divided and tumultuous France.

Charles X succeeded Louis XVIII to the throne and ruled France from 1824–1830. Charles, the Count d'Artois, was the younger brother of both Louis XVI and Louis XVIII and a grandson of Louis XV. An emigré from the Revolution in 1789, he conspired against the Revolution and spent several years in England. Unfortunately, he returned at the Restoration and led the Ultras, i.e., the ultra-Royalist party, after the Restoration. They were uncompromising believers in absolute monarchy and the supremacy of the church. His coronation at Rheims (May 29, 1825) was an occasion of great pomp, with so much religious emphasis that it shocked many people.

Hostility aroused by his anti-liberal, pro-Catholic policy culminated in the 27–29 July Revolution of 1830 that brought the rule of the elder branch of the Bourbons to an end. Charles X abdicated on July 31, 1830. Thereafter he spent his life in exile, partly in Edinburgh (at Holyrood) and partly in Prague. He died in 1836.

The proponents of conservatism and regressive government during Charles's brief reign could not cope with the massive economic changes that disturbed the core of French society and led to the revolutions of 1830 and 1848. Intellectuals, poets, dramatists, and choreographers sensed the

Fig. 59 Les Trois Divinités du Jour, Modes de 1830. Extravagance rules fashion aesthetics in the style of the day with wild hair styles, balloon sleeves, and bouffante skirts. Courtesy of the Cabinet des Estampes.

La Mode,

Janvier 1830

Pl. XX.

Vol 2 Liv 1er

Coiffure en rubans, par Mme Guichard-Pavy, Rue de Grammont, No 15; Robe de velours, manches à la Henri 3, manches de dessous en crêpe lisse; fourrure en martre.

L'Administration de la Mode est Rue du Helder, No 43; et chez Dureuil, Place de la Bourse.

Fig. 60 A fashionable lady wearing outrageous hair and sleeve styles. And what is that strange scarf around her neck? Courtesy of the Cabinet des Estampes.

disruptive influences reflected by a growing and angry labor force. Fashions reproduced outmoded beliefs in women's role as the decorative enchantress whose public role was at odds with her growing sense of autonomy and need for independence.

The heartlessness of the old régime found its revenge in the nefarious corset and the return of the waistline in the early 1820s. "Fashion in the streets disregarded the earlier pared-down, figure-clinging style of dress and a start had been made on the build-up of outer garments and even more, on the growth and variety of under garments."[1] Many petticoats gave width and weight to the skirts. Different sorts of stockings, body suits, or tights were popular. Ladies began to wear pantalettes for leg protection from the cold or from a sudden breeze that would lift their skirts and compromise their modesty. Warm outerwear consisted of *pelisses* (capes) that followed the normal lines, emphasizing a thin waist. Shawls and capes were large and meant to cover all the dress materials.

Gradually the tightening of laces became exaggerated. The unnatural *gigot* sleeves grew to an enormous size, while the hooped dress balanced these additions. Nineteenth-century fashion dictated that when the waist was constricted, the shoulders must be padded and the skirts must shoot out from the tiny waist as quickly and briefly as possible.[2] Sleeves were stuffed with pads of feathers. They may also have been spread out by steel springs, used to eliminate their interference in normal activities; they lifted up the voluminous material and attached it to the shoulder.

Dress was prompted by specific occasions and the time of day. In the morning, women spent time at home with household activities, often in a more relaxed, plainer style. When out visiting, women wore more stylish dresses, though they were of a more practical nature since walking demanded a freer fashion. *Mondaine* women would change their dress for dinner and evening wear.

If a dance were attended, the ball gown would be extravagant and *décolleté*. Evening colors became somewhat stronger, with magenta, purple, bright green, and blue among the favorites. Heavy types of fabric were also popular, among them plush, velvet, heavy woolen, silk, and brocade. Trimmings and embroidery, beads, fringes and all kinds of elaboration were in favor again. The picture of an elegant lady was completed by a precious cashmere shawl. The lady's shoe had a low heel, but that was not to last.

Women wore plaits in the back of their heads fastened with a comb. Ringlets at the sides of the face were often made of curls of red-dyed silk that hung in two puffs from the forehead and were fixed by means of a band tied around the head. Puffs were chosen to match the women's hair color and, though we may not see these curls as particularly attractive, it was an easy way to make the hair look dressed with little effort.

The width that was given to the face by the sausage-shaped curls was enhanced by cart-wheel hats replacing the soft bonnet that reached huge proportions with trimmings of grass, flowers, feathers, and stiff ribbon bows, especially for street wear. From 1824 evening hairstyles echoed this general shape in the Apollo knot, a virtual parody of classical curls, and "upstanding loops of plaited hair, decorated with feathers or skewered with Glauvina pins."[3]

By 1828, a profile consisting of huge sleeves with a maximum width around the elbow and a dropping waistline, began a downward look that was emphasized by a V-shape of pleated folds on the front bodice. The ballerina's tutu followed the fashion and emphasized the long line of the waist by becoming V-shaped. Smaller hats also began to find favor, with upturned brims "framing the face in a narrow oval."[4]

Buckram stiffened skirts and sleeves, and petticoats became heavier, wider, and more numerous. The ostentation of the Victorian woman was on its way and was much sought after by the middle classes. The poor could not compete, as they had been able to do in the brief time of simple cottons. In the August 1828 *La Belle Assemblée*, "The Cabinet of Taste," a correspondent from Paris bemoans the fact that:

> Never, I believe, was the mania for dress carried to the excess as it is at present: no expense is spared and even if a lady wish to be economical, and have the dresses which last year she put on but once, altered to the present fashion, her marchande de modes or her extravagant soubrette, takes care to assure her it is impossible.[5]

Writers criticized unserious trends in dress. In the paper "Manners, Fashion and the Power of Dress," Ernst Moritz Arndt argued convincingly for designs that enhanced dignity and humanity rather than frivolity.[6]

Fashion magazines contributed to nostalgia for other eras, now that neoclassicism had had its day. An appetite for Gothic literature and architecture spread throughout Europe. The Gothic style of architecture prevailed in the rebuilding of parliament buildings or cathedrals, and Renaissance palaces and banks brought this taste for the past into everyday living.

If fashion magazines promoted the longing for past times, they also provided valuable information about women's problems, such as how to find an appropriate husband or how women should spend their time. For example, the February 29, 1828, issue of *Petit Courrier des Dames* stresses the value of exercise for young women. The word dance is not mentioned, however, a recently published book entitled *Gymnastique des Jeunes Filles* is reviewed. An interesting quote from this issue concerns women's health and challenges Victorian attitudes that relegated women to a submissive inertia:

But if you are wise and sophisticated, you must know that one does very little for the physical education of young women. We do not accustom our young girls in exercises that would add to their physical strength without ruining their sense of grace and which would fortify their constitutions and would assure them all the advantages of good health. Also how often does one see in Paris, women whose pallor and exhausted and debilitated state, portray their weakness and their habitual malaise. Country folk are proud of their robust demeanor, as are provincials, and while admiring the elegance and good taste of Parisians, they consider them almost sickly.[7]

In Germany, fashion magazines wielded great power. The Napoleonic wars had stirred nationalistic interests and culture, encouraging other countries to compete with the modes of London and Paris. German national costumes were designed, but, unlike Paris, they remained national costumes rather than major fashion plates for the world to copy. Stronger economies depended upon healthy industry. Speaking about the importance of creating a more vigorous production of goods in German, many commentators stressed the fact that fashion journals "would, by instilling in consumers new desires for luxury goods, directly assist in the development of German-based manufacturing. Out of desire would come higher consumer demand, which would in turn produce a number of economic benefits."[8] Germany had watched the competitive relationship that developed between England and France in the late eighteenth century. The German fashion publication *Mode Journal* described fashion culture as a struggle between France and England. Germans were forced to rely on mediated representations and were therefore able to make more intelligent judgments about the fashion fads of the moment.

Women who lived in urban centers such as London and Paris, longed for dazzling and decorative effects that linked what they wore to exotic places and meanings. They sought elegance, ornamentation, and luxury in the newly manufactured and highly-advertised products of the industrial age. Illustrations of fashion plates vividly described the style of the moment. They demonstrated "how one style evolves into another and one social aspiration dissolves into another until women, within two generations or less, may seem almost to change into a different species."[9] They may not, however, disclose reality. Rather they allow us to glimpse the care-free young and exciting models. It never rains, someone else makes the beds, animals willingly give up their furs, and birds their feathers 'for our adornment.'[10]

The industrial age brought with it a fascination for machinery and gadgets. Inventions made possible by machines excited more interest than a beautifully hand-embroidered skirt. Fewer people knew the difference

Fig. 61 Caricature of corset tight-lacing, W. Heath, "New Machine for Winding Up Ladies," 1827. Courtesy of the British Museum Print Collection.

between good and bad clothing or a well-made garment. New methods of cutting men's frock coats gave a man with a narrow chest a broader girth. English tailoring became the most important influence in men's dress. London was the place for men to shop for fine wools and simple designs that suited the time. In England, as early as 1808, Heathcote's invention of a Bobbin Net machine introduced a cheaper alternative to handmade lace. Also invented were different kinds of canes and open-worked silk stockings. In America, Elias Howe invented a sewing machine that was marketed in Britain by the American firm of Singer. Soon after, hand sewing was almost completely replaced by machine work among the well-to-do.

The developing industry of manufactured fabrics contributed to women's interest in underclothes that helped to thin their waists. Soon fabrics became more elastic and "light steel wire replaced heavy whalebone."[11] Outcries against the corset's dangers to health continued. Years before in 1750, a veritable crusade was undertaken by doctors Winslow, Desessartz, and Vandermonde. These objections were signaled to the regular reading public by Rousseau, Locke, and Buffon. Joseph II published an edict against the use of stays in 1800 for impeding "the growth of the fair sex," especially in their obligations to childbirth.[12] But corsets did not have the rigidity and emphasis on changed body structure until the 1820s. The longer, less flexible corset "carried symbolic meaning about the virtues of a women who wore

Fig. 62 Marie Taglioni endorsed the amazing product, the mechanical corset, which allowed women to lace and unlace themselves automatically. This illustration is from *Le Petit Courrier des Dames,* March 25, 1833, p. 130.

them. They signified a woman's chastity and correctness; this symbolism is still alive in the word 'strait-laced.'"[13] Constructive revolt against corsets culminated in the movement of the Pre-Raphaelites in 1848. Dante Rossetti, the English poet and painter, and others wanted more natural lines. They contended that steel-boned corsets caused degeneration in the development of the female form as well as fatigue and deformation.[14] Today we know that it causes restrictive pulmonary disease.

Women at the time no longer had servants at their disposal at every moment. In order to eliminate this difficulty and to make the dressing a speedier affair, a mechanical corset was invented that was worn and promoted by the Romantic ballerina, Marie Taglioni. Recognizing the difficulties that women suffered in lacing themselves in the back, Monsieur Josselin invented a particular metal pulley system that permitted the woman to lace and unlace herself automatically.[15] The fashion magazine, *Petit Courrier des Dames—Journal des Modes* (March 25, 1833), described the fact that Mademoiselle Taglioni helped to advertise *les corsets mécaniques*. Since Taglioni's waist is the most graceful of all women:

> There is no doubt that the most elegant and supple forms will become perfection with the use of this new genre of corset. Of all others, this most celebrated artist would know how to appreciate the advantages of this corset *à la Taglioni* which does not interfere in the grace of her movements and with just a slight move of the finger instantaneously unlaces.[16]

The corset unlaced instantaneously, simply by the pull of a whale bone. Taglioni was an example to all women who understood the utility and desirability of corsets. Fashion writers predicted that young people would benefit from wearing them because they were more flexible and less expensive than the usual corsets.

By 1819, whale-boned corsets diminished as the highly fashion-conscious, latter-day *Merveilleuses* decided not to use them.[17] However, these women were but a few of considerable numbers of middle-class women wearing corsets. The mechanical or automatic corset was also called the "lazy woman's lacing," which enabled women to undress without the help of a servant, husband or lover. "Thus the mechanical corset contributed to self-reliance and to the democratization of the process of making socialized female bodies."[18] By the middle of the nineteenth century, corsets were being mass-produced in factories. In France, approximately 6,500 corset workers grew to 10,000 in 1855 and to 1,200,000 in 1861.[19]

The cult of neoclassicism survived in the form of a tendency to value the brilliance of a white body and a white face. Its meaning as a symbolic and stylish color prevailed during the Romantic era. The classical body adored the whiteness of the skin. "For the whiteness of the skin is also to be counterfeit, its color as artificial as the clothes' and the face's skin surface, as much a simulated concealing encasement as the elsewhere encasing robe."[20] Even women's faces were supposed to have a statue's effect. In Charles Baudelaire's "Eloge du Maquillage" ("In Praise of Makeup") (1863), he says that rice powder "grants a woman's face marble-like perfection," creating "an abstract unity that immediately coincides with the statue."[21] Gautier's "De la Mode" also extolled the virtues of white powder as a unifying and shiny marble-like adornment.

Although women were beginning to choose bright colors for evening wear, white continued to dominate. The March 11, 1832 *Journal des Dames* featured articles on the balls of the season, where one discovers the true "modes parisiennes." It mentioned that the predominant fashion for evening wear was "charmantes robes en gaze blanches brodées en soie de couleur" ("charming white gauze dresses embroidered in colorful silk").

In *Mademoiselle de Maupin* (1835) Gautier helps us to better understand attitudes toward beauty and women during the 1830s as well as the fantasies created on stage. It was Gautier who alerted us to the complex gaze of the male spectator and his preference for her white skin:

> The whole of her dear little person delighted me beyond all expression; I loved her frail, white, little hands through which you could see the light, her bird-like foot which scarcely touched the ground, her figure which a breath would have broken, and her pearly shoulders, little developed as yet, which her scarf, placed awry, happily disclosed.[22]

In the same novel, Gautier spoke of a paramour who had pretty legs and tiny feet, and he makes the revealing statement, "I am your virginity dear child; that is why I have a white dress, a white gown and white skin."[23]

Baudelaire found great insight in women's choice of clothing and makeup. In "Le Peintre de la Vie Moderne" he suggested that in describing women one must not separate them from what they wear. They are a "grand spectacle produced by a collectivity of forces. The urban woman is a *divinité*, a star whose radiance is due in part to her parure or her wardrobe. Everything that adorns a woman . . . is a part of her."[24] Like Balzac in his *Traité de la vie élégante*, Baudelaire explained that a woman depended on her toilette "for her very existence, to the point that she is virtually inseparable from her dress . . . thereby making of the two, of the woman and the dress, one indivisible totality."[25]

Baudelaire also was seduced by the excitement and beauty of exotic women and their clothing. In "Eloge du maquillage" he extolled the exquisite delicacy of the Orient and the way women dressed. He admired the artistry of the painter Constantin Guys, especially Guys' depictions of Turkey from his *voyage en orient*. Guys painted local scenes which evoked the prettiness of women and their "feminine glances," frenetic dances of eunuchs and "women who have preserved the national dress, embroidered vests, flowing scarves, wide pants, striped or gilded gauzes."[26]

Women with narrow waists and delicate frames were not the only inspirations for Romantic artists. They also found glory and excitement in the female warrior figures left over from the Revolution—women willing to risk their lives for freedom. The underdog, the weaker sex, the tiny country desiring sovereignty were causes taken up by the Romantics. In painting, *le Radeau de la Meduse,* by Géricault (1819), and *les Massacres de Chios* by Delacroix (1824) portrayed these struggles. Delacroix sympathized with the tragedy of the little island of Chios that, feeling isolated and secure with the waters all around it, stayed neutral in the Grecian war. But the Turkish fleet stopped at its harbor for repairs and saw the wealth of the country in crops, jewels, silks, and beautiful people spread within the range of its guns, practically unarmed. There followed a month of looting, arson, murder, enslavement, and rape that ended only when a group of Chios's men set fire to the admiral's ship. This provided the scene and set for Delacroix's remarkable *Massacre.*[27]

In music, the early works of Berlioz (messe, opera des Francs-Juges, 1825); in literature, the romantic novel par excellence, *Adolphe,* by Benjamin Constant in 1816, the first *Méditations* by Alphonse de Lamartine in 1820, the early poems by Alfred de Vigny in 1822 and Stendahl's *De l'Amour* (1822). In creating the Romantic imagination, artists brought excitement and color to the growing distress and despair of colonial wars and urban industrialization.

In the theater, the great poet Victor Hugo drafted a preface to his play *Cromwell* (1826). He validated the theater of the boulevards for the "common people" that for years played to the appetites and tastes of the growing middle classes. Few writers missed the stirring changes that Hugo was proposing, ones that dominated theatrical mores for the rest of the century. *La Préface de Cromwell,* the prime manifesto of the Romantic Movement in France, declared that authors must free the language of the stage, avoiding stilted verses and soliloquies. The new theater must mix genres, the grotesque with the noble or sublime, in order to better represent the way people think and feel. He also wished to abandon the classical rule of the three *unitiés,* which superficially impose rules unlike life's real experiences, or *la vraisemblance. La Préface* enunciated that local scenes and costume decor must suffuse the new performance style, rather than the stage picture looking artifically like a Greek palace.

At the famous performance of Hugo's play *Hernani* (1830), Gautier, devoted to Hugo's rather radical theatrical ideas which Gautier associated with truth and freedom, the faction that fought for the play to its success. That famous night he wore a scarlet doublet that, he claimed, he never removed from his body. The scarlet vest is forever linked to the fight for truth and freedom, showing how deeply connected clothing was to political stances. Hugo's language initiated a pointed identification with local issues, and he acknowledged that politics as well as aesthetics play an important role in performance. At the time he was lobbying for Turkish freedom. Hugo had an astounding success with his poems *Les Orientales* (1829), which consecrated the vogue in the Parisian imagination for local freedom as well as local art. Hugo's ideas reflected the growing changes and needs of middle-class audiences and France's growth as an industrial power.

As the 1830s progressed, street styles seemed to become increasingly decadent and unwieldy to the female figure. They "had become monstrosities in their excess of padding."[28] Reams of ruffles hid parts of the body such as the neck. Huge hats with "every conceivable ribbon, flower, fruit and feather was balanced precariously on the towering curled confection of hair dressing."[29] Skirts filled out, predicting the inflated hoop of later years. Starch was an indispensable additive to the wash; it puffed sleeves already stiff from wire supports or little feather pillows.

Fashion's perfect woman of the nineteenth century looked very much like the ballerina, albeit with heavier clothes. Some years later, the female reformer E. Ward pointed out how distorted the views were:

> Corsets, dresses, gloves, boots and shoes, are all made with a fixed idea of being smaller than nature would have them be . . . Not only women themselves, but many men, admire a feminine figure tilted forward on high heels, with a weasel waist and large hips.[30]

As small as the female body was, she was more covered up in the nineteenth century than ever before. The nineteenth-century middle classes hid their bodies in order to adhere to a changing sense of sexuality and attraction, although the French were always less serious than the English about veiling their physical beauty. Clothing illustrated the difficulty Europeans had in dealing with their bodies. At no other time in history was the human body, especially the female body, as distorted and hidden by clothing.[31]

In the English *Belle Assemblée* (April 1831), "National costume" became a top item. The author pointed out:

> France is no doubt the head and fountain of taste and fashion in dress, yet without any distinctive marks to tell the source from which their fashions spring. Whilst the French dispense all that is valued in dress to the whole world, it is amongst their peasantry alone that anything approaching to a national or characteristic costume may be seen.[32]

"National costumes" were adopted as masquerade dresses during the carnival and at masked balls in Paris, where of course, fashion reigned.

Gazing at beautiful women in exotic costumes was a major pastime of spectators at the ballet in Paris; they became as important as the stage performers. Many were members of the famed Jockey Club that was founded in 1833 by the son of Napoléon, Count Waleski. These avid visitors sat in the *loges infernales*, boxes that touched the stage. Their opera glasses allowed scrutiny of the ballerinas' bodies at close range. Many of these men spent hours lingering backstage in the corridors, where they could whisper to the dancers of their liking, inviting them out after the show or propositioning them in one way or another. In London, it was the Dandy who peeked with longing at the dancers.

The heyday of the English Dandy lasted from 1800 to 1830 and in France, a bit longer. His chief characteristics were *sang-froid*, polite impertinence, cold sarcasm, irony, taste, and elegance. These characteristics are still revered by members of the English upper classes. Their notable fashion qualities were studied and crafted until they seemed effortless. The Dandies who avidly watched the ballet dancers at the Paris Opéra became characters in a play of their own making. Much attention was accorded their bearing and their attire, which later in the century created a cult, a philosophical approach to life that glorified the Dandy's performance. "Artful manipulation of posture, social skill, manners, conversation, and dress were all accoutrements in the aestheticization of self, central to dandyism."[33] It is worth remembering that the aristocracy of the seventeenth and eighteenth centuries was frequently the most viewed event at a performance.

In a chapter from *Sartor Resartus* entitled "The Dandiacal Body," Thomas Carlyle contemplated the role of the Dandy:

> A Clothes-wearing man, a Man whose trade, office, and existence consists in the wearing of Clothes. Every faculty of his soul, spirit, purse, and person is heroically consecrated to this one object, the wearing of clothes wisely and well: so that as others dress to live, he lives to dress . . . he is inspired with cloth, a Poet of Cloth.[34]

Using the analogy of clothing and the polity, Carlyle gradually layered his metaphor, creating a whole fabric of societal arrangements. When discussing the Dandy, he did not describe the male fashion of his time; he did not dictate the importance or value of the color black, nor of the evident strength gathered from wearing a coat and trousers that matched, which were easy to wear and eminently smooth to move about in.

The Dandy practiced a devotion to fashion in a very serious way. One of the most notorious and most celebrated dandies was Bryan (Beau) Brummel (1778–1840). His reputation as a lion dresser (chic and debonair) preceded him wherever he went. The Prince of Wales watched him dress in order to understand the secret of his impeccable taste. Brummel's most important qualification resided in the elegance of his bearing and the simplicity of his attire. Nothing in excess—not in colors, fabrics, or jewelry. His impertinent manners eventually left him in deep trouble with the Prince of Wales. Unable to pay his bills, Brummel ran from London in May 1816 to find refuge in France. English talent for understatement became the Western European aesthetic for men's dress in the nineteenth century.

To be fashionable requires impeccable taste, not just money. Good taste, although usually represented as an innate faculty, is, in fact, generally learned. Brummel had a natural inclination for fine taste, but he was said to be lacking in moral responsibility. Ironically, in a book attributed to him, he developed a theory that clothing is closely related to character: "in costume, the conjunction of beauty, or kindness, or love, or virtue, with particular dresses produces a combined effect upon the mind, which the weak person is unable, and the enthusiast, perhaps, unwilling to unravel."[35]

In Charles X's short reign he managed to intensify the regressive measures of his brother Louis XVIII and to create a troubled and chaotic atmosphere. Romantic artists bravely fought against the revived tactics of the *ancien régime* as they spun their tales of escape and tragedy. In the audiences a dominant male presence grabbed attention from the spectacle. The culture of the Dandy gave license to their piercing gapes and criticisms, using binoculars to see their dancing beauties.

The neorevolution of 1830 was prefaced by a fascinating encounter between Charles X and the citizens of Paris when he attended a ball at the Tuileries. It was the site of waltzing couples in a dizzying display of wealth and abandon, an occasion celebrating the visit of the King of Naples. The evening was cool, and when Charles greeted the crowds from the balcony, a wind suddenly came up and women screamed from the rush of cold air. He jested that the winds would help guide his flotilla in Algiers, the French invading Algeria in the process of owning their *exotisme*. As a result of Charles's staunch monarchist, and backward policies, the crowds began to yell "à bas les aristocrats," "Down with the aristocrats." They burned benches in the Tuileries gardens and attacked the guards. It was a prescient moment. Charles had to go, but kings were in fashion, and one month later the Duc d'Orléans, Louis Philippe, became the next king of France, however not for long.[36]

CHAPTER 8

The Kingdom of the Opera

Pale Goddesses on the Stage (1824–1830)

The Romantic period's stage designers, writers, and choreographers under-stood the importance of escape from the dismal, urban streets. Ballerinas represented more than their immediate characters on stage. They were the intermediaries between the audience and the potentially hostile, increas-ingly industrialized urban world. By playing a part in fantastic stories, they tried to stave off the inevitable mechanization of their society. It was almost as if industrialism were a disease caught by everyone. By the time Degas painted their exhausted bodies, they too were caught in a worker's web, facing long hours in the studio and on stage, with little job security or financial stability.

Many dance historians cite the debut of the Romantic Ballet as the opening of Filippo Taglioni's *La Sylphide* in Paris in 1832. Others link it to major currents in early nineteenth-century music and poetry that were al-ready fully advanced in 1832. Trends in art, music, and literature preceded dance in the Romantic revolution. Perhaps ballet's earlier links to the aris-tocracy and the court made it a distinctively conservative institution.

Innovations introduced by the Romantic ballerina and her attributes are continuously being analyzed. Illustrations and images show her to have a rather remarkable combination of delicate and powerful traits. And her waistline was no small part of this presentation. Leading ballerinas mimicked what the fashion magazines dictated; they dreamed of dematerializing by achieving a thin silhouette. The best means to achieve the wasp waist was to lace themselves up more and more tightly. The Romantic ballerina adopted this shape and found this line to suit her beautifully. She enjoyed a waist the size of a ring and wore a bell-shaped skirt to the ankles and a pair of wings that seemed to replace the sleeves.[1] Minus the wings, her sister in the street went to balls in the same attire.

The Romantic ballerina, however, was not a simple fairy tale character, passive and ethereal. Scenarios depicted a complex range of female characters and their roles.[2]

Romantic dancing heroines mirrored the earthy and material side of women who ruled in their domestic universe as personalities with seductive verve and wit. The more realistic Romantic ballerina tended to represent specific places, with tutus decorated in the style of that region. Though she may not have aggressively won her man, she still represented the revolutionary woman, aware of her surroundings, resourceful, yet sometimes failing to achieve her goals.

The temper of Romantic Ballet sought images of a more seductive nature and turned to the East as they did to the supernatural worlds.[3] The ballet landscapes in which the ballerina roamed were the domain of pageantry as well as opulence. These sensual women wore the traditional tutu despite the oriental themes of the ballets. "While costumes for male dancers . . . might be splendidly, if in-authentically, Oriental, the ballerina always wore her bouffant knee-length or calf-length tutu garnished, perhaps with fugitively 'Eastern' trim."[4] The conventional tutu endured, no matter what the geography or historical period, just as court ballet costumes did in the past.

The "Ballet Blanc," or the White Ballet as it came to be known, developed from the early nineteenth century era of romance, demons, and mystery. Fairy tales replaced mythology and anacreontic interludes. "Dancing becomes a transcendental language, charged with spirituality and mystery; a celestial calligraphy, it admits nothing profane."[5] These were the fairy tale ballets in which numerous creatures in white flitted about the stage. The "Ballet Blanc" symbolized a reawakening of female worship, as well as a ritualized approach to the whole field of ballet. It coincided, to some extent, with the revitalization of interest in Christianity and in Medieval thought, with the chaste Virgin Mary serving as a distant goddess figure in literature.

In his preface to *Mademoiselle de Maupin* (1835), the poet/librettist/critic of Romantic Ballet Théophile Gautier discussed his frustration with early Victorian morality and conservatism: "But it is the fashion now to be virtuous and Christian." Gautier continued: "Christianity is so much in vogue, owing to the prevalent hypocrisy, that neo-Christianity itself enjoys a certain favor."[6]

Ballet Technique Flourishes

The ritualized approach to ballet was considerably enhanced by new pedagogies concerned with building stronger, more beautiful dancers. Changes in attitudes toward the way the body is trained led to a dependence upon innovations in costume at the end of the eighteenth century. After Noverre and Magri, two of the most important writers on technique were Carlo Blasis (1820, 1828) and E. Théleur (1831) (perhaps Taylor Frenchified). It is important to comment on the concepts put forth by both of these great and insistent teachers of the ballet technique.

In Carlo Blasis's *The Code of Terpsichore, A Practical and Historical Treatise on the Ballet, Dancing and Pantomime; with a Complete Theory of the Art of Dancing: Intended as Well for the Instruction of Amateurs as the Use of Professional Persons*, the contemporary reader is impressed by his prodigious knowledge of ancient Greek and Roman writings as well as of authors and artists throughout history whose works impart an aesthetic understanding of how we consider ourselves to be cultivated artists and how we approach art in its natural, most effective form.[7] An excellent dancer and performer, Blasis directed the Imperial Ballet Academy attached to La Scala Opera in Milan from 1838–1851, after a dancing career in many cities including Marseilles, Bordeaux, Paris, and London. Like Noverre, Blasis gave healthy attention to painting and sculpture and saw the ballet master following similar principles in the design and shape of movements. He became one of the preeminent teachers and proponents of a description and definition of the blossoming Romantic ballet. In his treatise, Blasis told stories, offered sage advice, described artists of past centuries, and tried to find the heart of his arguments in others' sayings and deeds.

Blasis's shaping of the body presupposed an awareness of certain eighteenth-century body placements, given the manner in which the torso had been typically confined by the corset, by the belief in the verticality of the spine in dance, and by the way the limbs and feet were used. Changes in costume during the 1790s rendered the body more free moving and gave the legs a chance to lift higher, turn more quickly, and jump higher. Blasis's theories profited from the lighter and looser clothing. The use of maillots (or tights) covering the legs created a more uniform look to the body, and they permitted the knees to bend easily in order to jump and move with speed. Coiffeurs of soft curls and minimal hair enabled the head to sway and turn, even snap around with alacrity. Heels were taken off shoes and sandals; ballet slippers were used to create a new technique for the foot, the heel, the instep, and the metatarsal, as well.

Blasis's chapter "The Study of the Body" described a manner that has clearly been enunciated since the Renaissance, that we must look tall and erect in order to display the body as it should be presented, with numerous references to verticality and length of neck and torso:

> Let your body be, in general, erect and perpendicular on your legs, except in certain attitudes and especially in arabesques, when it must lean forwards or back wards according to the position you adopt. . . . Throw your breast out and hold your waist in as much as you can. . . . Let your shoulders be low, your head high, and your countenance animated and expressive. . . . The elegance of the upper part of the body is chiefly to be attended to by a dancer, as in that, one of his principal merits consists. Carry your bust gracefully, impart to its motions and oppositions a certain abandon and by no means let it lose the beauty of its pose nor the purity of its design.[8]

He repeated himself: "Always draw your body well up, and especially your head, even in your minutest poses. Besides a graceful carriage, let the dancer acquire uprightness, by forming an exact counterpoise with every part of his frame, and thus enable him to support his body on one leg only."[9]

Blasis gave a detailed analysis of the arms, and hands, and wrists as they framed and supported the body. It took nearly thirty years (1790–1820) for the foot to become an important technical tool in the ballet technique. Blasis accentuated the foot's delicate, arched line while, at the same time, it was carefully worked with numerous exercises that created the correct shape and strength, a strength that carried the body rapidly in space as the feet darted here and there. Blasis advised the dancer:

> In all your *terre à terre* steps you cannot be too active about your instep, nor bend your feet too much downwards (arching, or pointing the foot); as the former gives your execution considerable brilliancy, and the latter renders it light and graceful.[10]

Blasis analyzed what the body must do in order to jump; previously a more difficult endeavor with heavier costumes. The dancer had to raise his shoulders along with the body and bent legs; the thighs, knees, and feet springing upward. The body moved forward and upward at the same time; "the motion intended to send the body forward places it so at the moment of the leap and that destined to carry it up, makes it describe a large segment of a circle."[11]

Blasis recognized and commented upon the changes in dance due to the "eminent perfection" of Dauberval, Gardel, Vestris, and other artists. But he accentuated the value of "modern artists," acknowledging that their performance were full of charm and that they executed variations of "perpendicularity and equilibrium, attitudes and arabesques" that were unknown to their predecessors. The new choreographers created a variety of dance combinations and pirouettes, and most importantly, they were no longer burdened with "those complicated embellishments" encircling the performer in narrow limits of simplicity.[12]

One of the most important contributions of the Romantic period to the ballet canon was the arabesque, a pose that Blasis was beginning to work on in his *Traité* of 1820. In their treatises, dancing masters such as Magri, Blasis, and Théleur described the way the arms worked with the extended leg balancing the perpendicular in equiponderence. Blasis based his theories of balance on Leonardo da Vinci's studies on equilibrium.[13]

Blasis made it very clear that sweat and hard work were involved in becoming a brilliant performer: "They are aware how much labour it costs to hold one's self on one leg, and how much greater to do so on one's toes. Imagine therefore what difficulty there must be in turning in such a position, without the slightest jerk in any part of the body."[14]

A chapter on the art of costuming revealed Blasis's rational approach to stage clothing. He made a plea for historical accuracy and guided taste: "Each performer should be obliged to wear that species of costume which is exactly appropriate and peculiar to the character he represents."[15] He described the importance of the art of costume design and how necessary it is that costume designers pay attention to the choreography: "They require, in short, to be lightly and elegantly habited; and their costume should be so arranged so as to add new charm to the art."[16]

Thinking practically about costume and choreography, Blasis cautioned the designer to create costumes that were not only historically accurate, but that were also conducive to moving in technically difficult ways. "If a character such as a Turk is introduced, why give that person an enormous costume? . . . The dancer would be imprisoned in his apparel and deprived of the means of displaying the simplest movements."[17] He elaborated on this point: "A certain resemblance to the particular national or period costume should be preserved but still remember to display so much only as is pleasing and decorous . . . Adorn the original model, and reject what is faulty in it."[18] He gave his nation, Italy, credit for making the most scrupulous and detailed costumes.

But he clearly disrespected the way dancers and actors in France were costumed. "In France, except at the Opéra of Paris, everyone had to find his own dresses; and he arranged them, consequently, according to the imperfect ideas he may have formed of peculiar styles in costume. Thus, the characters lacked truth and dignity."[19]

However, Blasis added that Paris was the place to learn about making and designing costumes by inquiring of men of learning,[20] and he cautioned young people to avoid the example of actors, finding fault with Talma, who was considered a great costume reformer. He criticized Talma for playing the role of Coriolanus in a fancy tunic and a Greek helmet. Talma also acted the part of Niomède in the costume of Orestes, confusing Greek and Roman habits. Blasis also found fault with Vestris as the lover who was a simple farmer in *La Fille mal Gardée* as he wore "one of those fashionable dresses in which an exquisite would go to some ball." In Vestris's *Barber of Seville*, the character of Count Almaviva, instead of disguising himself as a farrier, performed the amusing scene in an elegant officer's uniform wearing silk stockings. To add insult to injury, Vestris also danced in the opera *Aristippe* in a tunic and turban![21]

As a panacea, Blasis counseled the choreographer to give intelligent directions to his collaborators—to make sure that there was unison between the character of the dresses and that of the scenery; although the colors of the decor could be different, but not more splendid. He also suggested that careful attention be paid to the period and place "peculiar to a country."

> Costume, in short, may be defined to be a kind of epitome of history, geography, and chronology; for it not only determines the country, but if exactly adhered to, declares even the epoch of time to which the piece relates.[22]

Actors and dancers who were instrumental in changing the old way and in bringing in the enlightened way were praised. He cited Clairon as the first who banished the "ridiculous mode of costume" and praised Lekain, Chassé, and especially Talma. In England, where Blasis danced as a soloist for four years, he remembered the contributions of Garrick, Kemble, and Siddons, and he recalled Maximilian Gardel's heroic act of dancing without a mask, "throwing off the trammels that with ignorance and prejudice had long enslaved his art."[23] Finally, he spoke of Dauberval and Pierre Gardel who adopted a "proper natural costume."[24]

A paradoxical twist to Blasis's *Code* resided in his attitude toward the Romantic Movement. He identified himself as a classicist and an Apollonian rather than a Dionysian Romantic, saying that imagination cannot be the sole measure of invention: "The romantic system is the direct road to absurdity and the classic system leads to liberal and enlightened reason."[25] Blasis denied the mercurial, changeable literary values of the nineteenth century; and he was unable to appreciate the burgeoning developments in aesthetics that breathed new life into traditions and habits. At the very finish of his book, Blasis returned to the conflict between the "classic" and the "romantic" styles, but he modfied his former comments, recognizing the faults and virtues of both approaches. In the end, no strict ideology should rule over a choreographer:

The grand aim of the Ballet-master, the mime and the dancer, should be the embellishment and improvement of the art; to grace it with all the nobleness, the splendour, and beauty of which it is susceptible; to render it worthy of the place it occupies among the other fine arts, and to make them all contribute as much as possible to so laudable—so desirable an object.[26]

Blasis was still wedded to Noverre's classical principles. By referring to the artists of the theater, painters, and those loyal to nature, truth, and imitation of life, he repeated the master's words. "Why should we not act like those who are really under the influence of the passion which we are desirous of representing?"[27]

Plates of illustrations at the end of his book portray drawings of bodies in clear outlines wearing Greek attire, able to lift their legs and show the symmetry of the movements. We see in these illustrations the apotheosis of ballet technique and the realization of years of transition, where, at that point, costume and movement synchronized.

There were differences between Blasis's "Traité's" plates and the "Code's" plates; the latter included more women in the illustrations. "Although the thirteen plates from the 1820 'Traité' have been retained, the drawings in the *Code of Terpsichore* show female dancers, as well as male dancers, demonstrating the various steps and poses. Eighteen figures out of fifty-six have been modified, turning the [original] bare-breasted, bare-legged men into classically clad women."[28]

The fluidity and lyricism of the figures on the pages are evident—the freedom with which they moved their arms and framed their faces; the high extensions, or at least the suggestion that the hips are open and able to lift the legs beyond the ninety-degree angle; the flexibility of the feet and arches that stood high on the metatarsal and brought the body into a tall suspension and breathtaking place while the feet were manipulated into a more rapid or slow contact with the floor; the turn-out of the hips and legs that offered a picture of open presentation; and, perhaps most important of all, the sense that all of these men and women were flying and being swept in different directions, ever so slightly off balance, taking a chance of falling in another space, or going up into the air, turning, or falling. The woman dancer had sprung free, with her light skirts, more flexible bodice, and soft slippers.

Dance historian Lillian Moore commented in the *Practice Clothes—Then and Now*, "Once they discovered the delights of working in clothing which permitted ease of movement, they never relinquished the privilege. . . . "[29] She recalled that Carlo Blasis stressed the importance of practice clothes for the dancer. He had posed for the illustrations in his "Traité" himself, in which most of the figures were shown dressed only in ballet shoes and close-fitting shorts. The later English edition covered these bodies up with theatrical clothing. Blasis wrote that practice clothing for women should be simple, such as a bodice and skirt of white muslin with a black sash around the waist. He wanted the clothing to hug closely to the body so that no part of the outline would be concealed or be too tight so as to hinder steps or "embarrass any of the movements and attitudes."[30] When the celebrated Danish choreographer August Bournonville auditioned for the Paris Opera in 1826, he learned that the regulations had just been changed and that he would be wearing pre-revolutionary knee pants and silk hose instead of the long, loose trousers previously worn by aspirants. The directors had decided that the long pants hid too many technical faults and anatomical defects. Looking at Blasis's illustrations, one senses that there is a feeling of youth, energy, and drive that is not apparent in paintings or illustrations of eighteenth-century dancers who seem frozen in a position of glacial space.

Letters on Dancing (1831) by the reputable dance master E. A. Théleur also shed light on the evoluton of technique and costume in the early part of the nineteenth century. Without reference to Blasis's pioneering work in "le Traité," or the Code of Terpsichore, Théleur made it clear that his book using Noverre's title was intended to improve the present state of training in dance and to denounce, to some extent, the current "illiterate and mechanical" approach to ballet. Like Blasis, although he did not acknowledge Blasis's work, he wanted to take "the present style of execution" and to "reduce it to systematic principles."

In the tradition of the *Encyclopédie*, his book was meant for the inquiring mind but, he added, "the student must be guided by an enlightened teacher." Like the Encyclopedists, Théleur's approach helped the dance student "do it yourself," with careful attention to comportment and basic information about technique and anatomy. He called attention, as did Noverre and Blasis, to the respected dancers and dancing teachers of the time, namely, Noverre, Dauberval, Gardel, Milon, the Vestris, Didelot, Deshayes, D'Egville, Albert, Duport, Ferdinand, Aumer, the Coulonges, Paul, Mlles Gosselin, Fanny Bias, Clotilde, Bigottini, Brocard, Mercandotti, and Taglioni.

In his preface, Théleur stated that some people were old fashioned and did not want to change their dispositions. He quoted the journalist Sir Richard Steele from *The Spectator*:

> The low ebb to which dancing is now fallen, is altogether owing to this silence: The art is esteemed only as an amusing trifle; it lies altogether uncultivated, and has unhappily fallen under the imputation of illiterate and mechanic . . . and to set dancing in its true light would shew the usefulness and elegance of it with the pleasure and instruction produced from it, and also lay down some fundamental rules that might so tend to the improvement of its professors. . . . [31]

He also reiterated Noverre's comments about the vanity of virtuosity, "So well we may say that capering and tumbling are now preferred to, and supply the place of just and regular dancing in our theatres."[32] These remarks demonstrated a valued professionalism and conservatism that gave weight and respectability to the art of dancing.

The editor of these *Letters*, Sandra Hammond, pointed out that "Théleur's treatise represents the first work that pictures dancers on full pointe."[33] Like Blasis, whose "Code" was published the year before, Théleur's attitude toward pointe dancing was casual. His illustrations of women on pointe called attention to the proper placement of the arms rather than the use of the feet. But he spoke about training to strengthen the toes, advising the student "to keep the toes pressed together and straight, the strength of the ankles being used to lift the heels from the floor, rather than to try to roll up through the balls of the feet."[34]

Students were instructed to rise on the points of their toes, then to change the feet before lowering the heels and to execute "the pirouettes" on the points of the toes.[35] In addition, Théleur gave "clarification for the shapes and positions of the foot at the supporting ankle for various movements. He distinguished between the uses of the foot fully pointed touching the ground against the front or back of the supporting leg."[36] He expanded upon the use of specific *coupé* positions (creating a much more flexible and capable foot) with the fouetté and the pirouette. Théleur carefully described the "stations" or standing positions that had not been previously written about but were certainly included in the style of dancing of his time.

Théleur's text seemed to have more in common with Blasis's earlier work, the *Traité Élémentaire, Théorique Et pratique de l'Art de la Danse* (1820), as they both concentrated principally on technique for, and the attributes of, theatrical dance. Both of these enterprises were complicated, since they were writing during a period of vast changes, when once "distinctive dance styles—serious, demi caractère and comic—had blended together as to cause a confusion of styles."[37]

Théleur seconded Blasis's stipulations describing the way the softly curved arms worked in opposition to the legs. One should raise or open the arms by moving the elbows as the first part of the arm to move; they and the wrists should be well curved as they rise opposite the shoulders before extending to the final pose. In the same way, the elbows were the last part of the arm to descend. Théleur advocated the use of the curved fingers in most cases, but there was also the opening up of the hand to express "animated voluptuous poses." Blasis called for the arms to be raised higher than the head, but not Théleur, and both sets of illustrations showed the hands raised over the shoulders. Théleur specified the way the body was placed so that the head was erect but not stiff, and the upper part of the chest raised. This held the stomach in—enabling the dancer to breath more freely, and to give strength and control to the hip area. The higher the weight was placed, the easier it became to balance. The principle of holding a movement for a period of time influenced the way we train today, in adage, especially. No doubt, the corset holding the abdomen and ribs in place served as a keen reminder of these postulates.

For the upper body and arms, Théleur directed that the shoulders be pressed down in order to extend the length of the neck and to create an elegant figure. The arms were to be rounded and projecting outward, which caused the waist to appear small; the backs of the hands should be in a line with the points of the elbows, the little fingers pointing toward each other; the first joint of the thumbs should be placed on the first joint of the first fingers; the second fingers should cover about one half of the first, the third fingers about one half of the second, and the little fingers were extended.

With anatomical awareness, Théleur wanted the legs to be turned out from the hips, the caps of the knees (as much as possible) in line with the great toes; the little toes should grasp, as it were, the ground. He divided up the foot into three parts that bore the weight of the body rather than the commonly mentioned two parts of the metatarsal and heel.

By emphasizing the technique of the foot, Théleur explained the seminal importance of jumping to the technique. "The practice of the change of feet, with the knees and toe joints straight, executed by the force of the ankle joints, gives considerable elasticity and strength to the feet; it produces great firmness on the points of the toes, and equilibrium in the body."[38]

Théleur's *Treatise* contained plates or "Fancy Costumes" that illustrated the positions (stations) of the body as well as the shape of the arms, torso, and back. In addition, the artist dressed the men and women in attire that had a certain historical or regional attribution in order to educate the young pupil or choreographer about correct dress styles, knowing that costuming was always conducted in a rather off-handed way. They are as follows:

Grecian, Zephyr, Flora, with a Garland, Bayadère or dancer from In-dia), Indostan, Tyrolien, Neapolitan, Grecian (a Bacchante), Bacchus, Modern, French Troubadour, Spanish Lady and Gentleman, Soubrette, with Castanets, Figaro, with Castanets, Figaro, with Tambarine (sic.) Grecian: Zephyr, Flora, Cupid, Psyche, and Mercury, Venus, Adonis and the Graces.

It is my impression that Théleur had less breadth of understanding and knowledge than Blasis. Théleur described the basic training in a more detailed and sometimes more insightful manner. However, he had less

wisdom about the other arts and his writing represented the work of a careful, well-intentioned craft person, rather than the efforts of a person with a
distinguished background and career as a dancer and choreographer.

The Advent of Pointe Dancing

As mentioned before, the growth and development of ballet technique now
depended on the increasing use of pointe or toe dancing. With this extraordinary discovery came a revolution in the history of dance, for it was
the gradual adaption of the toe shoe that initiated the epoch of classical
ballet.[39]

One of the earliest pioneers in experimenting with the foot reaching onto
the toes was Mademoiselle Gosselin. She debuted at the Paris Opéra in 1809
and was spoken about later with great respect, although she was not a top
soloist. Many people remarked that no male dancer or ballerina had ever
approached her perfection. In the *Journal des Débats*, August 3, 1827,
Gosselin was remembered by stating, "The astonishing flexibility of her legs,
her powerful musculature, permitted her to remain suspended for a minute
on the tips of her toes." It is difficult to surmise when she did this, perhaps
in 1813 but surely before 1818, because in 1818 she died in labor. In 1827,
Taglioni was compared to her as holding herself with the same "aplomb" on
her toes.

Visitors to the Opéra from Scotland in 1815 wrote clearly and rationally
about French dancers and their passion for acrobatics and virtuosity. Sensing
that a balance needed to be struck between technical skill and beauty of
performance, they wrote that Parisian audiences were to blame. They saw
pointe work in the same light as we see 32 fouettés.

> The applause in the French opera seemed to us to be in direct propor-
> tion to the difficulty, and to bear no relation whatever to the beauty of
> the performances . . . but, when one of the male performers after spin-
> ning about for a long time, with wonderful velocity, arrests himself
> suddenly and stands   immovable on one foot; or when one of the
> females wheels around on the toes of one foot, folding her other limb
> nearly in a horizontal position—he breaks out into extravagant excla-
> mations of astonishment and delight: Quel Aplomb! Ah diable! Sacré
> Dieu! &c.[40]

Other dancers who explored this new genre and dazzled their audiences
were Amalia Brugnoli and Elisa Vaque-Moulin. Both deserve recognition
for their remarkable efforts with this technique. Amalia Brugnoli was trained
in Naples by Armand Vestris, the son of Auguste. When he brought her to

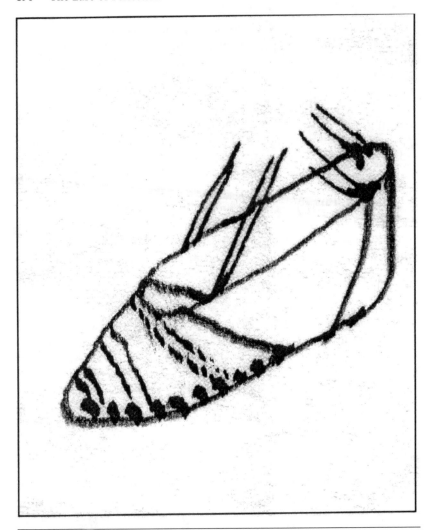

Fig. 63 Sketch of Fanny Ellsler's toe shoe from the Vienna State Opera Museum. "The dotted lines are meant to show double rows of stitching. The shoe is soft, made of pink satin. The stitching probably follows the hem of tape or ribbon inside the shoe, and the total effect, like quilting, gives structural support so that the toes do not splay as they normally would in a very high demi-pointe." Courtesy of Monica Moseley, Dance Collection of the New York Public Library.

Vienna in 1823, Marie Taglioni remembered in one of her journals that "Mlle Brugnoli was a dancer who brought to light a new genre; she did extraordinary things on the tips of her toes . . . In order to raise herself up, she was obliged to use great effort with her arms."[41]

When Brugnoli came to London in 1832, she was admired by Lady Blessington in her book, *The Idler in Italy*. She remembered Brugnoli in 1823:

> She advances rapidly across the stage on the extreme point of her toes, without for a moment losing her aplomb, cuts into the air, and alights again on the point of her feet, as if she were no heavier than gossamer.[42] Taglioni also gave Brugnoli credit for introducing this genre nouveau, but considered it lacking in grace.

The 1827 *Almanacco* of La Scala, described La Brugnoli:

> La Brugnoli, whom our directors hastened to present together with her husband, the dancer Samengo and the danseuse Vaque-Moulin. All the most perfect that can be seen in dancing in the way of strength and nimble footwork resides in La Brugnoli. Actually working on the point of her foot, her steps, her attitudes, her turns acquire an airy something which strikes and astounds the imagination.[43]

When Brugnoli returned to London in 1833, the *Morning Herald* wrote:

> Mme Brugnoli's toe is quite unequalled by anything within our recollection, except Paganini's bow or single string. She performs evolutions on it such as no other dancer could accomplish with their ten, with unerring precision and nonchanlance. Her pirouette is inconceivable; her abandon, when from her pinnacle of foot she is wafted like a zephyr to her companion's arms, is, as the French said of one of their Ministers, unspeakable; and her stacato on the tips of her two toes—![44]

Such a discovery was not to be ignored by other dancers. Taglioni found something to learn. In 1833 the *Morning Herald* articulated that "Taglioni, like the general corps de ballet, has since we last saw her, studied to emulate the wonders of Brugnoli's toe."[45]

Elisa Vaque-Moulin sensitized London audiences in 1829 to the startling feats of the new pointe shoe. The *Morning Post* wrote of Vaque Moulin: "She possesses certainly great muscular powers, and leaves nothing to be wished for on the score of agility, vigour, and grace; her manner of standing and walking upon her toes is truly astonishing."[46]

Pauline Montessu was observed at Covent Garden in 1833 performing a "gracefully slow tip-toe circumvolution." Then, in 1836, Angelica Saint-Romain succeeded in astonishing the public by "the most unnatural trick of performing capriccios on the tips of her toes." Several of her movements appeared quite novel: "She raises herself," wrote the *Morning Post*, "on the point of both toes, so as to form an acute angle, and then slides forward on the stage with a gentle undulating motion of the body."[47]

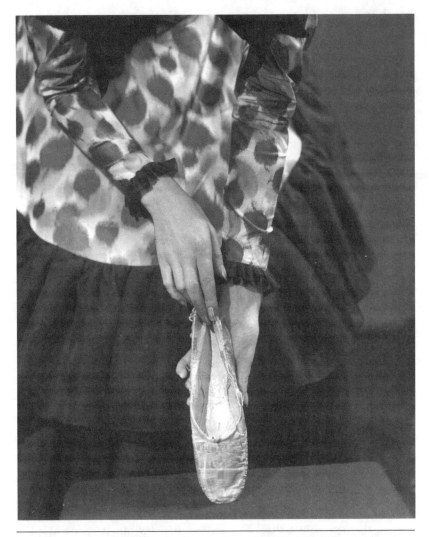

Fig. 64 Marie Taglioni's pointe shoe, held by Dame Alicia Markova. Unlike today's shoes, Taglioni's shoe was unblocked and had no shank. Ribbons emphasized the close relationship with the early nineteenth-century dress shoe. Photo by Gordon Anthony. Courtesy of the Theatre Museum, London.

The new foot technique took its toll on the little satin shoes that the principals wore. Fanny Ellsler wrote that she used up three pairs of shoes for any evening of performance.[48] Taglioni's shoes were made by the shoemaker Janssen who lived in Paris. Unlike today's pointe shoes, Taglioni's slipper was unblocked and had no shank.

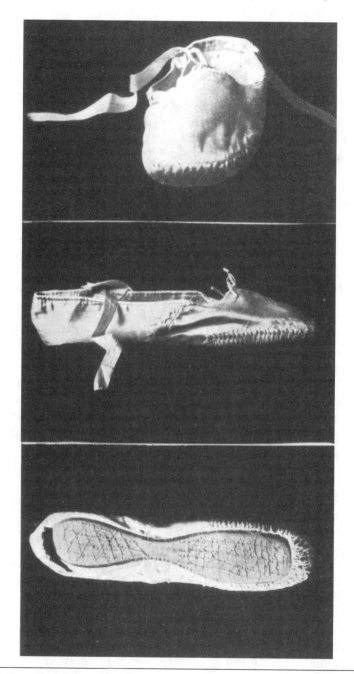

Fig. 65 Emma Livry's pointe shoe, early 1860s, reproduced from Cyril Beaumont, *Ballet Design Past and Present* (London: The Studio, 1946), p. 55. As in Taglioni's day, the shoe was unblocked and the pointes and sides strengthened by darning.

In his short story *Peau de Tigre*, Théophile Gautier wrote about the white "chaussons," or ballet slippers, as the most important item a ballet dancer wears. They looked like the ballroom dancing slippers of the early nineteenth century:

> The sole, which is very hollowed out in the centre does not reach the top of the foot, but ends squarely, leaving about two finger-breadths of material projecting. The purpose of this is to enable the dancer to perform pointe work by giving a sort of jointed point of support, but as the whole weight of the body is borne on this part of the shoe, which would inevitably break, the dancer has to strengthen it by darning, almost as old-clothes menders do to the heels of stockings to make them last. The inside of the shoe is lined with strong canvas and at the very end, a strip of leather and cardboard, the thickness of which depends on the lightness of the wearer. The rest of the shoe is chevronned on the outside by a network of ribbons firmly sewn on, and there is also stitching on the quarter, which is adjusted by means of a little tag of ribbon in the Andalusian manner.[49]

I used to darn my shoes. It is my understanding that toe shoes until the 1970s were commonly darned on the tips.

Both Taglioni's and Fanny Ellsler's toe shoes resembled Gautier's description. The leather sole did not cover the bottom of the shoe, leaving the heel and toe uncovered except for the satin, permitting more freedom to both the heel and the metatarsal. As Gautier notes, ballet slippers were strengthened by double rows of darning and stitching around the sides of the shoe. The stitching followed the hem of tape or ribbon inside the shoe and total effect like quilting gave structural support, so that the toes would not splay as they normally would in a very high demi-pointe.[50]

> Today the blocking of the top of a toe shoe gives strong support to the foot, especially the metatarsal and toe areas allowing the dancer to poise on her toes for long periods and to spin and balance. The material for blocking has varied, but to a large extent, has been the gluing together of densely-packed layers of paper and fabric that create a hard surface that is covered by the satin. The blocking softens with breaking in and wear. The shoe has a shorter outer sole made of flexible leather, while a strong insole of leather and fiber reinforces the dancer's instep. The shank is a strip underneath the insole extending from the middle of the heel to just under the ball of the foot is made of leather or synthetic fabric. These elements help the dancer to balance on her toes, as well as to move swiftly through space.[51]

One cautionary note concerns pictorial representations of dancers on pointe. Star ballerinas of the early nineteenth century in France were often depicted on their full pointes, but so were the social dancers of the period. Perhaps, rather than actually dancing on the toes, they were perceived that way as a painterly convention. The foot became much more important to the movements of the dancer when the high heels were removed and the whole foot carried the line of the leg.[52]

The white tutu and toe slippers of the "virginal" dancer still survive as talismans for the ballerina who was light, slight, and danced like a dream. In one of the early Romantic ballet scenes, she appeared as a dead nun, tossing off her habit and doing rather strange bacchanalian dances; or she appeared as a sylph floating through the forest with the help of wires lifting her from one tree to another; or as a wili again in darkly-lit and thickly-grown woods where she exercised her anger for having been abandoned by a loved one. Impersonating unreal creatures such as *houris* or insects was one of the imperatives. Some years later, in playwright Eugène Labiche's *Le Chapeau de Paille d'Italie* (1851), all the characters had insect bodies: female sultans, nymphs, sylphs, radiant butterflies, or golden ethereal beings, who basically scorned the real world, flying here and there in a perfumed and exotic atmosphere.

The kinds of magical spectacles in Pierre Gardel's mythological ballets that excited Parisians during the Revolutionary period were brought back in the guise of fairy tales. The talented painter and designer at this moment was Hippolyte Lecomte, who succeeded Garneray. The strength and vigor that was present in his painting was transferred to his designs for ballet and opera. He collaborated with Alexandre-Evariste Fragonard, son and student of both his father, the famous painter Fragonard, and Jacques Louis David. Although shorter than Garneray's, Fragonard's reign still produced remarkable costume designs. His popularity may explain why Fragonard also made many costumes for the Théâtre Italien (*Opera buffa e seria*).

Zémire and Azor, choreographed by Monsieur Deshayes, was listed as a *Ballet Féérie* in three acts and presented for the first time on October 20, 1824, at the Opéra, and, predicted events in *La Belle aux Bois Dormant*, or *Sleeping Beauty*, a tale of far away lands, magic spells, wicked fairies, passionate love, and extravagant costumes and scenery. Unfortunately, one month before the opening, Fragonard had an unresolvable dispute and left his position of costumier, fortunately, his work was largely completed.

Fragonard's costumes were extravagant and resplendent. Transported to the East, the characters of the Kings of Persia were bedecked with diamond headdresses, and silver-edged robes that gave them the look of huge insects.

A Pasha wore a turban of crimson velvet clasped with gold bands and a large red feather decorated with pearls; a series of pearls dangled from each side of the coiffure. A white cashmere scarf with gold threads and a necklace with three rows of pearls accompanied the robe. The silk waistband was also ornamented with crimson, gold thread, and a silver buckle. Pearl bracelets, red and green boots embroidered with silver adorned a yellow-brown satin robe with silver decorations. A black velvet belt held a red velvet sword sheath with a gleaming silver hilt.[53]

No doubt audiences were dazzled by the brilliance of the costumes, which seemed far too heavy for light dancing. The creature costumes were accentuated by floating scarves speckled with gold. The mermaid wore a silver vest and a long white dress with a blue scarf that rustled in the breeze. These were the fairies and genies that populated Arab and Persian tales. With the help of new machinery, costumes, and innovative transformations, the Opéra transported its audiences to a land of spectacular fairy tales.

Three years later, in a more restrained setting, a woman protagonist, *La Somnambule*, was featured with magical powers. In this scenario, we see a blending of the realistic and the mystical, as it tells the story of a young, female sleepwalker. *La Somnambule* was presented on September 19, 1827; its story provided by the famed writer of the well-made play, Eugène Scribe, and choreographed by Jean Aumer to music by Ferdinand Hérold.[54] The story was popular fare on the Boulevards, having been performed by the famed pantomimist Debureau in 1823. The sleepwalking ballet by Jean Aumer was regarded as a wonderful innovation.

It recounts the tale of a rich farmer, Edmond (Ferdinand), who was to marry Thérèse (Montessu). A young widow who runs an inn, Gertrude (Legallois), feels miserable, as she is also in love with Edmond. The new Lord of the Manor, Saint-Rambert passes through the village on his way to the castle with his servant, Olivier, played *en travesti* by Mademoiselle Brocard. At Saint-Rambert's first glimpse of Gertrude, he falls in love with her. Their tryst is interrupted by Thérèse who, trance-like, enters through the window in her nightgown with a lantern. Saint-Rambert surmises that she is sleepwalking and escapes. She is discovered in his room and the people in the village, as well as Edmond, are horrified by this impropriety. Edmond finally decides to marry the other woman, Gertrude. In the most dramatic scene of the ballet, the village gazes upon Thérèse walking toward the mill fast asleep. The theme of the beautiful sleepwalking *Somnambule* is not uncommon, even today. They watch her kneel and pray for Edmond's happiness. Gertrude adores Saint-Rambert, but in the end, Edmond decides to marry Thérèse, despite her strange sleep habits. The costume, designed by Hippolyte Lecomte, contributed to the mystical vision of a woman in a pale gown floating through the stage space asleep. Montessu's sleepwalking costume certainly contributed to the development of the tutu.

Fig. 66 In the ballet of the opera *La Muette de Portici* (1828) by Auber, La Femme Espagnole dansant La Quarache, Spanish woman dancing La Quarache. Here the costume designer Lecomte offers charm as well as regional color with a distinctive headdress and long scarves that move with the body. Courtesy of the Bibliothèque de l'Opéra.

One of the most enduring works, *La Fille mal Gardée*, known for its symbolic performance just one week before the storming of the Bastille, returned to the boards and the repertory of the Paris Opera in 1828. Costumes for this revision were based on the original designs that recollected with a certain nostalgia the simpler pastoral times before the Revolution. The choreographer Jean Dauberval had been the teacher of dancing master Jean Aumer. Aumer created a slightly revised version, adding new music by Ferdinand Hérold. The *Courrier des Théâtres* of the time recalled Dauberval's original premise for the ballet, his having seen a picture of a young peasant girl crying, her clothes in disarray, her mother hurling angry words at her while the lover escapes.

Another ballet of importance, *La Muette de Portici*, was hailed as a *succès fou*, an enormous success, and the March 5, 1828, *Petit Courrier des Dames* noted a big crowd for the debut, applauding the beauty of Mademoiselle Noblet in the pantomime as she revealed "the secrets of an art that she carried to such a high degree of perfection." Costume illustrations displayed the charm and well-chosen appointments of Lecomte's designs. His designs for *La Muette de Portici* were of considerable interest, as Lecomte used popular costumes from the seventeenth century, with hairdos and petticoats similar to those found at that time.

The *Courrier* revealed that the beautiful people in the audience wore "enchanting blue berets with white feathers and adorned in fabulous jewels." Again, on March 20, the costumes in *La Muette* were noted both on stage and in the audience. The *Courrier* also mentioned that the younger women did not wear the usual cashemere shawls or white feathers, but the older crowd touted turbans as a novelty.

Pierre Gardel's long and autonomous reign as Maître de ballet was coming to an end. Though he produced no more full-length ballets after 1818, he skillfully ran the company until 1829, ushering the dancers and choreographers into the new, more commercialized period of Romantic Ballet. The exquisite Marie Taglioni honored Pierre Gardel by dancing the title role in his ballet *Psyché* at his benefit performance February 23, 1829, the 561st performance of this popular ballet.[55]

Two ballet scenarios that survive today as important representatives of the Romantic era were commissioned from Eugène Scribe: *La Belle au Bois Dormant* (*Sleeping Beauty*) (Scribe, Aumer, Hérold) and *Manon Lescaut* (Scribe, Aumer, and Halévy). On April 27, 1829, *La Belle au Bois Dormant* had its first performance. It was originally presented as a *divertissement* by Gardel in the opera *La Belle au Bois Dormant* (1825), with music by Carafa. The fairy tale by Charles Perrault provided a light schema for the work. The audience at the Opéra adored the opulence of the scenery and the workings of the machinery created by Ciceri. Spectators delighted in what could not be found in real life, moments of transcendental magic. During a banquet

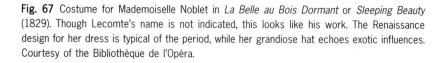

Fig. 67 Costume for Mademoiselle Noblet in *La Belle au Bois Dormant* or *Sleeping Beauty* (1829). Though Lecomte's name is not indicated, this looks like his work. The Renaissance design for her dress is typical of the period, while her grandiose hat echoes exotic influences. Courtesy of the Bibliothèque de l'Opéra.

Fig. 68 Marie Taglioni was the hit of *La Belle au Bois Dormant*. Her beauty and grace mesmerized an otherwise unimpressed audience. She emerges from the depths of the ocean in Naiad-like ball dresses. Courtesy of the Bibliothèque de l'Opéra.

Fig. 69 *Manon Lescaut* evoked the excesses and ornamentation of eighteenth-century ball gowns. Courtesy of the Bibliothèque de l'Opéra.

scene, at the wave of a wand, all of the dishes and flowers on the table turned into reptiles breathing flames of different colors. In a later production of *la Belle au Bois Dormant* (which is still performed today), one of the dancers, Monsieur Simon, asked his friend, the great romantic painter Eugène Delacroix, to design his costume. Delacroix created a Louis XVIII chevalier while the rest of the costumes were done in a Renaissance mode. The sketch, a sepia, used two tones of red and blue washed with white and showed a hand on the hip against the skirt, and a doublet with open sleeves with high soft boots, and a large felt hat with a scarlet plume.

The second scenario that Scribe presented was based on L'Abbé Prévost's novel *Manon Lescaut* (1733), which is also performed to this day and was choreographed by Jean Aumer and again starred Pauline Montessu. Premiering May 3, 1830, it capitalized on the continuing fascination for sentimental romances about women and love. The ballet featured eighteenth-century costumes and sets that had great nostalgic appeal. Scribe calculated that the heroine Manon needed different dramatic qualities and that she should no longer be played as a shrewd and ultimately dangerous young woman. Rather, he created a kind of Clarissa, a deeply emotional and provincial girl who encounters difficulties with wealthy and powerful suitors.

In this ballet, the composer Halévy discovered what soon became a common element of ballet music, the leitmotif, a recurring theme. Lecomte's designs for this bucolic production with its shepherds, sylvans, and nymphs, returned to the inventions of Boquet, Gillot, and Bérain, thus creating a light, fine, and amusing costume series. Noteworthy were the uniform costumes designed by Eugène Lami, whose costumes were conceived with clarity and imagination.

Soon after, Lami worked on *L'Orgie*, an absurd, light-hearted ballet choreographed by Coralli. Taking place in Seville in 1809, the heroine is kidnapped by don Carlos who goes off to war for three years. Upon his return he no longer recognizes her, apparently because she is wearing a different dress! Lami succeeded in making many fabulous uniforms for the numerous cavaliers, soldiers, and dragoons. The Parisian spectators gladly recognized these clothes from the recent Napoleonic wars as memories of heroic times now lost.

Manon Lescaut was the last ballet to be choreographed by the talented and underrated Jean Aumer. He decided to resign his position as dancing master in the spring of 1831, and the Director Véron replaced him with Jean Coralli. Aumer died two years later from a stroke. One of the problems with his tenure seemed to be that he feared for his job and his reputation because he lacked the enduring respect of his colleagues. Apparently, Aumer made the mistake of allowing the person who wrote the scenario equal billing with himself, and this decision put his creative abilities at a certain disadvantage. The wily, self-protective Gardel never experienced this humiliation.

Charles X's conservative and Victorian policies were mirrored at the Opéra in the appointment of the strait-laced Vicomte Sosthène de la

Rochefoucauld, who was superintendent from 1824 until 1830. It was he who ordered that the skirts of dancers should be lengthened by one-third "so that carnal thoughts should not occur to the gentlemen who sat close to the stage!"[56] He even covered up with ivy the private parts of statues that decorated various parts of the Opéra. Honoré de Balzac remarked upon this *pudeur* in his story "A Prince of Bohemia," adding that other prudish reforms of the 1820s ruined the ballet in Paris during those years, although he does not specify what was ruined.

Despite the longer dresses, the ballet became increasingly popular during these critical years in practically every way. The stage picture and costumes illuminated its stories of grandiose events with opulent transformations and the new gas lighting, as well as the dance technique, attracted more and more attention.

For years, Boulevard theaters presented evocative dancing scenarios that were situated in faraway countries. For that matter, so did the Paris Opéra and London's Kings Theatre. What changed were the visits to Paris of dancers from other countries and an emerging fascination for all things foreign. In 1830, it was especially an attraction for Spanish beauties and dancers, (Delorès Séral, an Andalusian, danced a bolero that Ellsler transposed into the cachucha.[57] This fascination for Spanish "gypsies" became known as *Espagnolisme.* Several years later, Spanish dancers danced in their exotic habits at the balls that drew all of haute société and helped propel the way for an uproarious popular phenomenon.[58] They encouraged choreographers to explore other regional dances; the *danses populaires* were performed with great zest and verve by all dancers; and their training had to include lessons in the music and dance forms of different nations. Dancer Taglioni enjoyed her various roles of other nationalities, dancing an animated tyrolian and a Russian peasant dance dressed in "une sarafane de satin bleu," creating a tasty cocktail of both folklore and classicism which was enchanting."[59]

Perhaps as a result of the poverty of the child dancer, Nestor Roqueplan, former director of the Paris Opéra, described a new or more recognized addition to the Opéra's population, *le rat.* "Rats" were child dancers working at the Opéra, the gypsies of the corridors backstage, and a symptom of the industrial age. According to Roqueplan, they were students of the dance school who "lived there, *grignote* (nibbled) there, *jabote* (chattered or prattled) there and *clapote* (feet made splashing noises) there." The *rat* was very young, seven to fourteeen years old, and became *a member of the chorus of amours,* or *sylphides.* She wore old ballet shoes from older dancers, old shawls, hats the color of soot *(suie),* and she warmed herself by smokey oil lamps. She carried bread in her pockets and asked everyone for pennies to buy bonbons. She made holes in the scenery to watch the show and ran behind the back drops, playing in the corners of the corridors. She earned twenty sous each night and got eight or ten francs a month and thirty kicks from her mom.[60]

In their desire for security and an acceptable place in society, nineteenth-century dancers sought marriage and propriety. Roqueplan discussed earlier times when upper-class men took actresses and dancers for their mistresses; only to discover pleasure and ruin with these women. He recalled a very interesting story about a powerful revolutionary terrorist who loved an actress. When she asked him what he would give her for her birthday, he answered, "I will give you your life" ("Je te donnerai la vie"). Roqueplan lamented that after the Revolution women performers were forced to make art and nothing more. He bemoaned the *embourgoisement* of the Opéra, ennumerating the lamentable changes for ballerinas at the Opéra. When the Opéra was privatized in 1830, it became an *affaire de commerce* or an *affaire bourgeoise*. No longer a state-run institution, it lost the glamour of former days and encouraged different standards of morality. Dancers married dancers and singers married singers. The sexual arrangements of former times became real marriages with contracts and women who swore fidelity to their husbands. They no longer dreamed of great town houses and rich wardrobes. They bowed to the husbands who did their *entrechats* along with them.[61]

The person responsible for the *embourgeoisement* of the Opéra was the entrepreneur, Louis Véron, who served from 1831 to 1835, during which time he enriched himself. Like his father, he later went into publishing and in 1844 took over *Le Consitutionnel*, an important newspaper at that time.[62] His spectacular reign was described by Charles de Boigne in *Petits Mémoires de l'Opéra*, offering a clear and unsympathetic picture of Véron's brief administration. Everything Véron did depended on how much commercial value and publicity he could wrest from any decision or possession. He learned to use the tools of the media by advertising, including his horse and carriage, his dinners in cafés, and especially his artists.

Money dominated all of his decisions. In four years, Véron personally made 900,000 francs. He retired before the finish of his contract, ceding his position and what he owed the Opéra to Henri Duponchel, who with Aguado became the next leaders of the Opéra. No longer dependent upon the monarchy for political direction, some thought there was more hope for the ballet. De Boigne emphasized that Véron, like a pasha, did everything in a big way. Backstage at the Opéra became an elegant club, not a place to be scorned or ashamed of.[63] The *foyer de la danse,* or the place where men went backstage to view the dancers, was described as a temple of voluptuousness without *volupté:*

It is a large hall that was once a part of the hôtel de Choiseul. All around, from top to bottom, there used to be mirrors displayed and panelling that was white and gilded; in the back, there is a marble bust of la Guimard; round wooden rods covered with old red velvet as equally spaced; there are a few gas lamps, some bench seats, a worm-eaten table. On top of this table lies the attendance sheet, embellished with arabesques and extraordinary signatures: such is the home of dance—before dance as we know it came to be—in the days when it was still busy in its dressing rooms wrapping itself up and applying white and red make up. Ballet! The season ticket holder only dreams of ballet! Thanks to ballet, this sad and depressing home of dance brightens up and is transfigured.[64]

Boigne goes on to describe the experience of the dancers in the *foyer de la danse*:

The first subjects appear with watering cans in hand. The place belongs to them. They are home. While devoting themselves to their usual exercises, they do the honors. The first subjects walk in steadfastly; their dignity does not allow them to run like someone playing a mere minor part. Taglioni is the only one who flies in; she cannot help herself. As soon as they enter, they continue to walk steadfastly toward the barre, hold on to it with one hand and, with the other, pour water on the floor from their watering cans, and rub their shoes on the wet floor; then with a gesture filled with authority, they hand over the already-mentioned watering can to their mother or to the sister in their service that is also holding their shawls.[65]

Albéric Second described in his *Les Petits Mystères de l'Opéra* the young ballet dancer in rehearsal; he did not find her practice clothing appealing or magical:

The women are bare-headed and low-necked; they have bare arms, their figures are imprisoned in tight bodices. A skirt, very short, very puffed out, either in gauze or striped muslin, reaches to the knee. Their thighs are chastely hidden beneath large calico knickers, as impenetrable as a state secret . . . I have no hesitation in asserting that a dancer at class is not at all captivating or poetic.[66]

Théophile Gautier in *La Peau de Tigre* (1866), gave a clear account of the young ballerinas in their classes, offering perhaps one of the most thorough descriptions of their dance dress. They wear "a short skirt of white muslin or black satin, a piqué bodice, white silk stockings and cambric knickers reaching to the knees which replace the tights, worn only on the stage."[67] One detects here the growing modesty that developed at different moments during the nineteenth century.

Descriptions of the English dancer's discreet costume were exciting fare for newspaper readers as seen in the April 6, 1845 issue of *The Satirist*:

> The soloists of the ballet envelop their dainty limbs in complete fleshlings, a privilege which seems denied to the ordinary members of the corps at Her Majesty's Theatre. The curious habit of swaddling their legs—the upper part at least—with white folds of calico is better calculated to defeat curiosity than to delight the eye of the pit spectator. But delicacy just now is at a higher premium than usual.[68]

The prudery of Charles X's reign spilled over into the corridors of the Opéra, while the scenic and technical designers exploited the brilliance of their new machinery. Though ballet spectacle and transformations astonished its audiences, the dancer's body and its technical expertise were soon to capture center stage.

CHAPTER **9**

The Turning Point
"The Ballet of the Nuns"
and La Sylphide

The Romantic imagination stirred up and enjoyed fearful adventures and nightmarish thoughts, especially of young women at risk. The movies of the early twentieth century, such as *The Perils of Pauline*, concentrated on similar themes. Fantastic and extreme, even brutal, mysteries became popular in the late eighteenth century with the Boulevard melodramas of writer Arnould-Musset.[1] In the nineteenth century, the short tales of writer T. E. Hoffman strongly influenced choreographers and dancers and their taste for the *fantastique*.

E. G. Robert practically invented the taste for the grotesque and weird. In 1797 he installed himself in a large, abandoned chapel in the middle of the Church of the Capucins in Paris. Cemeteries were often the settings for his scary stories. In one of his famous productions, *Young Enterrant sa Fille*, or *Young Burying his Daughter*, the protagonist Young, carrying the inanimate body of his daughter, enters a subterranean place where there are richly endowed tombs. He knocks on the first tomb where a skeleton appears and frightens him away. The same thing happens with another tomb, but by the third, a shadow rises and asks, "What do you want?" He responds, "A tomb for my daughter," and the shadow relinquishes his place for Young's daughter. Just as the cover is closing on this tomb, her soul rises to the sky and Young throws himself on the tomb, declaring his happiness at this event.[2]

Audiences loved le *merveilleux*, the realm of mystery and fantasy that Romantic Ballet provided, and, as a result, new technologies were discovered

Fig. 70 Third act ballet scene from *Robert le Diable,* portraying nuns who come alive from their tombs. It was the sensation of the season, with Taglioni as the Abbess. Courtesy of the Bibliothèque de l'Opéra.

to improve scenic design and create new special effects. Since popular theaters in Paris were pouring larger sums into scene design, the administration of the Paris Opéra realized they needed to do the same. A committee under the direction of Duponchel was formed in 1827 to supervise its efforts. One of its first decisions was to send designer Pierre Ciceri to Italy to study Italian scene painting.

The efforts of the brilliant Ciceri, photographer Daguerre and his diorama, or a stage backdrop without borders with subtle light that gives the illusion of a particular locale, the costumers Fragonard, Lecomte, and Lami and particularly the invention of gas lighting in 1817, enhanced the settings and thereby the glory of Romantic Ballet. "Helping the illusion considerably were the varied effects of illumination now possible because of the introduction of gas lighting."[3] In particular, the lighting was able to reproduce moonlight that became a vital ingredient of the Romantic ballet. Without the growth of scenic technology, in which magical illusions surpassed the transformations of the seventeenth and eighteenth centuries, romanticism could not have thrived. New scenic attributes enabled the choreographer to imagine more natural settings with storms of greater power; thick, dark forests; and gentler, more bucolic environs and village squares and interiors.

Shadowy and mysterious places with diaphanous costumes became scenic events that audiences adored. As décor became an optical feast, costumes followed suit. The costume most responsible for the birth of the so-called Romantic tutu is the white tunic style creation worn by the corps de ballet in Act III of the Ballet of the Nuns of Giacomo Meyerbeer's *Robert le Diable*. Long discussed by dance historians as the seminal Romantic representation, its influences derive from nordic spiritism as well as English gothic novels. In the cloister scene, spectres in white voile float above the funereal pavement stones and presage the "sylphs" of the ballet *La Sylphide* and the "wilis" of the ballet *Giselle*.[4]

Fig. 71 The ballet from Robert le Diable. Painting by Edgar Degas (1876). This production was a careful re-staging of the original Ciceri and Lamy designs and presents a dream-like version of the Bacchanale scene. Courtesy of the Metropolitan Museum of Art.

The historic importance of this opera and especially the "Ballet of the Nuns" is due in part to the choreographic inventions of Filippo Taglioni working with his daughter, Marie Taglioni. Taglioni's performance as the mother abbess Héléna captivated its audience and especially the composer Meyerbeer.[5] *Robert le Diable* premiered November 21, 1831; it had more than 750 French performances before it was finally dropped in 1893. In the Act III ballet scene, the Nuns divest themselves of their habits unexpectedly to reveal their light, white, tutu-like dresses that, according to illustrations, seem rather too bouffante to fit comfortably under their habits. The scene, which was reported to have cost nearly 50,000 francs, "was to be acknowledged as the precursor of the *ballets blancs* that would be such a feature of the new type of ballet that was to capture the imagination of the public for generations to come."[6] Marie Taglioni was responsible for its success to such a degree, that Meyerbeer refused to let her go when she wanted to be replaced in order to start work on *La Sylphide*. She only performed the role of Héléna six more times before Pauline Duvernay took over for her.

The visual documentation of the celebrated "Ballet of the Nuns" is curiously inconsistent. Some illustrations show a white costume that is softly flowing and closely touching the body; others, which may have been from later productions, display the look of an hourglass costume, with a tutu-like skirt that billows out from the waist. Perhaps the immateriality of the vision despaired designers and painters. Degas's vision of the ghostly scene remains the best suggestion of its mood; though he painted a much later version of the ballet scene in 1871, the program stated that the decor and costumes were based on the original Ciceri designs in the opera in 1871. No contemporary graphic representation of the ballet renders justice to the scene where Bertram, with his cavernous voice, evokes the vision of the nuns waking from their tombs. They were *les jolies damnées* who gave up their joys in heaven for voluptuousness on earth. Gautier describes this moment with the nuns in white chemise-like gauze dresses:

> One can vaguely see the coffin covers open up in the darkness, while hearing the beating palpitations of the wings of moths; then indistinct forms begin to emerge from the obscure scene detaching themselves from each standing tomb and climbing each flag stone, like smokey fumes. A ray of light from an electric jet shoots forth across the church-like vaults sketching in the bluish shadows the feminine forms which, under the whiteness of their shrouds begin to move with a deathly sensuality.[7]

The *Courrier des Théâtres*, on October 27, 1831, was quoted as saying, "It's admirable; it's frightening what one will see in *Robert le Diable*. What grace, what terror, what truth, what fantasy! A nun's Bacchanale in their

Fig. 72 The role of Abbess Hélène initially played by Taglioni, in a habit that, when torn off, exposed the ballet gown dress worn during the bacchanale scene that followed. Courtesy of the Bibliothèque de l'Opéra.

simple habits, and finally some things which will be admired from the loges for at least six months!"

Typical of the frivolities associated with the stage, the December 25, 1831, *Journal des Dames* advertised chocolate fantasies created in honor of the story of Robert de Paris by Walter Scott:

> It is going to rain Robert-le-Diable like candies and, regarding this opera, the confections are likely to play a famous part! Briefly speaking the candy-makers are going to make a mint during the holidays. The public should try not to remain indifferent as they walk by their shops decorated with these marvels and then everything will be for the best.[8]

The English journal, *La Belle Assemblée*, July 1832, also remarked upon the striking "Robert," but, as purveyors of gossip, they preferred to discuss the mishaps on stage: "Mlle Taglioni, while resting against a tomb in the front of the stage was exposed to a similar peril, by the sudden descent of another fragment of the scenery."[9]

Several puritanical critics objected to the power of this religious sabbath. An Englishman, Lord Mount Edgcumbe, in *Musical Reminiscences*, 1834, protested:

> The French stage, once the pattern of decency and propriety, is now become a school for profaneness and immorality, the most sacred subjects are exhibited, the most indecent exposed, almost without disguise in opera, melodrames and ballets; of this perverted type is *Robert le Diable*; yet I am sorry to say it had been translated and produced at our theatres. I saw it acted out at Covent Garden, and never did I see a more disagreeable or disgusting performance, the sight of the resurrection of a whole convent of nuns, who rise from their graves, and begin dancing like so many bacchantes, is revolting, and a secret service in a church, accompanied by an organ on the stage, not very decorous.[10]

The "Ballet of the Nuns" perpetuated the French fascination for the Gothic and women floating around tombs, especially as Taglioni was so convincing in her role as the Abbess. Gautier attributed part of this modish interest in the Gothic to a fascination for the Middle Ages, especially what was presented in the opera, ballet, and theater.

> . . . Who will deliver me from the Middle Ages, . . . from these Middle Ages that are not the middle ages? O the cathedrals with their ever full-blown roses . . . their lace work of granite, their open trefils, their stone chasubles embroidered like a bridal veil, their tapers, their chants, their glittering priests, their kneeling people . . . their angels hovering and flapping their wings beneath the vaulted roofs.[11]

La Silphide M.de Taglioni. (A.O.)
(opéra)
1832

Fig. 73 No single costume is more important than that worn by Marie Taglioni in *La Sylphide* (1832). Lami's conception led to the archetypal design for the tutu worn by all ballerinas. Courtesy Bibliothèque de l'Opéra.

The nun's *féerique* dress presaged the tutu, which was said to enhance the spirituality of the dancer. However, when the nuns tossed off their habits and danced a *bacchanale*, the spirituality evaporated and the dance titillated the spectators.

This was not the case in *La Sylphide*, when the angel Taglioni achieved an idealized perfection and gave the impression of never touching the earth. She flew, and one supposes that her new lilting and light costume helped her to create this seraphic vision.[12]

No single theatrical costume in the history of ballet is more important than that worn by Taglioni in *La Sylphide*, for of it was born the tutu, which is to ballet as the ermine to royalty. That costume is the prototype and elder sister of all tutus. As the costume designer, Lami's name is inextricably tied to the triumph of Taglioni and the first true Romantic ballet. Artists, and notably A. E. Chalon, recognized the visual excitement of Taglioni's performance, as well as Lami's charming costumes, and the link between the artist and his stage costumes became interchangeable. "Stage artists were deliberately serving the public taste and even elevating it, as art was now seen properly to do so."[13]

Lami's artistic invention of the tutu became the symbol and the uniform of the dancer. Although *La Sylphide* achieved fame for the tutu, its design could be seen in a sketch of Taglioni as the nymph or dryad Flore by Chalon.[14] The first sketch of the tutu as we know it was made by Lepaulle in 1834; a relatively short skirt made up of many layers of tarletan, a décolleté bodice with flowers placed on her low neckline, sleeves that bloom out as was the fashion, a clear silk floating belt (Vaillat said it was blue), pearl bracelets, a pearl necklace, a subtle crown of wild flowers, and two transparent wings. The effect became a fashion marker.

We do not really see the tutu as we know it until the performance of *La Péri* in 1843, when Paul Lormier designed the Péri costume. The shape of the tutu in *Robert le Diable* and *La Sylphide* was less flared and fell more naturally from the waist, so that the extravagant, expansive layering of tarletan or tulle or gauze came a bit later.

The most notable characteristics of the tutu are its lightness and floating qualities made possible because the material provides the ethereal elasticity necessary for the bell-shaped, layered skirts. At the end of the eighteenth century, the inventions of new machines made possible the manufacture of the tutu. The fabric, gauze, originally came from the Near East, but was manufactured in Lyon and Paris. Gauze is transparent and requires a complex process of production. Its usage for ballet costumes became intimately connected to the tutu's development during the nineteenth century.

Another extremely popular material in the making of the tutu, muslin or *mousseline*, saw a tremendous vogue during this time. French and English manufacturers made great efforts to create the fine and transparent muslin with the seeming lightness of spring clouds. Astonishingly, three hundred meters of material weighed no more than a pound.

Tarlatan also served as a tutu fabric. It was made of cotton and was the preferred material for ballroom dance dresses. It served as the underskirt because of its stiff texture as well as its suppleness. Manufactured in the city Tulle in the department of Corrèze in the Massif Central, the material tulle with a netted weave was also utilized as a light-weight fabric that was used for embroidery and lace. It was considered *le roi des tissus*, but in 1816 the first machine caused a battle between England and France for the sale of the product. Toward 1830, the various systems of manufacture, including Jaquard, allowed for a variety of designs and laces in this elegant fabric. Tulle was used commonly in many furnishings, etc. Today three different kinds of tulle are used for tutus. A similar fabric, voile, served as a material like the tutu costumes that Degas painted.[15]

La Sylphide opened March 12, 1832, with the elegaic Taglioni's arienne performance. The influence of the ballet *La Sylphide* on the development of audience taste and the direction of *danse d'école* cannot be overestimated. Adapted from Charles Nodier's story, *Trilby ou le lutin de l'Argail* (1822), Adolphe Nourrit's scenario satisfied a new interest in natural wonders and tragic and mysterious events. Ciceri and Lami both succeeded in creating the transformative atmosphere, while the original music by Schneithoffer did not necessarily satisfy, as a writer for the fashion magazine of March 25 *Journal des Dames* said, "The music is the weak link; it is too uniform."(*La musique est la partie faible; c'est trop uniforme.*)[16]

Théophile Gautier stated that this ballet initiated Romanticism in the dance world. He pointed to the rose-colored tights and satin slippers instead of the Greek cothurne as well as a "great abuse of white gauze and tarletan" and spoke of the shadowy creatures in transparent skirts who seemed to evaporate before our eyes. White was the color that dominated these romantic women.[17]

The story tells of James, a young Scotch farmer, who sits dreamily by the fireside on the eve of his marriage to Effie.[18] James's love for Effie vanishes when he sees the wispy Sylphide clad in a tutu and toe shoes, whose seductive dancing charms him. She leads him into the woods, where many other sylphs fly in the trees. The witch Madge offers him a magic shawl to catch the Sylphide, and when he wraps it around her body, her wings fall off and she collapses and dies. At the same moment, James observes Effie and his friend Gurn on their way to marry. This leaves James miserable and bereft forever.

The story had been created in an earlier production in 1822 by Louis Henry in Milan and had many subsequent versions with different scores.

costumes de M. TAGLIONI, rôle de la SILPHIDE, et de MAZILLIER, rôle de JAMES REUBEN, dans la Sylphide. Ballet.

Académie Royale de Musique

Malœuvre Sculp

Chez Hautecœur Martinet, Libraire, rue du Coq, N.º 3 et 15, Paris.

Fig. 74 Marie Taglioni partnered by Joseph Mazillier in *La Sylphide* (1832). Courtesy of the Bibliothèque de l'Opéra.

All of the dancers were excellent, but Taglioni excelled. Jules Janin wrote in *The Journal des Débats*, August 24, 1832:

> This is a danseuse! We need know nothing else when we see her so relaxed, so happy to dance, dancing like the bird sings . . . Look! She uses her hands when she dances! Look at her bending torso! Such novelty! Look at her two legs, they walk! Look at how she always remains on the ground! Look! There is not a pirouette, entrechat, or difficulty in sight—nothing but dance! This woman walks, performs dramas and idylls—as a woman! Oh, this ravishing girl! She has given us a new art and taught us one more pleasure.[19]

Taglioni's Sylphide brought a new slant on the widely popular literary conceit of the sylph. Unique was the modernization of this sylphide who was a romantic and lived in a world that combined folklore, Medieval Scottish themes, and magic. The winged-sylph dancer wore butterfly, beetle, or moth wings. Later (1836) peacock feathers, strangely enough, were attached to the other wings perhaps to overlay them with an iridescence as "they trembled and fluttered in the gas light."[20]

Marie Taglioni represented fashion's ultimate heroine, as a propagandist for mechanical corsets, and as a star of the fashion journals of her time. Their articles emphasized her entrancing qualities: The March 25, 1832, *La Belle Assemblée* noted:

> The success of *La Sylphide* has been enormous. Mlle Taglioni was never so radiant, light, coquettish, alive, but still gracious; this is a Sylphide who emerges from the hearth and begins to fly; a Sylphide who entices and then flees; a Sylphide who suffers and dies.[21]

The beauty of her tutu was transfigured and enhanced by the scene in the forest, where many similarly costumed women dancers, suspended on wires, were discovered flying through the trees.

The great feat of Taglioni in her performance of *La Sylphide* in 1832 was to promote the invention of toe dancing as it had never before been shown. Her use of pointe dancing, after apparently grueling hours of training from her instransigent father, dignified her performance and brought her ability to suspend and move more swiftly to a higher plane. Her ballet shoes helped her to physically impersonate the sylph as a muse who seduces and threatens at the same time.

Taglioni's effect upon her audiences caused the creation of a new verb *taglioniser* (to be "sylph-like") and a new turban. A Sylphide Turban was invented, as was the coiffure à la Sylphide, just as several generations earlier women wore the *robe à la Guimard*. Her success resulted from the imagination of the artists as well as the taste of the public. The word Sylphide also became an adjective.

As fashion magazines grabbed hold of representations of Taglioni and lionized her, she fomented an esthetic of the wasp waist, with the undulations and the suppleness of vines and the graceful, minute shapes of an ideal fragility. Hats and necklines were typically adorned with flowers and lace, but with the advent of Taglioni's successes, "women added all sorts of *fanfreluches* or ornamentations to offer the appearance of lightness and vaporousness."[22]

Taglioni's accomplishments in the ballet also created a new philosophy of the dance and its focus on beauty. She came from a long line of great Italian performers who traveled the world and made their names in Paris, London, and, of course, Milan. Italian dancers and choreographers contributed beyond all others to the extension of ballet movement, especially for their startling virtuosity and dramatic sensibility as their choreographers emphasized the expansion of technical invention. Such names as Angiolini, Onorato, Vestris, and Magri during the eighteenth century and Vigano, Blasis, Bigottini, Samengo, and Brugnoli in the early nineteenth century remain notable. Like Italian actors, Italian dancers were known for their dexterity, wit, charm, and serious training in various styles, especially the *grotteschi* or grotesque tradition. What was derived from the long history of dance and theater in Italy and its *commedia dell' arte* tradition was a rigorous physical, sometimes acrobatic, training relying on acting abilities, freeing the body and insisting that the performer learn a minimum standard of virtuosic steps. Performances never seemed inhibited by the clothing worn.

The prodigious amount of writing about Romantic Ballet exists for several reasons and concerns the ethos and the pictorial representation of the ballerina, her body, and her clothing. The "white goddess" became a kind of film star.

> Never before or since have so many 'presentation books' poured from the presses—albums of pictures with or without text; gift books (Keepsakes was the happy and homespun English expression), richly dight (sic) as a medieval Book of Hours with 'illuminations,' pictorial and ornamental, to enhance their often slender literary claims.[23]

The commercialization of ballet, both in London and in Paris, thrived with the visualization of its finest moments in portfolios, galleries, periodicals, etc. The stories of operas and ballets were included in these books so that the tales and their illustrations beguiled the new middle-class readers with escapist dreams. In addition, the iconography of Romantic ballerinas intrigued ballet lovers and created poetic images that told more about

Taglioni's genius than all the critics' words. Achille Deveria created a celebrated colored lithograph of the Sylphide bounding toward the footlights
with very high jetés. Chalon's series display a profound accuracy of observation, as do the sketches by the Russian artist Bassine. They all reveal
Taglioni's "imponderable flight," or *équilibres sur la pointe*. It was clearly
understood that under her diaphanous covering was a steel armature.[24]

The Romantic Ballet is the true ancestor of our ballets today. Choreographic and technical inventions of the period, along with the evolution of
the tutu and pointe dancing, were major developments that founded our
modern concepts of dance and costume. The "Ballet of the Nuns" and *La
Sylphide* remain as two of the most influential ballets of all time and were a
major turning point in the history of ballet.

CHAPTER **10**

The Dark Side of White

Important shifts in taste and tradition in fashion and ballet from the 1780s to the 1830s influenced the way women and dancers were perceived and had profound consequences on how they lived their lives, especially for ballerinas during the 1830s in Paris and London. Ballet dancers were poorly paid, forced to train in unhealthy ways, and were therefore at risk for prostitution and serious problems.

Corsets, stylish shoes, and odd-shaped sleeves distorted and disfigured the daily life of the woman in the street. The ballerina also suffered from fashion's caprices that dictated a tiny waist and exquisite feet that took the form of the toe shoe on stage. With the new tutu fashion, her legs were seen and admired, while choreographers capitalized upon the newly discovered limbs by calling attention to the quickly developing leg and foot technique. Strong turn out was becoming *de rigueur.* The opening of the hips and legs, facilitated by hours of daily stretching caused pain, and pain became an important aspect of the dancer's experience. Dancing masters also worked for the power of the legs and feet to such an extent that the dancer tended to become too thin. But the lighter she was, the easier it was to execute the difficult jumps, extensions, and lifts. Audiences could not take their eyes off the ballerina's legs; they barely saw the arms and face of the dancer. In this fragmented form, a few lost the sense of being a whole person.

One of the most cogent reasons for the woman dancer's lack of stability and personal strength occurred in 1830 during Dr. Véron's regime as Director of the Paris Opéra: he no longer provided the dancer with the security of a pension. This occurred at the time of the July Revolution, when there ceased to be support from the royal court. Nestor Roqueplan commented on the July Revolution which changed "la charte des théâtres."[1] When the

Opéra ceased to be a kingdom of divine rights, it fell into the hands of rapacious entrepreneurs with a fixed and regulated subvention. No longer were there aristocratic patrons and protectors from the court. Roqueplan saw this as a paradoxical revolution that was waged against gentlemen, sinecure, huge endowments, debauched viewers, and the executors of money. The consequences of the *embourgeoisement* of the Opéra were long lasting and far reaching. Driven by economics and capricious managers, the jobs of dancers at the Opéra became more flexible, but also dangerously unpredictable. Not long before, the ballet was divided into *premiers sujets*, *remplacements*, *coryphées*, *figurantes* et *comparses*.[2] Suddenly one sees *premiers sujets* or stars who replace others in the corps and the *coryphées* who become *premiers sujets*, forsaking the worn-out standards of an institution that formerly brought a sense of stability.

Consequently, Romantic ballerinas lived harsh lives, despite the picture they created on stage. Their penury was compounded by their backgrounds. "They came, almost without exception, from the poorest families."[3] After 1830, the dancers who already received pensions or whose contracts confirmed their retirement funds were assured of their rights by the government. But Véron decided to eliminate this liability and entered into contracts on whatever terms he wished. This practice lasted until the late 1850s, and it severely changed the perception of the dancer, even though the pension rights were then reinstalled.

In his *Mémoires*, Dr. Véron verified the distinctly low status of dancers, speaking about them as though they were some other species. He mentioned that after his tenure, Duponchel continued to recruit ballet girls from the slums.[4] "One cannot imagine the privations, suffering, fatigue and courage of those poor girls on whom fortune has not yet smiled."[5]

The difficult daily life of the corps de ballet, especially the lack of good food, often led to starvation. "It is as a result of enormous sacrifice and superhuman courage that poor dancers become figurantes or simple corps dancers."[6] Some found the means to teach and therefore earn some money while they were training. Generally, during the 1830s little ballerinas on their way up were poorly clothed and had to walk long distances to the Opéra, as they lived miles away in the poor districts such as La Bastille or Montmartre.

Working poor ballet dancers sought relief from male spectators in the infamous *foyer de la danse* made known by Degas. "In the 1830s . . . the backstage of the Paris Opéra became a privileged venue of sexual assignation, officially countenanced and abetted . . . For the millionaire libertines of the audience . . . performance [was] foreplay to possession" in the "private seraglio" the Opéra had become."[7] Interestingly, management in England developed a similar strategy ten years earlier as a means to attract more subscriptions for their presentations. The need for advance subscriptions was met by the charity of wealthy gentlemen. John Ebers, the Director of The Covent Garden Opera Ballet after its bankruptcy in 1820, opened the wings of the stage and a new green room where rich men could gaze and mix with the dancers and their agents—be they mothers or procurers.[8]

Many ballets during the Romantic period offered a contrasting picture from that of the ballerina as fallen woman. Rather, she called forth depictions of ethereality and chastity as shibboleths for the changing industrial world. "The dancer for women images woman as both cynosure of eyes and epitome of virtue, but both beauty and purity depend upon a sexuality refined to the vanishing point."[9] The ballerina projected a demure manner and a body of extraordinary prowess that was meant to "attenuate" and "disembody" her own sexuality. Both men and women of the 1830–1870 audiences liked the Romantic model, although the number of woman spectators was much fewer. The "ostentatious modesty" of the Romantic ballerina presides over the ballet world today as well: "Perhaps the imagery of ballet blanc has such staying power because it has entered a discourse of the body."[10]

> The ballerina's body is etherealized. She seems to scarcely rest upon the ground. She is, as it were, suspended just slightly above the earth so that we may see her better. She seems cut off from the sources of her being, or rather, those dark internal sources are shown by her as something light and white, brittle as are all baubles, all playthings that we can utterly examine; yet, at the same time, so perfect is her geometry that we feel this plaything which our minds may utterly possess, to be as well the veriest essence.[11]

No longer real, she represented the Platonic ideal:

> In the second act [of La Fille du Danube], the disembodied persons, colourless, wearing the white uniform of pure ideas [tutu], express themselves only in the secret tongue of classical ballet . . . 'It must be a terrible trial to follow that woman who flies like the wind.'[12]

This picture presents a rather intense and problematic description of a nineteenth-century heroine. It adulates her virtuosity and ability to suspend, while it emphasizes her innocence and virtue, which could be seen as victimization as well. There are threats to the chastity of all heroines in the ballet canon.

Perpetuating the view of the ballerina as either saint or sinner, or as having the Madonna/prostitute complex, Théophile Gautier designed an argument for the beautiful dancer Fanny Ellsler and compared her unfairly to Taglioni with the remark that Ellsler was the pagan dancer and Taglioni was the Christian dancer. Ellsler projected a more earthy, folksy impression and his reviews of her performances constantly refered to the beauty and sensuality of her body. Revived interest in a more sensual body as a result of the Spanish dancers performing in Paris did not necessarily contribute to the iconic purity of "the ballerina," even though Victorian messages penetrated Parisian as well as London life. As long as she sought the gaze of her audience members and was being watched by them, she and her body were open to their lascivious and scatalogical thoughts. "Newspaper critics described and compared female dancers' body parts in excruciating and leering details."[13]

Ballerinas wore their tutus, toe shoes, and maillots as standard parts of their performance uniform and they became fetishes for the spectators. Objects like the corset, the tutu, the toe shoe, and maillots—all accoutrements of women dancers—took on lives of their own with biographies that lived through history and related to events in their own way, often unknown to their wearers. They became much more in their significance than in their specific matter, and they became elements in shifting values that caused new meanings and difficult changes. Basically, a fetish represented "The individual displacement of private erotic feeling onto a non-genital part of the body, or onto a particular article of clothing by association with a part of the body, or onto an article of clothing in conjunction with its effect on the body."[14] Writers and artists viewing the exciting new tutu costume, with its singularly thin waist and transparent glimpses of voluptuous legs, relished the sexual charms with which it imbued the dancer. But the tutu also gave status to a dancer.

One explanation for the enduring significance of tutus and toe shoes is that they provided agency for the woman dancer; they signaled her abilities, talents, beauty, dedication, and fame. During the nineteenth century, the ballerina's celebrity status grew while her social status probably diminished. "In adopting a clothing metaphor to project an image of social status or position, one can express various degrees of identification with that position."[15] Wearing a tutu signifed that the dancer had trained vigorously and seriously in order to perform the romantic and classical repertoire.

The classical tutu "became a standard artifact for beauty, vigour, suppleness, vivacity, and harmony in its own right."[16] The costume endured because it was adopted by vaudeville and music halls, choruses of pantomime, as well as the corps de ballet. Though the boulevard dancer was not technically distinguished, the tutu and tights gave her much-needed professional credibility.

The diaphanous gowns worn by Marie Taglioni and others "enhanced the choreographic effect of Romantic plots, but it is clear from engravings and lithographs of danseuses that what was described as ethereality was seen as transparency"[17]—it was the bodies that were prized.

The voyeur/Dandy enjoyed the ballerina's perfection and imagined what great charms were hidden beneath those skirts and tights. To him, she represented "loose morals and easy virtue."[18] The ballerina's traditional role as a sexually available object persisted, but not because she lacked tight lacing. On the contrary, her corset enticed the eager viewer with her delicate neck and waist and tiny, fragile appearance.[19]

Erotic meanings abounded in Romantic ballet, not only because the lead ballerina wore transparent skirts and a décolleté neckline, but also because she was held and occasionally lifted by her male partner. Although nowhere nearly as developed as our understanding of lifts and partnering, the Romantic ballerina did find herself lifted into the air with her skirts flying. "Lifts made pas de deux more athletic and also more erotic, if their presence on five of the first thirty issues of the pornographic weekly *The Exquisite* (published in London between 1840–1842) is a reliable indicator."[20]

If the tutu brought the dancer a certain cachet as a svelte heroine, her toe shoes encapsulated fashion's appetite for the fleet-footed female. Her fragile feet mimicked the street shoe, whose skinny and delicate shape predominated as the look for all women's feet. There was a price paid for the dancer's use of the toe shoe that, as the century progressed, became a serious problem. In 1855, Roqueplan described the dancer's pain:

> The public thinks that the dancer's foot is so beautifully arched, so supple, so graceful when it is encased in a silk stocking and a piqué shoe. However when examining the nude foot of the dancer, one discovers a monstrous appendage with a fat lot of red and tumified skin as a result of the violent and continuous exercises of ossified articulation, which caused twisted toes, ingrown nails, corns, irritated skin and protrusions . . . This is what he thinks is caused by practicing *entrechats, pirouettes* and pointe work.[21]

The shoe fashion of the day, with its taste for higher heels, interacted with what was developing on stage. "The wearer of the high-heeled boot is in the position of one who is walking on tiptoe."[22] Dr. Treves described the physiological danger that high heels imposed on women's feet: the abnormally high arch of the shoe, and the unequal levels upon which the various parts of the sole are placed, tend materially to weaken the instep and natural curve of the foot. The muscles are unable to act as they should act; unequal strain is thrown upon the ligaments, and while some shorten under this false position, others become stretched and weakened. "The stability of the whole foot becomes in time impaired, its graceful outline is lost and the foot that has long been cramped by a fashionable shoe is rendered in time simply and distinctly hideous."[23]

The distinctly hideous foot trained to wear fashionable high heels was a close neighbor to the ballerina's toe slipper:

> In ballet, the tip-toe stance has semi-contradictory associations with the ethereal, spiritual, air-borne. The rising popularity of classical ballet and other forms of tip-toe dance in the nineteenth century represents a major public, artificially more or less sublimated manifestation of foot and leg fetishism. Some have seen an erectile symbolism in the high-flailing leg of the can-can dance, also a product of the nineteenth century. The ballet girl was the erotic priestess, a Terpsichorean hetaira, while the high heel gave to the woman of fashion the erotic lift of the dancer.[24]

The ballerina's fetishist toe shoe has also been seen as an extended phallus: "Then the pointe shoe, a recapitulation of the leg's length and line, forms a slightly bulbous tip at the end of the ankle's thinness."[25]

However sensual the meaning of her legs and feet, dancers dealt with daily pain. The foot was not only to be stood upon, but it was also to be thin and small in its shape. Ballerinas suffered from the unnatural consequences of a tight shoe, as they were encouraged to place their weight on a graceful and dainty foot. In China, the feet of the highbrow women suffered more than we could ever imagine.

Not only did the dancer struggle with the technique that drove her to stand on her toes, but she spent hours reshaping her body and developing strength as Roqueplan tells us:

> The young dancer prepares herself every morning with a thousand hideous contorsions, such as *pliés* and *battements* which stretch her as well as suffocate her and drown her in sweat for the sake of performance. She can be compared to a racehorse, buried in shawls as she runs through the halls and climbs in pain to her dressing rooms. Without vigor, lightness or smiles, she suffers all this for a tiny bit of applause.[26]

De Boigne also recounted the daily experience of classes for the ballet dancer. His descriptions are remindful of Charles Dickens's narrations of children in the workhouses.

> Dancing class has replaced the Inquisition, but with dancing classes one must pay 50 francs a month. The dancing master is without pity for his victims; he stretches them, torments them, shouts and hounds them. Never a moment of rest! Never a word of encouragement! He commands and they obey.[27]

When the dancer wishes to extend the height of her legs in the air, she must stretch even more than her normal exercises:

We must stretch our legs, almost to the breaking point. You see all these feet and all these arms executing a perfect ensemble maneuver. It is a question of holding on to the barre with the right hand, and on command, the hand holding the left foot lifts it higher. In the middle of these tortures, smile![28]

A tragically painful account about a young ballet dancer was reported by Albéric Second:

I was barely seven years old when I was sent to M. Barrez's class at 4 rue Richer. I went out in the morning with my stomach empty, except for a cup of what was said to be coffee. I had neither shoes on my feet nor a shawl on my shoulders, and, as often as not, my thin muslin dress was threadbare like lace.[29]

Her story continues:

I arrived shivering and often starving. Then began the daily suffering of which my description, however exact, cannot give you a real idea . . . Every morning my teacher imprisoned my feet in a grooved box. There, heel-to-heel, with knees pointing outwards, my martyred feet became used to remaining in a parallel line by themselves. They call this 'turning out.' After half an hour of the box, I had to endure another form of torture. This time I had to place my foot on the barre which I had to hold with the opposite hand to the foot in exercise. This was called 'breaking in.' When this toil was over, you might think I was allowed to rest. REST! Does a dancer ever rest? We were just poor wandering Jews at whom M. Barrez incessantly shouted, 'Dance! Dance!'[30]

With all this tortuous attention to bodily perfection, the dancer still had to have a beautiful face as well as a sweet disposition. Dancers became known for their beauty and manners, rather than their talents as moving performers. Confirming this dictum, Roqueplan cynically mentioned the fact that the corps de ballet were no longer beautiful, that the more attractive dancers had given it up to become army wives. "Now the corps is full of ugly and decrepit dancers. The situation at the Opéra became so desperate that the Minister of Police did a *levée en masse* (conscription) for beautiful women between the ages of eighteen and twenty-five."[31] Most of the draftees had no talent as dancers—that caused a general hilarity. Roqueplan tried to explain this dreadful condition by pointing out that military men divided up the corps de ballet among themselves.

Dancers who became mistresses of soldiers or businessmen were better off before 1815 and lost a considerable amount of money as the century progressed. "Under the Empire, one found that the love of a dancer cost 400,000 francs a month. The last years of the Restoration, she might get 30,000 a year."[32]

Offering themselves up to the men in tall black hats who came to observe their pre-performance exercises, the young dancers made their way to the famed *foyer de la danse* before the ballet. Roqueplan recounted that the dancers appeared ragged in their daily treks to the *foyer*, with warm-ups on their feet and arms, and that they walked with an odd turn out which only dancers have, looking like English chickens.[33]

Despite the shabby rehearsal clothes, ballerinas were considered beauteous and magical. Though thin, their bodies appeared attractive, especially their legs, which carried them to new heights. The legs that were revealed after centuries of hiding became an obsession that began in the early part of the century and climaxed with the Can-Can dancers in the late nineteenth century. In an amusing moment, Théophile Gautier, when discussing his career as a ballet librettist, despaired of hoping for more serious themes and quipped, "It is not easy to write for legs."[34]

The nineteenth century was priggish in its attitude toward the lower half of the body. Dancers with their transparent skirts and their flying legs created a great stir in the audience's imagination. Instances of excessive prudery involved the concealment of women's legs. Books on etiquette repeatedly advised their readers to avoid mention of "legs" or to use the less suggestive word, "limb." A story told about an Englishman who traveled to America in 1830 reported him seeing trousers covering the legs of a piano in a seminary for women. Men were easily aroused by a glimpse of a women's ankle. At this time there was a high incidence of fetishes involving shoes and stockings that further "testified to the exaggerated eroticism generated by hiding the lower half of the female body."[35]

From the beginning of the century, the fantasies of the subscribers to the Opéra were always of the same kind. During the Empire, Madame de Rémusat said of the Opéra audience, "The only thing they go to hear are Miss Goudet's legs."[36] Members of the Jockey Club asked a certain manufacturer to make binoculars that enlarged objects thirty two times. "With these awful binoculars underwear becomes a joke. They reveal as much of even the best harnessed legs as if the dancer had slipped out of her dress."[37]

Contemporary writers criticized the tendency for nineteenth-century audiences and writers to divide up the female body into parts, especially those parts with erotic meanings. Historiographers found fault with the visual arts for diminishing the woman's role as a model in paintings, i.e., women became dehumanized objects without agency. The ballet dancers, hairdressers, and "keyhole" nudes in Edgar Degas's paintings were the distant cousins of Vermeer's serving girls. By the nineteenth century they were manipulated like puppets and fragmented into their constituent parts. The notebook jottings of Degas stipulated:

> Of a dancer do either the arms or the legs or the back. Do the shoes— the hands—of the hairdresser—the badly cut coiffure … bare feet in dance, action, etc. Do every kind of worn object placed, accompanied in such a way that they have the life of the man or the woman; corsets which have just been taken off, for example—and which keep the form of the body.[38]

Degas was looking for artifacts of the body that had their own stories to tell, separate from the whole "beautiful picture." But he had not intended to deploy an antifeminine attitude.

There was a fascination with the ballerina's body as a symbol of the mystery and sensuality of femininity. Those who came to see the ballerina back stage played key roles in this theater within a theater. The Dandies' importance in London society life was so far reaching that when they attended the opera, they called attention to themselves by talking and using binoculars to study the dancers' bodies (see Degas's parody, fig. 71). Later, the demise of the Romantic Ballet in London might be attributed to the fact that the public became more serious about Victorian mores and rejected dancers for their lack of prudery.[39]

Comments from contemporary English papers emphasized the generalized appropriation of the dancer and her aching body by male society. The reporter for *The Age* on February 13, 1831 writes, "The ballet is a shade better than last year, but not in the figure, where the same cream-coloured divinities with their ancient faces and thick legs are still allowed to kick out the shoe maker's pumps without grace or agility."[40]

If the camera were to be our means of seeing the Romantic ballerina in nineteenth-century Paris or London, it would surely be focused on the dancers' legs. In *Illustrated London Life*, April 16, 1843, stated:

> The ominibus crowd studied and contemplated the 'new gal's legs'. . . . The legs at the Opera are selections from the best masters— we beg pardon—we mean mistresses, yes, mistresses is precisely what we mean. We perfectly recollect admiring the emotion of several ancient aristocrats in the stalls on the recent appearance of the legs of Fanny Ellsler . . . Oh the legs of Fanny displayed a vast deal of propriety, and frightened sober men from their prescribed complacency. Taglioni's leg encompassed a great deal of attention; Cerrito's leg magnified excitement; Duvernay possessed a magic leg, but to dilate is useless— the Opera is the bazaar of legs and a stall costs ten and sixpence.[41]

By the 1830s the pit of the Covent Garden Opera House known as Fop's Alley, "had become an unruly debauch in which the Dandies from White's and Crockford's loudly commented on the merits and deficiencies of the dancers' bodies, regularly interrupting the ballet with catcalls, obscenities, or the equal furor of their approbation."[42]

Later in the century, the Countess de Castiglioni, mistress to Napoléon III (Emperor of France 1852–1870), commissioned one of the earliest French photographic firms, Mayer and Pierson, to photograph her legs. This series of photographs, taken between 1854 and the 1860s, demonstrated the excitement, allure, and fetishistic value of the legs that ballet and music hall dancers were exposing to the public, a public that became aficionados of Can-Can legs and chorus line legs.[43]

In an article by Théophile Gautier for *Le Figaro* which belongs to a series entitled "Galerie des belles actrices," on October 19, 1837, Gautier calls attention to the inimitable beauty of Fanny Ellsler's legs:

> Which are purely and elegantly shaped, recall the strong, slender lines of those of Diana, the virgin huntress. The kneecaps are neat and well defined, and the whole knee beyond reproach. Her legs are very different from those of the ordinary dancer, whose body seems to have shrunk into her stockings and settled there. They are not the legs of a parish beadle or a knave of clubs that stir the admiration of the elderly gentlemen in the stalls and set them busily polishing the lenses of their opera glasses, but two beautiful legs from an antique statue worthy of being cast and lovingly admired.[44]

Ballet dancers wooed their audiences with the tremendous technical skills of their legs and feet, as well as with their beauty. They are, of course, blamed for the interest others took in these attributes. However, it was their talented legs that brought them their livelihood.

An interesting sidelight to the dancer's glamorous but hard-earned reputation is the effort she made to create the sylph-like impression to which the corset contributed. Her sister in the streets also wore the corset to impress society with her delicate frame.

Wearing a corset that was tightly boned and laced, heels, and large skirts (revived with a fury after Napoléon), a woman of means could neither move quickly, reach far, lift heavy objects, nor raise her arms at any distance. This fragile soul became the heroine of Romantic literature and often died of a broken heart.[45] She required assistance for any physical task and was carefully handed in and out of carriages because of her debilitation. She was trained from childhood to learn "ladylike accomplishments" such as those found in the novels of Thackeray, Dickens, and Disraeli. Her dresses reflected this frail ethos.[46] However, it was also true that the woman in factories or mines in Britain and France worked twelve or more hours a day in clothes that did not impede her ability to accomplish her work.

Another example of the masochistic behavior of the nineteenth-century woman was the practice of wearing hoops and crinolines on stages lit by oil lanterns. In a flash she could be surrounded by flames that could kill or cripple her as they twisted about her ankles, causing escape to be very difficult.[47] Thackeray spoke of the nineteenth-century woman as an "exquisite slave."[48] The tragic story of dancer Emma Livry highlights the dangers of wearing layers of flammable materials. Livry's tutu caught fire during a dress rehearsal at the opera and she suffered great pain for eight months before she died in 1862. Only the metal corset under her tutu went unscathed.

Though the corset "enslaved" women, it brought the torso into what women thought at the time was a favorable silhouette: "Waist or torso compression and breast-sculpture have been historically inseparable." The corset enabled the breasts to look round and as "succulent" as carnal apples.[49]

An opponent of the idea that corseting was a dangerous and common affliction is Edward Shorter, the author of *A History of Women's Bodies.*[50] Shorter debunked the idea that the corset was a dangerous device for the female body. He insisted that very few women, only the upper five percent of the population, from the thirteenth century on, wore corsets and that essentially they were harmless. The number of tracts against corseting, implying that the fashion was prevalent, seems to dispute Shorter's comments. Modern thinking is that corsets prevented full expansion of the ribcage and lungs, and thus caused Restrictive Lung disease.

The wasp waistline, defined by the corset also created a great deal of criticism for this fashion. In *The Absurdities of Stays; and The Evil Effects of Tight Lacing* (1845) by Henry Whitfeld, he pontificated about fashion's idiosyncracies:

> That man is born to trouble, none will deny; but it is equally true that the greater portion of his sufferings is the direct consequence of his own errors; and, although much alleviation cannot be expected till a proportionate improvement is made in his whole moral and intellectual condition, yet, as there is a large amount of misery which arises from the most trivial and absurd causes, to remove which would in no degree curtail even the temporary pleasures of life, I shall endeavor to direct the attention of the public to one of these causes the greatest folly in civilized life, and one of the chief sources of ill-health among females of every class of society—I allude to the use of stays; for so great is the evil, that I doubt if the ingenuity of man could have invented any instrument capable of inflicting on his fair partner a greater degree of suffering, or one that would tend so much to deteriorate the human race.[51]

Whitfield bemoaned the effect of the corset on reducing lung and breath power, sometimes associated with what is called chlorosis or "green sickness," anemia and a serious lack of circulation in the legs. In addition, he mentioned that the corset caused curvature of the spine and premature decay of the bones. He asked:

> But how is it that in this enlightened age this fashion is still a favourite amongst us? It is that man is a creature of habits; and so much is he under their sway that great exertion, and often considerable moral courage is required to set them aside; and as the study of the laws of nature is but little included in the education of the community, we cannot be surprised that they are almost wholly disregarded, while the laws of society are bowed to with submission, however frivolous their origin and painful their results.[52]

He cited a case study from the early 1840s of a woman who could only speak in a weak whisper, who in two years went from a waist of twenty eight inches to a waist of twenty three inches, who could not eat or sleep, had a cough, etc. She was directed to enlarge her stays and to abolish the busk immediately. She recovered her voice in five weeks and in three months was fine. No medicine was prescribed!

Children were especially susceptible to health problems, according to Whitfield, because they were growing:

> For while every other part of the body is increasing in size and growing into womanhood, the chest is confined to the proportions of infancy; and experience convinces me that to this may be attributed the immense number of cases of debility among females.[53]

Confirming the earlier opinion of Whitfield, Dr. Daumas wrote in 1861:

> The corset bruises the hips, creases and hardens the skin. Around the waist it causes a red, inflamed, wrinkled aureole. Some women in the evening, when they undress, are so tortured by burning sensations that they tear their flesh with their pink nails.[54]

In *Hygiène Vestimentaire*, Dr. Debay offered these statistics which averaged forty years of observation: "Of 100 young girls wearing a corset: 25 succumbed to diseases of the chest; 15 died after their first delivery; 15 remained infirm after delivery; 15 became deformed; 30 alone resisted, but sooner or later were afflicted with serious indispositions."[55]

Suffering became a necessity for fashion in the Romantic era. Maigron, quoting from "unpublished documents," described the purpose of the couturier as "one who makes the body conform to a columnar shape."[56] The female martyr must submit to untold tortures to be thin enough, dainty enough or small enough for the finesse of fashion. In addition to a meager diet, the 1830 journal *La Mode* told us that the supreme distinction was to appear languorous, expiring, without vivacity or gaity. Women must walk like shadows without limbs.[57]

In addition to causing poor health, corsets represented another aspect of fetishistic behavior. Like women's legs, the sylph-like delicacy of body and fragility of waist appealed to man's erotic imagination and offered men "visions of his superior socio-sexual power as he is so much larger."[58]

Both women on stage and on the street affected a quality of evanescence and wispyness. The flowing and floating tulle skirts contributed to the woman's look of lightness and vulnerability. If she were a thin soul, as apparently Marie Taglioni was, this picture of sylph-like buoyancy grew.

The intense and demanding life of the dancer could easily be compared to a religious vocation. Since living for the stage and the dance career have often seemed as serious as a religious creed, it seems appropriate to find analogies to ballet in religious orders. Strenuous exercises, harsh hours, and fatigue led to unhealthy eating habits and, in some cases, anorexia. There is a curious relationship between skinny women and the nineteenth-century literary craze for gothic melodrama. A fascination for Medieval Christian thought, fueled by the writings of Chateaubriand and the worship of martyred women, was to some extent reflected in the Romantic ballet scenarios as well as in the image of the ballerina. Young women of the Romantic era starved themselves in order to appear beautifully thin and pale as the novels portrayed. "She aspired to look as pale as her friend Marguerite, so she drank vinegar, and ate lemons . . . she died at nineteen years of age, 'd'une maladie de langueur.' By dint of depriving herself of nourishment and by eating acidic foods, she ruined her body."[59]

In addition, the Romantic yearning for a "sublimely emaciated female body" (later envisioned by Aubrey Beardsley) looked to the sylph as "female desire unborn," somehow satisfying some bizarre ideals purveyed by the professional white male world.[60]

Devotées of Saint Catherine of Siena began to be seen at the end of the eighteenth century. Saint Catherine is said to have died of Holy Anorexia, a phenomenon not unknown to religious women as long ago as the fourteenth century.

> In Medieval society, a woman subjecting herself to starvation to cleanse her sins and achieve greater holiness was respected, and her behavior was not discouraged. Instead of being seen as an illness, starvation was considered a virture, as evidenced the reverence of Catherine of Siena.[61]

Holy Anorexia was a term used to describe self-starvation in an attempt to achieve a greater spirituality and closeness to God. Though religious mysticism flourished since the earliest days of Christianity, it often gains prominence during times of economic transition, civil strife, and chaos. Whether or not the Romantic ballerina intentionally denied herself important nutrition, it appeared that thinness was an attribute. "In order to achieve this state of thinness so cherished by dancers, she worked and perspired all her life."[62] Those who aspired to follow in Taglioni's footsteps became thinner than those who attempted to imitate Fanny Ellsler. Symbolically, the Taglionists wore wings while the Ellslerists emphasized their footwork in shoes fashioned to permit pointe dancing.

During this period it was thought that the dancer's bony structure held no need for a thoughtful brain because she was but a body doing intricate leaps and jumps. Unfortunately, she was too often an uneducated and pitiful creature, easily intimidated by the management of the Opéra.

This was due in large part to the narrow life of the dancer. As Roqueplan said, "why stuff their heads with facts about geography when they spend all their time trying to do entrechats? They knew little of the world when they marry and it is their husbands who take charge of all serious matters, her costumes and her roles. He is the one who bothers directors with her injuries and illnesses."[63] The young uneducated dancer, too young to be married, relied upon her mother for direction and, at the same time, her body became the livelihood by which the mother survived.

The injustices and suffering of the ballet girl, her exploitation, as well as her complicity in the web of her relationships to her mother, to each other, to management, and finally to predatory gentlemen who visited the Opéra, were astonishing and complex. She used them as they used her. The mother of a daughter owned her until she was twenty-one; she legislated and procured for her. She covered her daughter's shoulders when she was finished dancing; she gave her a carafe full of cold bouillon that fortified her. She also propositioned men to subsidize her and she asked for three or four thousand livres for the rent.

The young ballerina who turned twenty-one years of age was considered an adult and ready to be free of her mother. In order to get rid of the omnipresence of the stage mother, the administration of the Opéra chose "protectors" for the sixteen-year-old dancers to free them earlier from "maternal tyranny." Sixteen years was the legal age when one was considered an adult, but a protector was needed for signatures on contracts until she became twenty-one years of age.[64] In the mid-nineteenth century the word *danseuse* was considered a pejorative term equal to *courtisane* and was replaced by the term *artiste* in various kinds of contracts.

The dancer as sexual object retained its powerful allusion despite remarkable progress in the professionalization of ballet. "First it was the prostitutionalization of the dance." Then there was "the eclipse of the male dancer, if not banishment, by the female travesty dancer due to the new economics, and a free-market economy."[65] However, the male dancer in Copenhagen and in Russia, where the ballet was completely supported by kings, retained his substantial role in ballet. The corps also held on to their legal right to work, while in England and France and their free-market economies, the corps became debased and ballet trivialized. This situation seemed to imply that patriarchal, autocratic governmental systems were more protective of the female dancer.

Whether in the corps or as soloists, male dancers in Paris were not adored and appreciated in the same way as their female counterparts. On the contrary, both Théophile Gautier and Jules Janin spoke cruelly about the ugly male body and denounced its presence on the stage. The absence of men from the ballet stage and their revilement were indications of an intentional strategy. Men were effectively banned from engaging in performance during the height of Romanticism, not because they were subordinate to the women on stage, but "rather because Gautier and Janin wished to uphold the male's virile image—his dominance—untainted by the feminine."[66]

As privileged in their places as they sometimes seemed, ballerinas were often unable to keep their jobs or to make ends meet. Those not able to dance in theaters consistently throughout the year were considered seasonal dancers. In desperation and in order to survive, they often became prostitutes. From 1816 to 1831, 12,700 prostitutes were registered in Paris. Over one-third were natives of the capital and the rest were young provincial migrants; about 30 percent were former servants. In any one year, about 3,800 prostitutes were registered to work in the 180–200 licensed brothels graded according to "luxury" and cost.[67]

In the first third of the nineteenth century, a system of legal prostitution existed that included registration and police regulation. (The total estimated number tripled in the first three decades of the century.)[68] One step above the prostitute were the courtesans or avowed kept women. "They are lodged in rooms which the respectable woman could not pay for with the fruits of her industry nor of her talent, however exceptional that might be."[69] Ballet dancers were often relegated to the status of courtesan. Leon Abensour described the working girl/dancer's inability to survive on her salary alone. "She must look for financial solace from men in order to lighten her burden."[70] "As brilliant as she is on stage, her daily life is humble and modest. A crowd of singers, dancers, and actresses who earn meager salaries must also buy sparingly and at the same time depend on masculine generosity."[71]

An English study of the period confirmed the likelihood of poor dancers becoming prostitutes. *London Labour and the London Poor*, Henry Mayhew's four-volume study, represented an important contribution to social history. The author conducted interviews, writing down verbatim what the interviewees said. In one series, he spoke with street musicians and dancers who were given money by passersby. There were dancing dogs, acrobats, street clowns, harp players, jugglers, street players, tom-tom players—the so-called dregs of humanity.

Mayhew also described "houses of ill-fame" that were often controlled by families; the women who ran them had to be at least 25 years old, so as to exert authority over the younger women. In 1857 there were more than 80,000 prostitutes in London. One explanation was that there were, according to Mayhew, too many girls born, five more per hundred than boys.

Mayhew investigated the trades of women who became prostitutes. They were milliners, dress-makers, straw bonnet-makers, furriers, hat-binders, silk winders, tambour-workers, shoe-binders, slop-women, or those who worked for cheap tailors, those in pastry shops, those in fancy and cigar-shops, bazaars, and ballet-girls.[72]

Mayhew commented on the reasons for the ballet girls' poor reputation:

> Ballet-girls have a bad reputation, which is in most cases well deserved. To begin with, their remuneration is very poor. They get from nine to eighteen shillings. Columbine in the pantomime gets five pounds a week, but then hers is a prominent position. Out of these nine to eighteen shillings they have to find shoes and petticoats, silk stockings, etc., so that the pay is hardly adequate to their expenditure, and quite insufficient to fit them out and find them in food and lodging. Can it be wondered at, that while this state of things exists, ballet-girls should be compelled to seek a livelihood by resorting to prostitution? Many causes may be enumerated to account for the lax morality of our female operatives. Among the chief of which we must class—low wages, natural levity and the example around them, love of dress and display, coupled with the desire for a sweetheart, sedentary employment and want of exercise, low and cheap literature of an immoral tendency, absence of parental care and the inculcation of proper precepts. In short, bad bringing up.[73]

In many cases, prostitution in London from 1827 to 1835 involved girls from eleven to sixteen years old, who were often subject to diseases from which they died. Diseases also threatened the lives and professions of dancers. One in seven adults died of tuberculosis, or the "white disease," in the first half of the nineteenth century. Fashion magazines described the demise of young beauties of the time as succumbing to the "mode romantique", i.e., they died of tuberculosis.[74]

Ballerinas were vulnerable to this illness since it was more vicious in crowded urban environments, especially during the winter. Often they ate poorly and were subject to exhaustion from exercising and late night performances. Fashion journals did not hide from topical discussions of contemporary health issues, though the supercilious tone of the writing detracted from real social consciousness. The fashion magazine *La Mode*, April 14, 1832, spoke of the closing of major Paris theaters due to a cholera epidemic that lasted nearly one year and praised the Opéra for continuing to stay open despite a terrible cold snap during which period, horror of horror, no one could wear the latest spring styles:

> In the middle of the most virulent terrors of the epidemic, *Robert le Diable* and *la Sylphide* still attracted a crowd . . . Mlle Taglioni, our ravishing Sylphide, left town for a short time in order to charm the inhabitants of Berlin. Many thanks to M. Véron; without you and the Opéra, life would be truly unbearable.[75]

Several pages later, the magazine spoke about "how the poor suffer, the ill die, and how contagion spreads its ravages and engenders death" (*"étend ses ravages et répand la mort"*). Finally the epidemic abated, and the journal *La Mode* in May celebrated its departure.

There was also the likelihood of dancers contracting gonorrhea and syphilis; various painters and illustrators seized upon the dramatic quality of the latter. The taste for the macabre during the second half of the nineteenth century was manifested especially in the work of Félicien Rops, who painted "The Dancing Death" (1865) with its grotesque image of a horribly thin dancer, her tutu lifted displaying a flabby behind and her scrawny chest. In the painting the immodesty of the dancer/prostitute was compounded by her "companion," the disease syphilis which haunted her.[76]

In spite of the litany of the deleterious effects of ballet dancing, many young girls wanted to become dancers. Being on stage offered opportunities for an exciting life with more stature and social standing than a shop girl. She might have desserts, turbans, and umbrellas named after her or new words invented for her such as *taglioniser* (meaning to be beautiful, to be light, to be vaporous as a sylph, like the dancer Taglioni). If she achieved the coveted position of a principal dancer, she would be paid extremely well and invited all over the world. Fanny Ellsler appeared in Washington, D.C., and the United States Congress adjourned early in order to attend her performance. She also received the grand sum of $10,000 for one performance in Havana, Cuba. The dancer's picture would appear in all the important newsworthy journals and people would recognize her name, face, and legs. She might meet a young man of upper station, someone she would never have encountered as a shop girl or industrial worker. Her motivating hope was that she would become an extraordinarily beautiful dream girl, an ethereal being, wearing costumes of rich fabrics and embroideries and that she would live in a gloriously romantic world.

Conclusion

Weaving a history of fashion and ballet from 1780 to 1830 has been an engaging and, occasionally, improvisational effort of synthesis—of meshing together changes affecting fashion with those developments in dance costume. Fashion for the aristocracy during the late eighteenth century brought a fresh respect for the body as the ideas of the *Philosophes* penetrated the salon and encouraged women to loosen up their garments. A newly discovered interest in archeology encouraged theatrical, operatic, and dance productions of Greek and Roman myths. Individual actors and dancers thought historical costumes important to the story and wore them on stage. Classical themes dominated the Paris Opéra. In the century after the French Revolution, classical themes gradually disappeared from the stage as middle-class audiences sought stories and tales that made money and marriage central themes. Despite reform, stage costumes continued to take liberties with history so that it seemed there was a mixture of so many epochs that resulted in an amusing "cacophony."[1] While revolutionary thought jarred and stirred up new ideas that were reflected in ballet scenarios and stage expression, costumes still displayed the body as prescribed by street fashion. The period of the French Revolution may be seen as a moment of extreme transition that resulted in change, even in such traditional institutions as the Paris Opéra. However, neoclassicism and the trend toward middle-class themes in ballet did not necessarily change habits at the Opéra. Even in times of revolution, the ballet had its aesthetic way. Costumes had to look elegant, bright, shiny, and richly produced. Illusion and escape still meant splendor. Neoclassical lines simplified stage imagery, but ornaments were still important.

   The literary critic Peter Brooks made the point that the violence of the Revolution and the Terror, in concert with the secular and anticlerical ideas of the Enlightenment, naturally resulted in new attitudes toward the body. Each person has the possibility during a lifetime of achieving a personal destiny through good works, ambition, and hard work. Could this new concept of the body have affected the development of dance and the approach to the dancer's body? The dancer's conquest of space became a metaphor for the consequences of the French Revolution and the progress of ballet as a technique. The body previously was enclosed and ensconced in a prescribed and limited geography; then, with costumes that allowed the legs, feet, and full arms to move with speed and freedom, the body took over the space it was in. This new concept of the body as its own achievement, as a physiology of signification no longer doomed to corruption from the moment of conception, helped to create the technique that permitted the body to suspend itself and linger in one position perched on one foot, taking its time, to fly across the space, to move more quickly, or to be held and balanced by a man.

As is often true of change, it is more easily accepted and promoted by the young. Youth and youthful values began to wield significant influence during the revolutionary period. As mentioned before, writer Elizabeth Ewing pointed out that the beginning of the nineteenth century, when neoclassicism ruled, was the first time that there was such a comprehensive revival of an old fashion and that it reflected the values of a young, fresh society whose idealism looked back to better times. In fact, Ewing saw the neoclassic mode as something that was "especially attuned to the young," who had hoped that after the Revolution the world would be a better place. Indeed, the Revolution bred a cadre of young generals, technocrats, and administrators, including Napoléon, who thought they were fighting for the ideals of Liberty, Equality and Fraternity.[2]

Equality for women would eventually free them from the nefarious influences of the corset and wide skirts, but it would be a long process. In *Fashion in Underwear*, Ewing commented that the most important contribution to changes in fashion would come later from the movement for the emancipation of women, especially in England and eventually in France. To some extent, starting with the outspoken *Vindication of the Rights of Women*, by Mary Wollstonecraft in 1792, it was with the passing of the Infant Custody Bill in 1839 that the first results of the efforts of Mrs. Caroline Norton were achieved. "The bill secured recognition of the human rights of the female, half of the human race." In the middle years of the nineteenth century, John Stuart Mill advocated women's suffrage; but at first, this did not affect the "tyranny of tight lacing, crinolines, bustles, voluminous petticoats."[3]

The plight of women found its metaphor in a ballet scenario of the 1830s, *La Révolte des Femmes* (*The Revolt of the Women*), or *La Révolte au Sérail*

(*The Revolt of the Harem*), as it is known today. Writer Joellen Meglin, in "Feminism or Fetishism," stitches together a discourse on the radicalization of women during this time as they responded to social pressures epitomized by the growing interest in Saint-Simonisme led by Prosper Enfantin. Ballet dancers lived out their own wished-for destinies by playing harem women who revolted against the men and the system that tyrannized them. It was a playful story but had profound messages for the time.[4]

Meglin alerted us to the semiotic importance of the costumes. She revealed that the costume rendering of the dutiful self-effacing Negress Mina, displayed a woman in black makeup whose certain tilt of the head and body represented "blackness." The costume for Zulma, the heroine, demonstrated her prowess as general-in-chief of the "army." Wearing fanciful armor plate over her torso and hips, along with a helmet whose feather suggested a phallic fetish. Zulma brandished a sword as she pointed her steely breasts at her victims.[6] Meglin also described the presence of gender ambiguity during the Romantic period by calling attention to a design for Zéir the page, a male role played by a shapely woman dressed in pantaloons, a short coat and a Turkish-like turban that showed her curls.[7] I pointed out that in the late eighteenth century there were many women playing men's roles, but the number of women dancing male roles at the beginning of the nineteenth century is also truly astonishing; it was well known that later in the century this was a popular practice.

The physical culture movement that developed toward the end of the nineteenth century would soon help women in the momentum for women's rights. As women in the late 1880s went outdoors to play and find excitement in sports and movement, they needed to be rid of heavy, constricting skirts and bodices for a freer body in order to bicycle, play tennis, run, and jump.[8] Many threw away their corsets, wore divided skirts or bloomers, and began to think about their bodies as effective, physically able instruments. Dance led the way for this particular emancipation in the early part of the century.

The rising industrial age gave birth to a constant stream of inventions that affected both fashion and the ballet stage. Neoclassic styles encouraged the use of cotton and cotton-type materials. Cotton was washable, and with an increasing interest in health and social welfare in crowded urban centers, clean clothing became important. The inventions of the cotton gin and the spinning jenny facilitated the development of the cotton industry, creating cheaper materials for the rising middle classes and, unfortunately, perpetuating slavery in the New World.

The corset continued to hold its commanding position as underwear. Various fads in corset style mirrored a fascination for the new and the mechanical, such as the mechanical corset. There was also the Divorce Corset that separated the breasts with a padded triangle of iron or steel that was inserted, point upwards, into the center front of the corset. The title Divorce Corset is interesting in itself, as it reminds us that the men who made corsets found what they thought was a cute advertising phrase to objectify a woman's body. There were also metal eyelets for lacing by 1823, while steel busks continued to be used through the 1820s. In 1832, the Frenchman Jean Werley took out a patent on women's corsets made from a loom. His invention remained popular through 1890.[9] Presumably, if women had designed the corsets and underwear, they would have created a less painful article of clothing, yet women corset makers were slow in coming into the industry.

Underwear covering women's private parts was late in winning the acceptance of women in society. When the younger set wore Greek-style fashions, they wore body stockings underneath. Drawers were frowned upon by health advisors, as they prevented the free circulation of air. Little girls from 1810 to 1820 wore white pantaloons that showed just beneath the skirt. That fashion was also practiced to some extent by adult women, but the fad did not last. Drawers were often split and held together with laces, as anything that covered the groin was considered unhealthy. It was not until the twentieth century that women wore underpants.

Ballet dancers and actresses, however, had to cover their lower parts as early as the 1750s with *caleçons de précaution*, as management worried that men in the audience would use their binoculars to view women's legs and thighs. Reeling to some extent from the nakedness of the female body in neoclassic tunics in the early nineteenth century, the prudish La Rochefoucauld, who managed the Opéra, insisted on longer skirts. Dancers' rehearsal clothes from the late eighteenth century to the mid-nineteenth century seemed to be what normal people wore under their everyday clothes. Their skirts and light bodices were less heavy and more practical. In other words, as early as the 1780s, the dancer in the studio was stripped of much of the material that covered most people.

On stage, the creation of the tutu and toe dancing dramatically changed how the woman dancer moved and was seen. Though not made of steel or mechanical materials (save for the corset), the tutu and toe shoe reflected a thirst for change and a passion for invention. They allowed her to appear to glide and fly and contributed to the development of the ballet technique. These new technological tools wielded tremendous power as part of a uniform, and in their symbolic meanings they represented the secret desires of the audience for escape from the strictures of everyday life. Even today, the young woman in the audience, as well as the young dancer, dreams of wearing a tutu.

The toe shoe was originally a soft and supple device to raise the body higher, perhaps an attempt to rise closer to the gods who descended during earlier mythological ballets. Eventually, that shoe turned into a hard-edged, often noisy apparatus that provided more support and more technical help. It too took on meaning, both as a fetish and as an ingenious method of extending the body's capabilities, like stilts or the bicycle. As the nineteenth century progressed, the female toe shoe became more and more important as a way of communicating balletic values on stage. Men were denied this advantage.

It was during the period of the mid-nineteenth century that ballet costumes and their transformation of the body changed to an aesthetic tool from a mere representation of the upper classes and nobility. Costumes began to contribute to better dancing and gave dancers the opportunity to discover what the body could express.

With the remarkable discoveries of gas lighting and the diorama, the stage became a seductive environment. The tutu-clad ballerina integrated herself into this imaginative space—acting and dancing romantic stories in a more convincing manner. It was also during this time that the now-visible legs of the dancer took on extra importance. The *maillot* exposed the legs from the instep to the thigh, creating a uniform look on stage. The dancer's neck and thinly-waisted bodice called attention to the long line of the torso rather than to the uplifted, compressed breasts of the eighteenth century. The viewer's eye wandered down rather than up. Naturally, the ballerina's toe-dancing foot attracted much attention. It took her to new heights, lifted her in suspended balance, and gave her movements a smoother, more flowing quality. The arms, as well, were much freer and more flexible in their circular and gestural moves. The vocabulary of the arms increased, describing fuller circles and more extended lines in front and in back of the body. As the body moved into big jumps and turns, the arms were necessary to initiate momentum and control. Now that the hair was coiffed closer to the head and ears, the head seemed much smaller and the eyes and mouth could be better used as expressive tools.[10]

As costume liberated the dancer, so did scenarios that explored women's power. Romantic poetry ennobled the beautiful woman, but she and those who loved her were haunted by tragedy. Perhaps the high rate of women's deaths due to disease and childbirth motivated distressing stories during the Romantic period. Audiences no longer expected ballet to be thoughtless and trivial, though some scenarios still perpetuated this tendency.

Writers such as Théophile Gautier and, later, Stéphane Mallarmé were more attracted to ballet costume and its semiotic meanings than to the choreography itself. In Deirdre Priddens's *Art of the Dance in French Literature*, she quotes Gautier's vivid remarks in an 1837 article in *La Presse*. Inspired by his interest in art for art's sake and the Parnassian poets, Gautier emphasized form: "We no longer love pure form and beauty enough to endure them unveiled."[11] Gautier preferred the almost-naked bodies of Grecian maidens, but he was realistic enough to realize this as an impossibility. He felt that the dancer's costume could redeem a poor libretto. "The costumes are so fresh and charming that the eye is diverted and the mind is forgotten."[12]

Apparently during the period of Romantic ballet, audiences were less entranced by the bell-shaped tutu than by its color. The color white made its real mark with Taglioni and her effervescent purity. However, the marked presence of dancers dressed in white soon wearied critics such as Gautier.

Gautier's ideas about ballet later developed into a more abstract and airy description in the work of Mallarmé. "He is not absorbed by the great ballet personalities. Rather he thinks of dance as pure ideal. In his eyes the dancer is less a concrete reality than an idealized symbol of the imagination, and as such she remains his "inconsciente révélatrice," or "his revealing unconscious." For Mallarmé the filmy tutu represents a levelling and a generalizing of the stage picture and its transparency intrigues the poet. This "near nudity" attracts attention to the legs which are transfigured, divinized, in the light of the Idea."[13] Like Baudelaire, Mallarmé considered white a color of immense value as well as signification for women. He compared the stage to his *page blanche* or "white page" and black writing. White paints an aura of abstraction; it becomes "an absolute colour, and therefore a fitting dress for the icy glistening star of the dance in the purity of her abstraction, the whole intensified by the 'blancheurs extracharnelles de fard' or 'the extracarnal whiteness of powder.'"[14]

Mallarmé also commented (in his *Coup de Dés*) on the constant presence of the corps de ballet in white tutus, bringing to the stage a sense of wholeness and unity, and a lessening of the leading ballerina's star quality. She is inseparable from the group, just as a poetic line is inseparable from the surrounding words in clauses. The famed leading Romantic ballerinas of then and now leave little of themselves on the stage. Rather they fuse with the corps and the orchestra in a greatness undistinguished from the group. Here the costume as tutu serves as a ritual object, a mask of identity clearly emblematic of the moment and its evocation of beauty.

At the end of the nineteenth century, the dancer in the tutu lived and breathed as a gift to the age of industrialism. With its iron structures, steaming trains, telegraph, and telephone poles, she existed as an image from an ideal imagination, suggesting a spirit free from "concrete and steel elements." The dancer, in her beauty, layers of net and whiteness floating across the stage offers the audience an escape from the industrial urban world. Something unfortunate happened to the dancer of the music halls, dance halls, and pantomimes. She was pushed into the tough times described in the works of Dickens, de Maupassant, and later Zola, which resulted in her demise, her loss of self and respect, and a life which drove her into penury and sadness.

It was an era of syncretism when the French stage appropriated new breaths of life coming from other countries. In the areas of performance and literature, we witnessed the intensity of France's complex love and aversion for English taste. English theories of stage acting, pantomime and costume were gradually absorbed by dance and theater companies in France. Expressive gesture became a vital element in the *ballet pantomime*, known as the *ballet d'action*. Parisian society was also deeply attracted to German Romanticism which evoked a fascination for mysticism and the dark musings of German literature. Several duchies in Germany heralded changes in the *ballet d'action* in advance of Parisian ballet companies. The Viennese court provided opportunities for experimentation in dance and welcomed traveling dancers and actors. Influences were also imported from the South. When Spanish dancers came to Paris, the passion and sunlight of meridional Spain created further interest in the sensuality of Spanish dance and costume. Their colorful, sequined costumes and strong dance technique caused tremendous interest, to a large extent inspired by the way their dancing stressed the hips and torso.[15] Italian performers remained the finest in Europe. They were not, like the French, bound by rules of etiquette and could freely experiment with new steps and basic technique. These qualities brought them the reputation of being the best dancers during the nineteenth century. Other travels to Turkey, the Middle East, and Eastern European countries extended the appetite for the exotic and foreign.

Our discussion of women, fashion, and ballet ends at the threshold of Romantic Ballet. The subject of women and their bodies during the period of Romantic Ballet has recently caused much discussion and has become a fashion in itself. The last line of Goethe's *Faust* epitomizes the moment of the reign of women in Romantic Ballet: "The Eternal-Feminine Lures to perfection."[16] Indeed, the attraction that ballet has had for the eternal feminine continues today. Its roots are interestingly explored during the whole period of Romanticism.

It is impossible to know exactly what took place. Did fashion create the ballet costume, or did the ballet designer create a fashion style hitherto undetermined and unimagined by society? For the most part, fashion determines the designs on stage. But both ideas do eventually work in tandem, and style on stage and in the street evolve through a complex, interwoven web of experiences. Such is the narrative I have tried to describe.

Endnotes

Introduction

1. Purdy, *The Tyranny of Elegance*, 83.
2. Cavallaro and Warwick, *Fashioning the Frame* (quotes Barthes, 97). Existentialism promotes the ephemerality of the body's boundaries and frames and alerts us to the fact that what and how we see is inscribed in societal formations that paradoxically deploy the body's physical facilities at the same time that they strive to translate them into immaterial laws. It should not have surprised me to relearn that Sartre initiated the classic definition of the Other in his *Being and Nothingness*. The watcher is in turn watched—the observed of all observers. The viewer becomes spectacle to another's sight. 20.
3. Ibid., 3
4. Treves, *The Dress of the Period in its Relations to Health*, 1.
5. Ibid., 4.
6. Steward and Janovicek, "Slimming the Female Body?", 174.
7. See Angela Latham, *Posing a Threat*.
8. Geneviève Vincent in Catalogue of the Exhibition *Costume à danser* by Carole Rambaud, Centre Culturel de Boulogne-Billancourt, April 1989.
9. Elias, *The Civilizing Process*.
10. Jullian Offray, La Mettrie, *Man, a Machine*.1748 (La Salle, IL: Open Court, 1993), 93.
11. Private conversation with Richard Martin at the Met Costume Institute in 1998.

Chapter 1

1. de Graffigny. *Letters from a Peruvian Woman* (1752), 121.
2. Ibid., 123.
3. Hollander. *Sex and Suits*, 73.
4. Lee, *Ballet in Western Culture*, 105.
5. Martin, *The Ceaseless Century*, 27.
6. Roseann Runte, "Woman as Muse," in *Women in the Age of Enlightenment*, ed. Samia Spencer, Bloomington: Indiana University Press, 1984, 144.
7. Madame de la Tour du Pin, 1770–1853. *Memoirs* (London: Century Publishing Company), 67, 68.
8. Ibid., 69.
9. Delpierre, *Dress in France in the Eighteenth Century*, 93, 94.

10. An Elegant Art: Fashion and Fantasy in the Eighteenth Century. Los Angeles County Museum of Art, 1983.
11. Browne, *The Eighteenth Century Feminist Mind*, 35.
12. Boucher, *Histoire du Costume en Occident*, 296.
13. Browne, 32.
14. Forman, *Georgiana, Duchess of Devonshire*, 118.
15. Buruma, *Anglomania*, 39.
16. Schama, *Citizens*, 34
17. Carré, *Divertissements*, 247.
18. Cobban, *History of Modern France*, 114.
19. Ibid.
20. For a description of Rose Bertin's beautiful factory and showplace, see Leon Abensour *La Femme et le Feminisme avant la Révolution* (Paris: Editions Ernest Leroux, 1923).
21. Karbalova, Herbenova, and Lamarova, *A Pictorial Encyclopedia of Fashion*, 220.
22. De l'Éloffe, *Modes et Usages au Temps de Marie Antoinette*, 224.
23. Ribeiro, *Fashion in the French Revolution*, 27.
24. Schama, "Modes of Seduction," 103.
25. Jullien, *La Comédie à la Cour*, 1.
26. Karbalova, Herbenova, and Lamarova, *Pictorial Encyclopedia of Fashion*, 208.
27. Jullien, *La Comédie à la Cour*, 268.
28. Ibid., 287.
29. Carré, *Divertissements*, 249.
30. Cobban, *History of Modern France*, 116.
31. Carré, *Divertissements*, 260.
32. Ribeiro, *Visual History of Costume in the Eighteenth Century*, 15.
33. Vigée-Lebrun, *Memoirs*, 17.
34. Delaney, Lupton, and Toth, *The Curse*, 206.
35. Boucher, *Histoire du Costume en Occident*, 70.
36. Ribeiro, *Dress in Eighteenth-Century Europe*, 175.
37. Boucher, 296.
38. Fontenel, *Support and Seduction*, 25.
39. Ribeiro, *The Art of Dress*, 19.
40. Hogarth, *The Analysis of Beauty*, 65.
41. McCormick, "Notes on the Design of the Costumes."
42. Alice Annas, "The Elegant Art of Movement," *An Elegant Art* (1983), 37.
43. Ibid., 48.
44. Ibid., 47.
45. Ibid.
46. Gallini, *Treatise of the Art of Dancing*, 114.
47. Schama, "Modes of Seduction," 39.
48. Guest, *Ballet of the Englightenment*, 140.
49. Wynne, "Complaisance, An Eighteenth-Century Cool," 25.
50. Ibid., 27.
51. Molière, *Théâtre Complet*, vol. II, 439.
52. Franko, *Dancing as Text*, 123.
53. De Pure, *Idée des Spectacles, Anciens et Nouveaux*, 180.
54. Du Bos, *Reflexions critiques sur la poesie et sur la peinture*, 505.
55. Rameau, *The Dancing Master*, xii.
56. Ibid.
57. Batteux, *Les Beaux Arts Réduits à un même Principe*, 3 text-fiche, 291.
58. Ibid., 259.
59. Ibid., 275.
60. Magri, *Theoretical and Practical Treatise on Dancing*, 71.
61. Ibid., 72
62. Ibid., 75
63. Ibid., 128.
64. Murphy, "Ballet Reform in the Mid-Eighteenth-Century France. The Philosophes and Noverre," 33.

Chapter 2

1. Hollander, *Seeing Through Clothes*, 275.
2. Ibid., 274.
3. Balme, "Cultural Anthropology and Theatre Historiography: Notes on a Methodological rapprochement," 76.
4. La Clairon, *Mémoires*, 262–63.
5. Ibid., 262–63
6. Carlson, "The Eighteenth Century Pioneers in French Costume Reform," 39.
7. Collins, *Talma*, 43.
8. Clairon's effect on her profession went beyond costuming. She also waged a difficult battle against largely church-initiated statutes carried through to the French Parliaments and the courts. Actresses were reputedly immoral because they had been legally forced to live outside social and economic margins since the early Middle Ages. Regarded by the state until the Revolution as a nonperson, a woman entertainer could not inherit property or bequeath it. She was excommunicated from the Christian church and could not legally marry. If she gave birth, the children were illegitimate and could not be baptized. Upon death, rites were denied unless she abjured her profession. Unfortunately, La Clairon sacrificed her career by speaking out against the institutionalized prejudice against performers and subsequently she was sent to prison. After that La Clairon never went back to work. On the other hand, since she was no longer an actress, she could then be buried with full honors. (Jeffrey Ravel in *American Society for Theater Research Journal*, May 1994, vol. 35, no. 1.)
9. Jullien, *L'Histoire du costume au theatre*, 310.
10. Carlson, *Theatre of the French Revolution*, 101.
11. Ibid., 28.
12. Christout, *Le Merveilleux et le theatre du Silence*, 93.
13. Noverre, *Lettres sur la Danse et Les Arts Imitateurs*, 145.
14. Christout, *Le Merveilleux et le theatre du Silence*, 95.
15. Capon, *Les Vestris, le dieu de la danse et sa famille*, 214.
16. Christout, *Le Merveilleux et le theatre du Silence*, 95.
17. Flament, "Le Sourire de la Camargo," 503.
18. Sieur Clément, Lettre sur L'Opéra Comique, "Origine du caleçon," 1754, 395.
19. Christout, *Le Merveilleux et le theatre du Silence*, 95.
20. Jullien, *L'Histoire du costume au theatre*, 63.
21. Ibid.
22. Guest's *Ballet of the Enlightenment* describes the Byzantine, often insidious house politics of the Opéra.
23. Duplain, *Guimard, ou l'Art de la Danse Pantomime*, 18.
24. De Goncourt, *La Guimard*, 158.
25. Ibid.
26. Ibid., 152.
27. Ibid., 147.
28. Vaillat, *Histoire de la Danse*, 133.
29. De Goncourt, *La Guimard*, 150.
30. Ibid., 226.
31. Ibid., 251.
32. de l'Éloffe, *Modes et Usages au Temps de Marie Antoinette*, 313.
33. Curzon, *Articles Biographiques sur La Guimard*, n.p.
34. Toepfer, *Theatre, Aristocracy and Pornocracy*, 64.
35. Rousseau, *Julie or La Nouvelle Héloise*, 210.
36. Ibid., 213.
37. Rousseau. *Emile or on Education*, 356.
38. Rousseau, *Politics and the Arts: Letter to M. D'Alembert on the Theatre*, 82–83.
39. Ibid., 88.
40. Ewing, *History of Women's Underwear*, 52.
41. Rousseau, *La Nouvelle Héloise*, 122.
42. Brooke, *Western European Costume*, 110.
43. Ribeiro, *The Art of Dress*, 3.

44. Quoted in Joan Landes, *Women and the Public Sphere in the Age of the French Revolution* (Ithaca, NY: Cornell University Press, 1988), 72.
45. Trouille, *Sexual Politics in the Enlightenment*, 8.
46. Rousseau, *Julie or The New Heloise*, translated by Stewart and Vaché, 235.
47. Diderot, *Oeuvres Complètes. Troisième Entretien sur le Fils Naturel*, 146.
48. Ibid., 157.
49. Denis Diderot, *Rameau's Nephew*, translated by L. W. Tancock (Middlesex: Penguin, 1966), 105.
50. Diderot, vol. 7, 159.
51. Ibid., vol. 7, 161.
52. Diderot, vol. 10, 208.
53. Ibid., 20.
54. Hollander, *Seeing through Clothes*, 280
55. Collins, *F. Talma*, 44.
56. Voltaire, *Correspondance* LIII, 76.
57. Ibid., LIV, 18–85.
58. *Biographie Universelle ou Dictionnaire Historique*.
59. Cahusac, "Ballet," In *Encyclopédie ou Dictionnaire Raisonné des Sciences des arts Métiers*, (Stuttgart: Facsimile bad Canstatt Friederich Frommann Verlag Gunther Holzboog, 1966), 45.
60. Cahusac, *La Danse Ancienne et Moderne ou Traité Hostorique de la Danse*, 1754, 149.
61. Cahusac (1754) Ibid., 170.
62. Noverre, *Lettres sue la Danse et les Arts Imitateurs*, 108.
63. Ibid., 94.
64. Quoted in Selma Jeanne Cohen, *D ance as Theatre Art*, 36.
65. Jullien, *L'Histoire du costume au theatre*, 196.
66. For a thorough and enlightening study of eighteenth century dance techniques, see Edmund Fairfax's *The Styles of Eighteenth-Century Ballet*, Scarecrow Press, 2003.

Chapter 3

1. Karbalova, Herbenova, and Lamarova, *Pictorial Encyclopedia of Fashion*, 225.
2. Lynn Hunt quoted in Meltzer and Norberg, *From the Royal to the Republican Body*, 230.
3. Delpierre, *Dress in France*, 105.
4. See J. C. Flugel's chapter on the "Great Male Renunciation," in *The Psychology of Clothes*.
5. Harris in "The Red Cap of Liberty" quotes John Moore describing David's designs for revolutionary wear in *Eighteenth-Century Studies*, 300.
6. De l'Éloffe, *Modes et Usages au Temps de Marie Antoinette*, 427.
7. Boucher, *Histoire du Costume en Occident*, 335.
8. Ibid., 117–19.
9. De l'Éloffe, *Modes et Usages au Temps de Marie Antoinette*, 411.
10. Laver, *Costume and Fashion*, 151.
11. See Carle Vernet's grotesque renderings, "les Incroyables," 1797, and his son Horace Vernet's "les Incroyables et Merveilleuses," 1810–1818.
12. Brooks's *Objects of Desire in Modern Narrative* has a fascinating discussion of Marie Antoinette's body in the chapter "Marking out the Modern Body."
13. Hunt, "The Many Bodies of Marie Antoinette," in her book, *Eroticism and the Body Politic*, 123.
14. Hunt quoting Dorinda Outram's book, *The Body and the French Revolution*, 125.
15. Jules Michelet, *Women of the French Revolution*, 256–57. Before her death Corday was known for her wonderful taste in dress. The fashion historian Aileen Ribeiro described one of Corday's charming costumes as a spotted Indian muslin dress, a rose-colored fichu, and a natty tall, black hat with green ribbons.
16. Ibid., 137.
17. Hufton, *The Prospect Before Her*, 461–62.
18. Sennet, *Flesh and Stone*, 287.
19. Ibid.,285.

20. See Ozouf's *Les Fêtes Révolutionnaires* for a thorough study of the Revolutionary Festival.
21. Parker, *The Cult of the Antique* (Chicago: Chicago University Press, 1937), 129–32.
22. Harris, *Eighteenth Century Studies*, 302.
23. Ibid., 300.
24. Chazin-Bennahum, unpublished dissertation, 258.
25. Winter, *Pre-Romantic Ballet,* 168.
26. Starobinski, 1789, *Emblems of Reason,* 166.
27. Cobban, *History of Modern France,* vol. 1, 232.
28. Hunt, *From the Royal to the Republican Body*, 235.
29. Harris, *Eigteenth Century Studies*, 285.
30. Dickens, *A Tale of Two Cities*, 275–76.
31. Gontaut, *Mémoires of the Duchesse de Gontaut,* vol. 1, 30.
32. Recent information about costumes has come to light in the English Bedford Opera papers found in Woburn Abbey. Six cartons filled with documents describe the wardrobe situation and all the costumes during the seasons of 1790 and 1791 at the Pantheon Theatre, where Dauberval held control over productions of ballet. Large sums of money were spent on ballet costumes and, therefore, careful records were kept pertaining to all aspects of costume design and their materials. Judith Milhous, Gabriella Dideriksen and Robert D. Hume have written *Italian Opera in Late Eighteenth-century London, Vol. II, The Pantheon Opera and its Aftermath 1789–1795,* Oxford: Clarendon Press, 2000. It is very likely that Dauberval would have used similar costume materials to copy the original designs.
33. Ibid., 578–81.
34. Ibid., 568.
35. Ibid, 611.
36. Garafola, "The Nineteenth Century Travesty Dancer," 35–40.
37. For a lively discussion of transvestism and the theatre, see Garber's Chapter I in *Vested Interests.*
38. *Biographical Dictionary of Musicians, Dancers, Managers, and Other Stage Personnel in London 1660-1800* (Carbondale, IL: Southern Illinois University Press, 1978).
39. Goncourt, *Histoire de la Société Francaise pendent la Directoire*, 139.
40. Boulenger, *De La Valse au Tango*, 2.
41. Aldrich, *From the Ballroom to Hell*, 32.
42. Wallace, *Dance, a Very Social History*, 68.
43. Byron, *The Complete Poetical Works*, 22–31.
44. Carlson, *The Theatre of the French Revolution*, 247.
45. For an expansive and meticulous study of dress during the French Revolution, see Richard Wrigley's *The Politics of Appearances: Representations of Dress in Revolutionary France,* Berg, 2002.
46. Hunt, *Freedom of Dress in Revolutionary France*, 243.

Chapter 4

1. Libron and Clouzot, *Le Corset dans l'Art et les Moeurs*, 71.
2. Porter, *Constructions of the Classical Body*, 13.
3. See Aileen Ribeiro, *The Art of Dress: Fashion in England and France.*
4. Ribeiro, *Visual History of Costume in the Eighteenth Century*, 15.
5. Starobinski, *Emblems of Reason*, 166.
6. Hollander, *Seeing Through*, 276.
7. Ibid., 277.
8. Ibid., 117.
9. Laver, *Costume and Fashion*, 152.
10. Hunt, "Freedom of Dress in Revolutionary France," 245.
11. Not unlike Rousseau, John Locke's propensity for liberal philosophical ideas did not prevent him when wearing his doctor's hat from narrow notions. Apparently Locke felt that women suffered more from nervous disorders than men: their heads are weaker and so are their nerves. Their lives should be easy in order "to perform the tender offices of love." See Wayne Glausser's "Locke and Blake as Physicians," in *Reading the Social Body*, edited by Catherine Burroughs, 228.

12. Browne, *The Eighteenth-Century Feminist Mind*, 52.
13. Mercier, *New Picture of Paris*, vol. 1, 181.
14. Ewing, *A History of Women's Underwear*, 54.
15. Ibid., 56.
16. C. Willet and Phyllis Cunnington, *The History of Underclothes*, 108.
17. Ewing, *History of Women's Underwear*, 56
18. See June Swann's fascinating study, *Shoes*.
19. Squire, *Dress, Art and Society*, 153.
20. Brydon and Niessen, *Consuming Fashion*, 2.
21. Ibid., 13.
22. Such as Susan Foster's, *Corporealities: Dancing Knowledge, Culture and Power*.
23. Guest, *The Ballet of the Enlightenent*, 331–32.
24. Ibid.
25. See rope dancers in illustrations for Marian Hannah Winter's *Theatre of Marvels* and Marie-Françoise Christout's *le Merveilleux et le Théâtre du Silence*.
26. Swift, *A Loftier Flight*, 43.
27. Beaumont, *Ballet Design, Past and Present* XXII.
28. Ibid.
29. Starobinski, *1789: Emblems of Reason*, 143.
30. Vigée-Lebrun, *Memoirs*, 38–40.
31. Ibid.
32. Description from Exhibition at the British Museum, April 1996 on Sir William Hamilton.
33. Falcone, "The Arabesque," 244.
34. Boucher, *Histoire de Costumes en Occident*, 344.
35. Ribeiro, *Fashion in the French Revolution*, 127.
36. For an excellent study of Berthélémy see Marc Sandoz's biography *Jean-Simon Berthélémy*.
37. Guest, *Ballet Under Napoleon*, 109.
38. Guest, *The Ballet of the Enlightenment*, 325.
39. Guest, *Ballet Under Napoleon*, 110.
40. Christout, *Le Merveilleux et le theatre du Silence*, 205.
41. Ibid., 96.

Chapter 5

1. Cobban, *History of Modern France*, vol., II, 19.
2. Ibid., 22.
3. Martin, *2wice*, 101–02.
4. Erving Goffman quoted in Roberts, "The Exquisite Slave," 555.
5. Wilton, *The Book of Costume or Annals of Fashion, From the Earliest Period to the Present Time*, 254.
6. I saw a sketch for this gown at an exhibition in New Orleans, "Jefferson in America and Napoléon in Paris," April 2003.
7. See Preface to Vernet's *Incroyaables et Merveilleuses*.
8. Brooke, *Western European Costume*, 138.
9. The dance historian Carol Teton mentioned that she owns three pairs of early nineteenth-century dancing shoes whose soles were foreshortened like contemporary ballet shoes, so that they were sewn until the metatarsal begins and did not cover the heel.
10. Perrot, *Fashioning the Bourgeoisie*, 8.
11. Hunt, "Freedom of Dress in Revolutionary France," 237.
12. Cobban, *History of Modern France*, vol. II, 49.
13. Deane, *The First Industrial Revolution*, 92.
14. Cobban, *History of Modern France*, vol. II, 49.
15. The journal was issued from 1801 to 1822, "Observateurs sur les Modes et les Usages de Paris." There were all sorts of illustrations, for example, one showing women looking in the mirror putting on breast falsies to enhance their figures.

16. One particularly amusing plate drew portraits of the three graces who happened to be men dressed as women, all wanting to be in style.
17. *The Mirror of the Graces*, 185.
18. Ibid., 159–60.
19. Libron and Clouzot, *Le Corset dans l'Art et les Moeurs*, 75.
20. Ibid.
21. Browne, *The Eighteenth-Century Feminist Mind*, 32.
22. Ibid.
23. Ibid.
24. Beaumont, *A Miscellany for Dancers*, 25.
25. Ibid., 26.
26. Chateaubriand, *The Memoirs of Chateaubriand*, 46.
27. Ibid., Frontispiece.
28. Ibid., 344.
29. Herold, *Mistress to an Age*, 388.
30. Also, Brantôme, another writer, described the idea of "climates."
31. See Arkin and Smith, "National Dance in Romantic Ballet."
32. Milhous, "Vestris-Mania and the Construction of Celebrity," 41.
33. Quoted from the program booklet from the Paris Opéra on the occasion of restaging *La Dansomanie* at the Opéra in 1985.
34. This letter is described by Marian Eames (1957) in a New York Public Library pamphlet, *When All the World was Dancing*.
35. Ibid., 12.
36. Brewer, *Brewer's Dictionary of Phrase and Fable*.
37. Chazin-Bennahum, "Livrets of Ballets and Pantomimes 1787–1801," 224.
38. Guest, *Ballet Under Napoleon*, 119–20.
39. Ibid., 171.
40. Ibid., 177.
41. Bernardin de Saint-Pierre, *Paul and Virginia*, 170.
42. *Paul et Virginie* Libretto for the performance at Saint Cloud, June 12, 1806.
43. Guest, *Ballet Under Napoleon*, 229.
44. Ibid., 325.
45. Ibid., 330.
46. Ibid., 355.
47. Ibid., 344.

Chapter 6

1. Sorel, *L'Europe et la Révolution Francaise*, 416.
2. Boucher, *Histoire du Costume en Occident*, 355.
3. See Sarah Davies Cordova, *Paris Dances*.
4. Purdy, *The Tyranny of Elegance*, 151.
5. Ibid., 157.
6. Cobban, *History of Modern France*, vol. II, 82.
7. Ibid., 84.
8. Noted by Ribeiro in *Fashion and the French Revolution*, 154.
9. Harris, "Red Cap of Liberty," 308.
10. Fischer, *Costumes de l'Opéra*, 234.
11. Ibid., 233.
12. Guest, *The Romantic Ballet in Paris*, 19. Also, see Second's *Les Petit Mystères de l'Opéra*.
13. Guest, *Ballet Under Napoleon*, 433.
14. Fischer, *Costumes de l'Opéra*, 174.
15. Clark and Crisp, *Design for Ballet*, 85.
16. Guest, *Romantic Ballet in Paris*, 43.
17. Ibid., 49.
18. Aldrich, *From the Ballroom to Hell*, 159.

Chapter 7

1. Ewing, *Dress and Undress*, 60.
2. Brooke, *Western European Costume*, 139.
3. Foster, *Visual History of Costume*, 13.
4. Ibid.
5. *La Belle Assemblé* (August 1828), 77.
6. Karbalova, Herbenova, and Lamarova, *The Pictorial Encyclopedia of Costume*, 244.
7. *Petit Courrier des Dames*, 94.
8. Purdy, *The Tyranny of Elegance*, 2.
9. Moore, *Fashion Through Fashion Plates*, 9.
10. Ibid.
11. Perrot, *Fashioning the Bourgeoisie*, 151.
12. Waugh, *Corsets and Crinolines*, 130.
13. Browne, *The Eighteenth Century Feminist Mind*, 32.
14. Perrot, *Fashioning the Bourgeoisie*, 150.
15. Libron and Clouzot, *Le Corset dans l'Art et les Moeurs*, 81.
16. *Petit Courrier des Dames* (March 25, 1833), 130.
17. Libron and Clouzot, *Le Corset dans l'Art et les Moeurs*, 68.
18. Perrot, *Fashioning the Bourgeoisie*, 152.
19. Ibid., 159.
20. Downing, "Anti-Pygmalion," 239.
21. Baudelaire, "Le Peintre de la Vie Moderne," *Oeuvres Complètes*, 1185.
22. Gautier, *Mademoiselle de Maupin*, 275.
23. Ibid., 158.
24. Baudelaire, "Le Peintre de la Vie Moderne," 1182–1183.
25. Ibid.
26. Ibid., 1173.
27. Hersch, *To Seize a Dream*, 123.
28. Brooke, *Western European Costume*, 139.
29. Ibid.
30. E. Ward, *The Dress Reform Problem, A Chapter for Women* (London: Bradford, 1886), 10.
31. Stephen Kern, *Anatomy and Destiny: A Cultural History of the Human Body* (Indianapolis: The Bobbs Merrill Company, Inc., 1974), 10.
32. *La Belle Assemblée* (April 1831), 157.
33. Garelick, *Rising Star: Dandyism, Gender and Performance in the Fin de Siècle*, 3.
34. Carlyle, "The Dandiacal Body," *Sartor Resartus*, 217.
35. Henderson, "Passion and Fashion in Joanna Baillie's Introductory Discourse," 206.
36. Boulenger, *De la Walse au Tango*, 13.

Chapter 8

1. Libron and Clouzot, *Le Corset dans l'Art et les Moeurs*, 75.
2. Banes, *Dancing Women*, 4.
3. Jowitt, *Time and the Dancing Image*, 49.
4. Ibid., 53.
5. Levinson, *Marie Taglioni*, 42.
6. Gautier, *Mademoiselle de Maupin*, XIII.
7. Blasis, *The Code of Terpsichore*, which I consulted, published by Dance Horizons contains two title pages: the first lists 1828 as the London publication date; the second page, which is entitled *The Art of Dancing*, lists the date as 1831.
8. Ibid., 65.
9. Ibid., 72.
10. Ibid., 77.
11. Ibid., 80.
12. Ibid., 82.
13. Falcone, "The Arabesque," 86.
14. Blasis, *The Code of Terpsichore*, 83.

15. Ibid., 193.
16. Ibid.
17. Ibid., 194.
18. Ibid.
19. Ibid.
20. Ibid., 195
21. Ibid., 196.
22. Ibid., 197
23. Ibid., 534.
24. Ibid.
25. Ibid., 215.
26. Ibid., 541.
27. Ibid., 537.
28. Poesio, "Blasis, the Italian Ballo, and the Male Sylph," 137.
29. Moore, "Practice Clothes—Then and Now."
30. Ibid.
31. Théleur's, *Letters on Dance and Dancing*, edited by Sandra Hammond, preface V.
32. Ibid.
33. Ibid., 2
34. Ibid., 2.
35. Years ago when I studied with Margaret Craske at the Metropolitan Opera Ballet School, at an early point during the barre, she had us push up to the tips of the toes facing the barre, instructing us carefully to hold our toes straight and to develop the metatarsal muscles under the foot. Craske was considered a celebrated teacher of the Cecchetti method.
36. Ibid., 3.
37. Ibid., 2.
38. Théleur's, *Letters on Dance and Dancing*, 57.
39. Vaillat, *Histoire de la Danse*, 150.
40. Guest, *Ballet Under Napoleon*, 370.
41. Prudhommeau, "Naissance des Pointes: Deux Petits Chaussons," 49.
42. Guest, *The Romantic Ballet in England*, 48.
43. Quoted in Migel, *The Ballerinas*, 118.
44. Quoted in Guest, *The Romantic Ballet in England*, 49.
45. Ibid.
46. Guest, *The Romantic Ballet in England*, 48.
47. Quoted in Guest, *The Romantic Ballet in England*, 49.
48. Hawkins, *Archives Internationales de la Danse*, 7.
49. Gautier, *Peau de Tigre*, 335–36.
50. I am grateful to Monica Moseley for this description and a sketch of Fanny Elssler's shoe at the Vienna State Opera.
51. Barringer and Schlesinger, *The Pointe Book*, 12.
52. Prudhommeau, "Naissance des Pointes: Deux Petits Chaussons," 50.
53. Fischer, *Costumes de l'Opéra*, 183.
54. Winter, *Pre-Romantic Ballet*, 114.
55. Guest, *The Romantic Ballet in Paris*, 93.
56. Ibid., 22.
57. Vaillat, *Histoire de la Danse*, 164.
58. Arkin and Smith, "National Dance in Romantic Ballet," 20.
59. Vaillat, *Histoire de la Danse*, 165.
60. Roqueplan, *Les Coulisses de l'Opéra*, 45.
61. Ibid., 85.
62. McPhee, *A Social History of France 1780–1880*, 127.
63. De Boigne, *Petits Mémoires de l'Opéra*, 9.
64. Ibid., 16.
65. Ibid, 17.
66. Second, *Les Petits Mystères de l'Opéra*, 175.
67. Gautier, *La Peau de Tegre* (1866), 335.
68. Guest, "Dandies and Dancers," 45.

Chapter 9

1. See Chazin-Bennahum's unpublished dissertation "Livrets of Ballets and Pantomimes 1789–1801."
2. Winter, *Pre-Romantic Ballet*, 38.
3. Cohen, *Dance as Theatre Art*, 67.
4. Christout, *Le Merveilleux et le Théâtre du Silence*, 229.
5. Guest and Jürgensen, *Robert le Diable*, 1.
6. Ibid., 2.
7. Théophile Gautier, *Feuilleton du Journal Officiel* (1870), 153.
8. *Le Journal des Dames* (December 25,1831), 714.
9. *La Belle Assemblée,* (July 1832), 54.
10. Lord Mount Edgcumbe, in *Musical Reminiscences,* (1834), 215.
11. Gautier, *Mlle. de Maupin*, XXI.
12. Fischer, *Costumes de l'Opéra*, 208.
13. Hollander, *Seeing through Clothes*, 284.
14. See photo essay "Women of Faint Heart and Steel Toes," in *Rethinking the Sylph*, 129.
15. Kahane and Pinasa, *Le Tutu: petit guide*.
16. *Le Journal des Dames*, (March 25, 1832), 357.
17. Gautier, *La Presse* (June 29, 1844), 34.
18. See Banes, *Dancing Women*, for an insightful analysis of this ballet.
19. John V. Chapman, "Jules Janin: Romantic Critic," *Rethinking the Sylph* (Middleton: Wesleyan University Press, 1997), 216.
20. George Chaffée, "Three or Four Graces: A Centenary Salvo." *Dance Index*, New York, Sept.–Nov. 1944, 145.
21. *La Belle Assemblée* (March 25, 1832), 357.
22. Maigron, *Le Romantisme et al Mode*, 32.
23. Chaffée, 141.
24. Levinson, *Marie Taglioni*, 47.

Chapter 10

1. Roqueplan, *Les Coulisses de l'Opéra*, 27.
2. Ibid., 27.
3. Guest, *The Romantic Ballet in Paris*, 25.
4. Véron, *Mémoires d'un bourgeois de Paris*, 207
5. Ibid., 211.
6. Robin-Challan, *Danse et Danseuses à L'Opéra de Paris 1830–1850*.
7. Garafola quoted in Banes, *Dancing Women*, 39.
8. Solomon-Godeau, "The Legs of the Countess," 289.
9. Alderson, "Ballet as Ideology: Giselle, Act II," 297.
10. Ibid., 298.
11. Adrian Stokes (*Tonight the Ballet*, 1935) is quoted in *What is Dance? Readings In Theory and Criticism*, 1983 edited by Marshall Cohen and David Levin, 246.
12. Levinson, *Marie Taglioni*, 59.
13. Foster, *Corporealities: Dancing Knowledge, Culture and Power*, 6.
14. Kunzle, *Fashion and Fetishism*, 1.
15. Joseph, *Uniforms and Non-Uniforms*, 17.
16. Davis, *Fashion, Culture and Identity*, 110.
17. Davis, *Actresses as Working Women*, 109.
18. Ibid.
19. Kahane and Pinasa, *Le Tutu: Petit Guide; Petit Histoire du Tutu*, Opéra Nationale de Paris, 1997.
20. Davis, *Actresses as Working Women*, 122.
21. Roqueplan, *Les Coulisses de l'Opéra*, 53.
22. Treves,*The Dress of the Period in Its Relations to Health*, 27.
23. Ibid., 26.

24. Kunzle, *Fashion and Fetishism*, 17.
25. Susan Foster, "The Ballerina's Phallic Pointe" (Bloomington and Indianapolis: University of Indiana Press, 1996), 13.
26. Roqueplan, *Les Coulisses de l'Opéra*, 7.
27. De Boigne, *Petits Mémoires de l'Opéra*, 35.
28. Ibid.
29. Second, *Petits Mystères de l'Opéra*, 149.
30. Ibid., 150–51.
31. Ibid., 20.
32. Roqueplan, *Les Coulisses de l'Opéra*, 29.
33. Ibid., 59.
34. Jowitt, *Time and the Dancing Image*, 54.
35. Kern, *Anatomy and Destiny: A Cultural History of the Human Body*, 2.
36. Robin-Challan, *Social Conditions*, 25.
37. Ibid., 26.
38. Robinson, *Sex Class and Culture*, 41–42.
39. Guest, "Dandies and Dancers," 48.
40. Ibid., 33.
41. Ibid., 45.
42. Solomon-Godeau, "The Legs of the Countess," 288.
43. In Peter Wollen's *Raiding the Ice Box*, 1993, he describes the phenomenon of the chorus line that arrived with the Tiller Girls, "who offered the spectacle of (female) bodies in movement, duplicating the alienated form of the Fordist Labour process, its instrumental rationality," 56. The Tiller Girls were an English troupe of women from Lancashire who were a hit in Berlin in the 1920s.
44. Gautier, *Gautier on Dance*, 23.
45. The heroines of *Adolphe*, *Elénore*, and *Giselle* died of broken hearts.
46. Bell, *Dress and Human Finery*, 90.
47. Roberts, "The Exquisite Slave: The Role of Clothes in the Making of the Victorian Woman," 557.
48. Ibid.
49. Kunzle, *Fashion and Fetishism*, 20.
50. Edward Shorter, *A History of Women's Bodies* (New York: Basic Books, 1982).
51. Henry Whitfield, *The Absurdities of Stays and the Evil Effects of Tight Lacing*, 3.
52. Ibid., 7.
53. Ibid., 14.
54. Daumas, "Hygiene et Médicine," 1803.
55. Debay, *Hygiène Vestimentaire*, 153.
56. Maigron, *Le Romantisme et la Mode*, 182.
57. *La Mode* (vol. 2, 1830), 177.
58. Kunzle, *Fashion and Fetishism*, 21.
59. Maigron, *Le Romantisme et la Mode*, 198.
60. Bordo, *Unbearable Weight*, 206.
61. Saraf quotes Bynum in *The Pharos*, 3.
62. De Boigne, *Petits Mémoires de l'Opéra*, 37.
63. Roqueplan, *Les Coulisses de l'Opéra*, 89.
64. Robin-Challan, *Danse et Danseuses à L'Opéra de Paris 1830–1850*. 394.
65. Solomon-Godeau, "The Legs of the Countess," 289.
66. Daly, "Classical Ballet: A Discourse of Difference," 60.
67. McPhee, *A Social History of France 1780–1880*, 142.
68. Moses quotes A. J. B. Parent-Duchâtelet in *French Feminism in the Nineteenth Century* (New York: SUNY Series in European Social History, 1984), 30.
69. Ibid.
70. Abensour, *La Femme et le Féminisme avant la Révolution*, 228.
71. Ibid.
72. Mayhew, *London Labour and the London Poor*, vol. 4, 255.
73. Ibid., 257.
74. Maigron, *Le Romantisme et la Mode*, 199.

75. *La Mode* (April 14, 1832), 56–57.
76. Ducrey, *Corps et Graphies*, 150.

Conclusion

1. Maigron, *Le Romantisme et la Mode*, 10.
2. Ewing, *Fashion in Underwear*, 44.
3. John Stuart Mill wrote his prophetic "The Subjugation of Women" (1869), in which Mill brilliantly describes the oppressed state of English women.
4. Meglin, "Feminism or Fetishism: *La Révolte des femmes* and Women's Liberation in France in the 1830s."
5. Ibid., 73.
6. Ibid., 77.
7. Ibid., 79.
8. Ewing, *Fashion in Underwear*, 63.
9. Ibid., 46.
10. I remember hearing Antony Tudor remark that the perfect dancer had to have a long neck and long arms and legs. He went on to joke that the dancer was easier to work with if she did not have too many brains rattling around in her little head. His sarcasm was known throughout the ballet world.
11. Deidre Priddens, *The Art of the Dance in French Literature* (London: Adam and Chas. Black, 1952), 46.
12. Ibid.
13. Ibid., 72.
14. Ibid.
15. Ibid, 15.
16. Goethe, *Faust*, 503.

Chronology
A Brief Chronology 1780–1830 France

1770   Marriage of Dauphin and Marie-Antoinette

1774   Death of Louis XV, Accession of Louis XVI

1778   France enters War of American Independence

1783   Treaty of Versailles ends War of American Independence

1784   Beaumarchais's *Marriage of Figaro* first produced

1787   Meeting of Notables Anglo-Prussian intervention in Dutch Republic

1788   Convocation of States-General
December: Royal council approves decree doubling Third Estate

1789   Bread and Grain riots in spring and early summer
May: Meeting of States-General
June 17: Third Estate adopts title of National Assembly
July 14: Fall of the Bastille
August 4–11: Decrees abolishing feudal rights and privileges

1790   Civil Constitution of the Clergy

1791   Death of Mirabeau
June 21: King and family flee to Varennes and are arrested
September: Constitution of 1791, Dissolution of Constituent Assembly
October: Meeting of Legislative Assembly

1792   April 20: France declares war on Austria
June 20: Popular demonstrations in Paris
August 10: Attack on Tuileries
August 19: Flight of Lafayette
September 2–6: September massacres including political prisoners and clergy

1792	(*continued*)
	September 20: Valmy: First victory of Republican forces
	September 21: Meeting of Convention
	September 22: Abolition of monarchy
	November: Victory at Jemmapes, occupation of Belgium
	November 19: Decree of Convention offering help to all peoples seeking liberty
	December: Trial of Louis XVI
1793	January 21: Execution of Louis XVI
	February 1: Declaration of war against Great Britain
	March: Declaration of war against Spain
	Revolutionary Tribunal set up
	April: Establishment of radical Committee of Public Safety
	May 31: Rising in Paris
	June 24: Constitution of 1793 voted
	July 13: Assassination of Marat by Charlotte Corday
	Robespierre enters Committee of Public Safety
	August: National Draft inaugurated
	October Execution of Marie-Antoinette
	Execution of Girondins
	Dechristianization campaign
1794	March 24: Execution of Hébertistes
	June 8: Fête of Supreme Being
	June 26: Reconquest of Belgium
	July 27–28: Fall of Robespierre Thermidor period of renunciation of radicals
	November: Jacobin Club closed
1795	May: Peace with Holland
	August: Constitution of Year III voted
	October: Dissolution of the Convention
	November: Rule of the Directoire or Directory begins
1796	November: French victory at Arcola
1797	January: French victory at Rivoli
	May: Napoléon occupies Venice
	September 4: Coup d'état of 18 fructidor, Napoléon seizes power
1798	May: Departure of French Expedition to Egypt
	July: Victory at Battle of the Pyramids
	August: Aboukir Bay: Nelson destroys the French fleet
1799	March–July: Austrian and Russian successes
	September–October: Russian army defeated in Switzerland
	October: Napoléon returns to France

1799	(*continued*)

1799 (*continued*)
November 9–10: Coup d'etat
December: Bonaparte First Consul, Constitution of Year VIII
1800 June: Napoléon takes Marengo
December: Royalist Bomb plot
1801 August: French army in Egypt capitulates to English
Chateaubriand's *Le Génie du Christianisme*
1802 April: Concordat promulgated—pact between Napoléon and the
Pope
May: Napoléon made Consul for life
1803 April: British ultimatum
May: Renewal of war with Great Britain
Sale of Louisiana to the United States
1804 Coronation of Napoléon
December 2: Battle at Austerlitz
1806 July: Battle at Maida
October: Battle at Jena
1807 October: Invasion of Portugal
November, December: Milan decrees
1808 Establishment of the University of Paris
May: Joseph Bonaparte, King of Spain
December: Napoléon invades Spain
1809 March: Invasion of Portugal
April: Austrian Offensive
Disgrace of Talleyrand
May: Annexation of Papal States
Imprisonment of Pius VII
1810 Divorce of Joséphine
Marriage of Napoléon to Marie-Louise
Mme de Stael's *de l'Allemagne*
1811 Economic crisis
1812 September 14: Occupation of Moscow
1813 October: Wellington crosses the Pyrenees
1814 January: Allied invasion of France
March 31: Capitulation of Paris
April 6: Abdication of Napoléon
April 10: Toulouse Defeat of Soult by Wellington
April 11: Treaty of Fontainebleau
May 1: First Treaty of Paris
June 4: Constitutional Charter of Louis XVIII
September: Congress of Vienna meets

1815	March 20: Napoléon enters Paris
	June 18: Waterloo
	June 22: Second abdication of Napoléon
	July 8: Second Restoration
	November: Second Treaty of Paris
1816	September: Election of New Chamber
1818	November: Occupation of France ends
1819	Géricault's *The Raft of Medusa*
1820	Recall of Richelieu
1821	Death of Napoléon
	December: Fall of Second Richelieu ministry. Ultras take over government
1823	April: Expedition into Spain
1824	June: Dismissal of Chateaubriand
	Delacroix's *The Massacre of Chios* first exhibited
	September: Death of Louis XVIII
	Succession of Charles X
1825	May: Coronation of Charles X at Reims
1827	Victor Hugo's *Cromwell* debuted
1830	Victor Hugo's *Hernani*
	Berlioz's *Symphonie Fantastique* premiered
	July: Capture of Algiers
	July 28–30: Revolution in Paris
	August 2: Abdication of Charles X
	Louis-Philippe takes over until 1848
1831–	
1832	Cholera epidemic

Bibliography

Abensour, Léon. *La Femme et le Féminisme avant la Révolution*. Thèse de Doctorat. Paris: Éditions Ernest Leroux, 1923.

Alderson, Evan. Ballet as Ideology: *Giselle*, Act II. *Dance Chronicle* 10 (1987): 290–304.

Aldrich, Elizabeth. *From the Ballroom to Hell: Grace and Folly in Nineteenth-Century Dance*. Evanston, IL: Northwestern University Press, 1991.

"A New Look at an Old Dance," Conference Proceedings, World Dance Alliance, Hong Kong International Dance Conference, July 15–18, 1990.

An Elegant Art: Fashion and Fantasy in the Eighteenth Century. Los Angeles: Los Angeles County Museum of Art in Association with Harry N. Abrams, Publishers, New York, 1983.

Aries, Philippe, Georges Duby, and Michelle Perrot, eds., *History of Private Life, From the Fires of Revolution to the Great War*. Cambridge, MA: The Belknap Press of Harvard University, 1990.

Arkin, Lisa C. and Marian Smith. National Dance in Romantic Ballet. In *Rethinking the Sylph: New Perspectives on the Romantic Ballet*, ed. Lynn Garafola. Hanover, NH: Wesleyan University Press. 1997, 11–68.

Aschengreen, Erik. The Beautiful Danger: Facets of the Romantic Ballet. *Dance Perspectives* 58, Summer, 1974.

Austen, Jane. *Northanger Abbey*. Boston: Little Brown, 1892.

———. *Persuasion*. Boston: Little Brown, 1892.

Balme, Christopher. Cultural Anthropology and Theatre Historiography: Notes on a Methodological Rapprochement. *Journal of the American Society of Theatre Research* 35 (May 1994): 33–54.

Banes, Sally. *Dancing Women: Female Bodies on Stage*. London: Routledge, 1998.

Barnett, Dene. *The Art of Gesture: The Practices and Principles of Eighteenth Century Acting*. Heidelberg: C. Winter, 1987.

Barringer, Janice and Sarah Schlessinger. *The Pointe Book*. Hightstown, NJ: Princeton Book Company, 1998.

Barthes, Roland. *Critical Essays*. Translated by Richard Howard. Evanston, IL: Northwestern University Press, 1972.

———. *The Fashion System*. Translated by Matthew Ward and Richard Howard. London: Cape, 1985.

Batteux, Charles. *Les Beaux Arts réduits à un même principe*. 1746. Microfiche. Paris: Archives de la Linguistique Française, 1972.

Baudelaire, Charles. *Oeuvres Complètes*, Edited by Claude Pichois. Paris: Gallimard, 1961.

Beaumont, Cyril. *Ballet Design, Past and Present*. London: The Studio, 1946.

———. *A Miscellany for Dancers*. Compiled and translated. London: C. W. Beaumont, 1934.

Bell, Quentin. *Dress and Human Finery*. London: The Hogarth Press, 1948.

Bergler, Edmund. *Fashion and the Unconscious.* Madison, CT: International Universities Press, 1987.

Bernardin de Saint-Pierre, Jacques-Henri. *Paul and Virginia.* 1789, Translated by Clara Bell. New York: F. M. Lupton, 1887.

Berry, Lord William. *Freaks of Fashion: The Corset and the Crinoline.* 1868. Mendocino, CA: R. L. Shep, 1993.

Biographie Universelle ou dictionnaire historique. Paris: F.X. de Feller, Meguignon Junior et J. Leroux, 1864.

Blasis, Carlo. *The Code of Terpsichore, A Practical and Historical Treatise on the Ballet, Dancing and Pantomime: with a Complete Theory of the Art of Dancing: Intended as Well for the Instruction of Amateurs as the Use of Professional Persons,* Translated by R. Barton. Unabridged republication of the first edition published for James Bullock, London, 1828. Brooklyn: Dance Horizons, 1976.

Boigne, Charles de. *Petits Mémoires de l'Opéra.* Paris: Librairie Nouvelle, 1857.

Bordo, Susan. *Unbearable Weight: Feminism, Western Culture and the Body.* Berkeley: University of California Press, 1993.

Boucher, François. *Histoire du Costume en Occident.* Paris: Flammarion, 1983.

Boulenger, Jacques. *De la Walse au Tango; La Danse Mondaine au Premier Empire à nos Jours.* Paris: Devambez, 1920.

Brainard, Ingrid. The Speaking Body: Gasparo Angiolini's Rhétorique Muette and the Ballet d'Action in the Eighteenth Century. In *Critica Musica: Essays in Honor of Paul Brainard,* ed. John Knowles. Amsterdam: Gordon and Breach, 1996.

Breward, Christopher. *The Culture of Fashion.* Manchester: Manchester University Press, 1995.

Brewer, Ebenezer Cobham. *Brewer's Dictionary of Phrase and Fable.* London: Cassell, 1970.

British Museum. Department of Prints and Drawings. *Catalogue of Political and Personal Satires Preserved in the Department of Prints and Drawings in the British Museum.* London, 1978.

Brooke, Iris. *Western European Costume: Seventeenth Century to Mid-Nineteenth Century.* London: George Harrap, 1940.

Brooks, Peter. *Objects of Desire in Modern Narrative.* Cambridge, MA: Harvard University Press, 1993.

Browne, Alice. *The Eighteenth-Century Feminist Mind.* Brighton, Sussex: The Harvester Press, 1987.

Brownmiller, Susan. *Femininity.* New York: Linden Press/Simon & Schuster, 1984.

Brydon, Anne and S. A. Niessen, eds. *Consuming Fashion: Adorning the Transnational Body.* Oxford, UK: Berg, 1998.

Burroughs, Catherine B. and Jeffrey David Ehrenreich, eds. *Reading the Social Body.* Iowa City: University of Iowa Press, 1993.

Buruma, Ian. *Anglomania: A European Love Affair.* New York: Random House, 1998.

Bynum, Caroline Walker. *Holy Feast and Holy Fast: The Religious Significance of Food to Medieval Women.* Berkeley: University of California Press, 1987.

Byron, Lord. *The Complete Poetical Works,* Edited by Jerome J. McGann. Oxford, UK: Clarendon Press, 1981, 22–31.

Cahusac, Louis de. *La Danse Ancienne et Moderne, ou Traité Historique de la Danse* 1754, Geneva: Slatkine reprints, 1971.

Calder, Angus. *Byron and Scotland: Radical or Dandy.* Edinburgh: Edinburgh University Press, 1989.

Capon, Gaston. *Les Vestris, le dieu de la danse et sa famille.* Paris: Mercure de France, 1908.

Carlson, Marvin. *Theatre of the French Revolution.* Ithaca, NY: Cornell University Press, 1966.

———. "Eighteenth Century French Costume Reform," *Theatre Survey: American Journal of Theatre History,* vol. 28, May 1987, 37–48.

Carlyle, Thomas. *Sartor Resartus, the Life and Opinions of Herr Teufelsdrockh* 1838. New York: AMS Press, 1969.

Carré, L. C. Henri. *Divertissements: Sports et Jeux des Rois de France.* Paris: Gallimard, 1937.

Cavallaro, Dani and Alexandra Warwick, eds., *Fashioning the Frame: Boundaries, Dress and the Body.* Oxford, UK: Berg, 1998.

Chateaubriand, François-René de. *The Memoirs of Chateaubriand.* Translated by Robert Baldick, New York: Alfred A. Knopf, 1961.

Chazin-Bennahum, Judith. "Cahusac, Diderot and Noverre: Three Revolutionary French Writers on Eighteenth Century Dance." *Theatre Journal*, vol. 35, May 1983, 168–178.

———. *Dance in the Shadow of the Guillotine*. Carbondale, IL: Southern Illinois University Press, 1988.

———. "Livrets of Ballets and Pantomimes 1787–1801." PhD dissertation, University of New Mexico, 1981

Christout, Marie-Françoise. *Le Merveilleux et le Théâtre du Silence*. The Hague: Editions Mouton, 1965.

Clarke, Mary and Clement Crisp. *Ballet Art: From the Renaissance to the Present*. New York: Clarkson, N. Potter, 1978.

———. *Design for Ballet*. London: Studio Vista, 1978.

Cobban, Alfred. *History of Modern France*. 2 vols. Middlesex, U.K.: Penguin Books, 1961.

Cohen, Selma Jeanne. *Dance as a Theatre Art* (2nd ed.) with a new section edited by Katy Matheson. Princeton, NJ: Princeton Book Company/A Dance Horizons Book, 1992.

Collins, Herbert. *F. Talma*. New York: Hill and Wang, 1964.

Copeland, Roger and Marshall Cohen, eds.,. *What is Dance? Readings in Theory and Criticism*. New York: Oxford University Press, 1983.

Cordova, Sarah Davies. *Paris Dances: Textual Choreographies in the Nineteenth-Century French Novel*. San Francisco: International Scholars Publications, 1999.

Cronin, Vincent. *Louis and Antoinette*. London: Collins, 1974.

Cunnington, C. Willet and Phillis. *The History of Underclothes*. New York: Dover, 1992.

Curzon, Henri. *Articles Biographiques sur La Guimard*. Rondel Collection, Bibliothèque de la Arsenal.

Dacier, Émile. "Une danseuse française à Londres au début du XVIII (1725–1735)." *Mercure Musical*, July 15, 1907, 746–765.

Daly, Ann. "Classical Ballet: A Discourse of Difference." *Women and Performance*. Issue 6 (vol. 3), 1987/1988, 57–64.

Daumas, Dr. "Hygiène et Médecine." *Fashion-Théorie* Issue 33, March 1861.

Davis, Fred. *Fashion, Culture and Identity*. Chicago: University of Chicago Press, 1992.

Davis, Tracy C. *Actresses as Working Women*. London: Routledge, 1991.

Dayot, Armand. *Histoire Contemporaine par l'Image, 1789–1872*. Paris: Flammarion, 1905.

Deane, Phyllis. *The First Industrial Revolution*. 2nd ed. London: Cambridge University Press, 1979.

Debay. A. *Hygiène Vestimentaire*. Paris: E. Dentu, 1857.

Delaney, Janice, Mary Jane Lupton, and Emily Toth. *The Curse*. New York: E. P. Dutton, 1976.

Delpierre, Madeleine. *Dress in France in the Eighteenth Century*. Translated by Caroline Beamish. New Haven: Yale University Press, 1997.

De Pure, Michel. *Idée sur des Spectacles, Anciens et nouveaux* (1668), Geneva: Minkoff, 1970.

Dickens, Charles. *A Tale of Two Cities*. (1859). Signet Classic, 1960.

Diderot, Denis. *Oeuvres Complètes, Troisième Entretien sur le Fils Naturel*. Paris: Garnier Frères 1875, vol. 7. Nendeln, Liechtenstein, Kraus Ltd. 1966.

———. *Rameau's Nephew*. Translated by L. W. Tancock. Middlesex: Penguin: 1966.

———. *Recherches Philosophiques sur l'Origine et la Nature du Beau* 1751, vol. 10. Nendeln, Leichtenstein, and Kraus, 1966.

Downing, Eric. "Anti-Pygmalion" in *Constructions of the Classical Body*. Edited by James Porter. Ann Arbor: University of Michigan Press, 1999.

Dubos, Abbé Jean Baptiste. *Réflexions sur la Poésie et la Peinture* 1733. Microfiche. Paris: Archives de la Linguistique Française, 1973.

Ducrey, Guy. *Corps et Graphies: Poétique de la Danse et de la Danseuse à la Fin du XIXe Siècle*. Paris: Honoré Champion éditeur, 1996.

Duplain, M. *Guimard, ou l'Art de la Danse Pantomime*. Paris: Chez Mérigot, 1783.

E. Ward & Co. *The Dress Reform Problem, A Chapter for Women*. Bradford, London: 1886.

Eames, Marian. *When All the World Was Dancing*. New York Public Library pamphlet. New York: Arno Press, 1957.

Elias, Norbert. *The Civilizing Process*. Translated by Edmund Jephcott. New York: Urizen Books, 1978.

Encyclopédie ou dictionnaire raisonné des sciences, des arts métiers, 1752, rpt. Stuttgart Facsimile bad Canstatt, Friederich Frommann, Verlag (Gunther Holzboog). 1966.

Erickson, Carolly. *To the Scaffold: The Life of Marie Antoinette.* New York: Morrow, 1991.

Ewing, Elizabeth. *Dress and Undress: History of Women's Underwear.* London: Bibliophile, 1986.

———. *Everyday Dress: 1650–1900.* London: B. T. Batsford, 1984.

——— *Fashion in Underwear.* London: B. T. Batsford, 1971.

——— *History of Women's Underwear.* New York: Drama Books, 1978.

Fairfax, Edmund. *The Styles of Eighteenth-Century Ballet.* Lanham, MD: Scarecrow Press, 2003.

Falcone, Francesca. "The Arabesque." *Dance Chronicle*, vol. 19, 1996, 231–253.

———. "The Evolution of the Arabesque in Dance." *Dance Chronicle*, vol. 22, 1999, 71–118.

Faust, Drew Gilpin. *Mothers of Invention: Women of the Slaveholding South in the American Civil War.* Chapel Hill: The University of North Carolina Press, 1996.

Fischer, Carl. *Costumes de l'Opéra.* Paris: Librairie de France, 1931.

Flament, Albert "Le Sourire de la Camargo." Conférence aux Annales le 21 fevrier 1927. *Journal de l'Universite des Annales*, No. 22, 1927.

Flugel, J. C. *The Psychology of Clothes.* New York: International Universities Press, 1930.

Fontenel, Beatrice. *Support and Seduction: A History of Corsets and Bras.* New York: Harry Abrams, 1992.

Forman, Amanda. *Georgiana, Duchess of Devonshire.* New York: Random House, 1998.

Foster, Susan Leigh. *Choreography and Narrative: Ballet's Staging of Story and Desire.* Bloomington: University of Indiana Press, 1996.

———. "Dancing the Body Politic: Manner and Mimesis in Eighteenth-Century Ballet." In *From the Royal to the Republican Body.* Sara E. Melzer and Kathryn Norberg, eds. Berkeley: University of California Press, 1998, 162–182.

———, ed. *Corporealities: Dancing Knowledge, Culture and Power.* London: Routledge, 1996.

Foster, Vanda. *Visual History of Costume: The Nineteenth Century.* London: B. T. Batsford, 1984.

Foucault, Michel. *Discipline and Punish: The Birth of the Prison.* Translated by Alan Sheridan. New York: Vintage Books, 1979.

Fraisse, Genevieve and Michelle Perrot. *History of Women: Emerging Feminism from Revolution to World War.* Cambridge, MA: The Belknap Press of Harvard University Press, 1993.

Franko, Mark. *Dancing as Text: Ideologies of the Baroque Body.* New York: Cambridge University Press, 1993.

———. *The Dancing Body in the Renaissance (1416–1589).* Birmingham, AL: Summa Publications, 1986.

Gallini, Giovanni-Andrea. *Treatise on the Art of Dancing* 1762. New York: Broude Brothers, 1967.

Garafola, Lynn. "The Nineteenth Century Travesty Dancer." *Dance Research Journal*, Fall 1985–Spring 1986, 35–40.

———. *Rethinking the Sylph: New Perspectives on the Romantic Ballet.* Middletown, CT: Wesleyan University Press, 1997.

Garber, Marjorie. *Vested Interests: Cross-Dressing and Cultural Anxiety.* New York: Routledge, 1992.

Garelick, Rhonda K. *Rising Star: Dandyism, Gender and Performance in the Fin de Siècle.* Princeton, NJ: Princeton University Press, 1998.

Gautier, Théophile. Bénéfice de Melle Taglioni, June 29, 1844. *La Presse*, July 1, 1844.

———. *Gautier on Dance.* Translated and edited by Ivor Guest. London, Cecil Court: Dance Books, 1986.

———. *Mademoiselle de Maupin.* New York: The Heritage Press/London: The Nonesuch Press, 1944.

———. *La Peau de Tigre.* Paris, 1866.

Goethe, Johann Wolfgang von. *Faust.* Translated with an Introduction by Walter Kaufmann. Garden City, NY: Doubleday Anchor Books, 1962.

Goncourt, Edmond et Jules. *La Guimard.* Paris: Charpentier, 1893.

———. *Histoire de la Société française pendant la Directoire.* Paris, 1855.

Gontaut, *Mémoires of the Duchesse de Gontaut.* Translated by J. W. Davies, 2 vols. London, 1894.

Graffingny, Françoise de. *Letters from a Peruvian Woman* 1752. Translated by David Hornacker. New York: Modern Language Association, 1993.

Guest, Ann Hutchinson and Knud Arne Jürgensen. *Robert le Diable: The Ballet of the Nuns.* London: Gordon and Breach, 1997.

Guest, Ivor. *The Ballet of the Enlightenment.* London: Dance Books, 1996.

————. *The Ballet of the Second Empire*. London: Pitman Publishing, Middletown, CT: Wesleyan University Press, 1953, 1974.

————. *Ballet Under Napoleon*. London: Dance Books, 2002.

————. "Dandies and Dancers." *Dance Perspectives* 37, Spring 1969.

————. *The Romantic Ballet in Paris*. London: Pitman, 1966.

————. *The Romantic Ballet in England*. Middletown, CT: Wesleyan University Press, 1972.

Harris, Jennifer. "The Red Cap of Liberty: A Study of Dress Worn by French Revolutionary Partisans." *Eighteenth Century Studies*, vol. 14, Spring 1981, 283–312.

Harvey, John. *Men in Black*. Chicago: University of Chicago Press, 1995.

Hawkins, Charles W. "Taglioni et Elssler." *Archives Internationales de la Danse* (Paris), January 15, 1933, 7–9.

Hersch, Virginia. *To Seize a Dream*. New York: Crown Publishers, 1948.

Henderson, Andrea. "Passion and Fashion in Joanna Baillie's Introductory Discourse." *PMLA* from March 1997, vol. 112, 198–213.

Herold, J. Christopher. *Mistress to an Age*. Alexandria, VA: Time Life Books, 1981.

Highfill Philip, Jr., Kalman A. Burnim, and Edward A. Langhans. *A Biographical Dictionary of Musicians, Dancers, Managers, and other Stage Personnel in London, 1660–1800*. Carbondale: Southern Illinois University Press, 1978.

Hilton, Wendy. *Dance of Court and Theatre: The French Noble Style 1680–1725*. Princeton, NJ: Princeton Book Company, 1981.

————. *Dance and Music of Court and Theatre: Selected Writings of Wendy Hilton*. Stuyvesant, NY: Pendragon Press, 1997.

Hogarth, William. *The Analysis of Beauty*. Oxford: Clarendon Press, 1955.

Hollander, Anne. "Dress and its Image in Art." In *New Perspectives on the History of Western Dress*. Mary Ellen Roach and Kathleen Ehle Musa, eds. New York: Costume Institute of the Metropolitan Museum of Art, 1980, 42–51.

————. *Seeing through Clothes*. Berkeley: University of California Press, 1993.

————. *Sex and Suits*. New York: Alfred A. Knopf, 1994.

Hufton, Olwen. *The Prospect Before Her*. New York: Alfred Knopf, 1996.

Hunt, Lynn. "Freedom of Dress in Revolutionary France." In *From the Royal to the Republican Body, Incorporating the Political in Seventeenth- and Eighteenth-Century France*. Sara E. Melzer and Kathryn Norberg, eds. Berkeley: University of California Press, 1998, 224–249.

————. *Politics, Culture and Class in the French Revolution*. Berkeley: University of California Press, 1984.

————. *Eroticism and the Body Politic*. Baltimore: Johns Hopkins University Press, 1991.

Hurlock, Elizabeth B. "Arbiters of Fashion." In *Dress, Adornment and the Social Order*. Mary Ellen Roach and Joanne Bubolz Eicher, eds.. New York: Wiley, 1965.

Joseph, Nathan. *Uniforms and Non-Uniforms: Communication Through Clothing*. New York: Greenwood Press, 1986.

Jowitt, Deborah. *Time and the Dancing Image*. Berkeley: University of California Press, 1988.

Jullien, Adolphe. *La Comédie à la cour: les Théâtres de Société Royale pendant le Siècle Dernier*. Paris: Librairie de Firmin Didot et Cie, n.d.

————. *L'Histoire du costume au Théâtre*. Paris: Bibliothèque Charpentier, 1880.

Kahane, Martine and Delphine Pinasa. *Le Tutu, Petit Guide; Petit Histoire du Tutu, Opéra National de Paris*, 1997.

Kern, Stephen. *Anatomy and Destiny: A Cultural History of the Human Body*. Indianapolis and New York: Bobbs-Merrill, 1974.

Kirstein, Lincoln. *Movement and Metaphor*. New York: Praeger Publishers, 1970.

Kochno, Boris. *Le Ballet en France: du Quinzième à Nos Jours*. Paris: Hachette, 1954.

Kunzle, David. *Fashion and Fetishism: A Social History of the Corset and Other Forms of Body Sculpture in the West*. Totowa, NJ: Rowman and Littlefield, 1982.

Kybalova, Ludmilla, Olga Herbenova, and Milena Lamarova. *The Pictorial Encyclopedia of Fashion*. Translated by Claudia Rosoux. London: Paul Hamlyn, 1968.

La Clairon. *Mémoires* 1822. Genève: Slatkine, 1968.

La Gorce, Jérôme de. *Fééries d'Opéra. Décors, Machines et Costumes en France 1645–1765*. Paris: Éditeur de Patrimoine, 1997.

La Mettrie, Julien Offray. *Man a Machine*. 1748. La Salle, IL: Open Court, 1993.

Landes, Joan B. *Women and the Public Sphere in the Age of the French Revolution.* Ithaca, NY: Cornell University Press, 1988.

Laqueur, Thomas. *Making Sex: Body and Gender from the Greeks to Freud.* Cambridge, MA: Harvard University Press, 1990.

Latham, Angela. *Posing a Threat: Flappers, Chorus Girls and Other Brazen Performers.* Hanover, NH: Wesleyan University Press, 2000.

La Tour du Pin, Madame de. *Mémoires de Madame de la Tour du Pin* 1913. London: Century Publishing, 1913, 1985.

Laver, James. *Costume and Fashion.* London: Thames & Hudson, 1995.

Lee, Carol. *Ballet in Western Culture: A History of Its Origins and Evolution.* Boston and London: Allyn and Bacon, 1999.

Lehmann, Ulrich. *Tigersprung: Fashion in Modernity.* Cambridge, MA: MIT Press, 2000.

L'Eloffe, Comtesse de. *Modes et Usages au Temps de Marie Antoinette: Livre-journal de 1787–1790.* Paris: Firmin Didot, 1885.

Levinson, André. *Marie Taglioni.* London: Dance Books, 1977.

Libron, F. and H. Clouzot. *Le Corset dans l'Art et les Moeurs.* Paris: Chez l'auteur F. Libron, 1933.

Maeder, Edward. Curator of Textiles and Costumes. *An Elegant Art: Fashion and Fantasy in the Eighteenth Century.* Los Angeles County Museum of Art in association with Harry N. Abrams, 1983.

Magri, Gennaro. *Theoretical and Practical Treatise on Dancing* 1779. Translated by Mary Skeaping, London: Dance Books, 1988.

Maigron, Louis. *Le Romantisme et la Mode.* Paris: Librairie Ancienne Honoré Champion, Éditeur, 1911.

Martin, Richard. *The Ceaseless Century: 300 Years of Eighteenth-Century Costume.* New York: The Metropolitan Museum of Art, 1998.

———. *2wice*, vol. 2, 101–102, New York, 1998.

Marx, Karl. *Capital: A Critique of Political Economy,* Translated by Samuel Moore and Edward Aveling. Edited by Frederick Engels. New York: Random House/Modern Library, 1936.

Mayhew, Henry. *London Labour and the London Poor.* 4 vols. London: Griffin, Bohn, 1862.

McCormick, Malcolm. "Notes on the design of the costumes." *Baroque Dance 1675–1725,* Film made under the sponsorship of the Department of Dance, University of California at Los Angeles, 1977.

McPhee, Peter. *A Social History of France 1780-1880.* London and New York: Routledge, 1992.

Meglin, Joellen A. "Feminism or Fetishism: La Révolte des femmes and Women's Liberation in France from the 1830s." *Rethinking the Sylph: New Perspectives on the Romantic Ballet.* Lynn Garafola, ed. Hanover, NH: Wesleyan University Press, 1997, 69–90.

Melzer, Sara E. and Kathryn Norberg. *From the Royal to the Republican Body: Incorporating the Political in Seventeenth- and Eighteenth-Century France.* Berkeley: University of California Press, 1998.

Mercier, Louis-Sébastien. *New Picture of Paris,* 6 vols. 1798. 2 vols.1800.

Michelet, Jules. *The Women of the French Revolution.* Philadelphia: Henry Carey Baird, 1855.

Migel, Parmenia. *The Ballerinas.* New York: Macmillan, 1972.

Milhous, Judith. "Vestris-Mania and the Construction of Celebrity: Auguste Vestris in London, 1780–81." New Series Winter 1994–1995 vol. 5. Cambridge, MA: Harvard University Library, 30–64.

——— "Italian Opera in Late Eighteenth-Century London," Unpublished manuscript, 2000.

The Mirror of the Graces. By a Lady of Distinction. London, 1811.

Molière. *Théâtre Complet,* vol. 2, Édition de Robert Jouanny, Paris: Classiques Garnier, 1962.

Moore, Doris Langley. *Fashion through Fashion Plates 1771–1970.* New York: Clarkson N. Potter Inc., 1971.

Moore, Lillian. "Practice Clothes—Then and Now." Prepared and printed for Capezio, New York, 1960.

Moses, Claire Goldberg. *French Feminism in the 19th Century.* SUNY Series in European Social History. New York: State University of New York, 1984.

Murphy, Patricia. "Ballet Reform in Mid-Eighteenth-Century France: The Philosophers and Noverre." *Symposium, A Quarterly Journal.* Syracuse: Syracuse University Press, vol. 30, Spring, 1976.

Nixon, Nicola. "Men and Coats; or, The Politics of the Dandiacal Body in Melville's 'Benito Cereno.'" *PMLA*, vol. 114, May 1999, 359–372.

Norris, Herbert. *Costume and Fashion*, vol. 3, New York: E. P. Dutton, 1938.

Noverre, Jean Georges. *Letters on Dance and Dancing*. Revised and Enlarged Edition, published at St. Petersburg, 1803. Translated by Cyril Beaumont. Brooklyn, NY: Dance Horizons, 1966.

———. *Lettres sur la Danse et les Arts Imitateurs* 1760. Paris: Editions Lieutier, 1952.

Outram, Dorinda. *The Body and the French Revolution*. New Haven, CT: Yale University Press, 1988.

Ozouf, Mona. *Fête Révolutionnaire*. Cambridge, MA: Harvard University Press, 1988.

Parker, Harold. *The Cult of Antiquity and the French Revolutionaries*. Chicago: University of Chicago Press, 1937.

Perrot, Philippe. *Fashioning the Bourgeoisie*. Translated by Richard Bienvenu. Princeton, NJ: Princeton University Press, 1994.

Poesio, Giannandrea. "Blasis, the Italian Ballo, and the Male Sylph." In *Rethinking the Sylph: New Perspectives on the Romantic Ballet*. Edited by Lynn Garafola. Hanover, NH: Wesleyan University Press, 1997, 131–141.

Porter, James I. *Constructions of the Classical Body*. Ann Arbor: University of Michigan Press, 1999.

Prudhommeau, Germaine. "Naissance des Pointes: Deux Petits Chaussons." *Danser*, No. 18, Décembre 1984, 48–50.

Purdy, Daniel. *The Tyranny of Elegance: Consumer Cosmopolitanism in the Era of Goethe*. Baltimore and London: Johns Hopkins University Press, 1998.

Pure, Michel de. *Idée des Spectacles, Anciens et Nouveaux* 1668. Geneva: Minkoff, 1972.

Rambaud, Carole. Catalogue of the Exhibition, *Costume à Danser*. Centre Culturel de Boulogne-Billancourt, April 1989.

Rameau, Pierre. *The Dancing Master 1735*. Translated by Cyril W. Beaumont. Brooklyn NY: Dance Horizons Republication, 1970.

Ravel, Jeffrey. "Actress to Activist: Mlle Clairon in the Public Sphere of the 1760s." In *Theatre Survey*, vol. 35, May 1994, 73–86.

Reade, Brian. *Ballet Designs and Illustrations, 1581–1940*. London: Her Majesty's Stationery Office, 1967.

Regency Etiquette: The Mirror of Graces (London, 1811), By a Lady of Distinction. Mendocino, CA: R. L. Shep, 1997.

Ribeiro, Aileen. *The Art of Dress: Fashion in England and France 1750–1820*. New Haven, CT: Yale University Press, 1996.

———. *Dress in Eighteenth Century Europe*. New York: Holmes & Meier, 1985.

———. *Fashion in the French Revolution*. London: B. T. Batsford, 1988.

———. *Ingres in Fashion, Representations of Dress and Appearance in Ingres' Images of Women*. New Haven, CT: Yale University Press, 1999.

———*Visual History of Costume in The Eighteenth Century*. London: B. T. Batsford, Drama Book Publishers, 1983.

Richardson, Jane and A. L. Kroeber. "Three Centuries of Women's Dress Fashions," *Anthropological Records*, Berkeley: University of California Press, 1947.

Roberts, Helene E. "The Exquisite Slave: The Role of Clothes in the Making of the Victorian Woman." *Signs*, Spring 1977, 554–569.

Robin-Challan, Louise. *Danse et Danseuses à L'Opéra de Paris 1830–1850*. Thèse de Troisième Cycle, l'Universite de Paris VII, 1983.

———. "Social Conditions of Ballet Dancers at the Paris Opera in the Nineteenth Century." *Choreography and Dance*, vol. 2, No. 1, 1992, 17–28.

Robinson, Lillian. *Sex, Class and Culture*. Bloomington and London: Indiana University Press, 1978.

Roqueplan, Nestor. *Les Coulisses de l'Opéra*. Paris: Librairie Nouvelle, 1855.

Rousseau, Jean Jacques. *Emile or On Education* 1762. Translated by Barbara Foxley. London: J. M. Dent, 1948.

———. *Julie or La Nouvelle Héloise*. Translated by T. McDowell, University Park, PA: Pennsylvania State University Press, 1968.

———. *Julie or The New Heloise*. Translated by Philip Stewart and Jean Vaché, Hanover, NH: Dartmouth College and University Press of New England, 1997.

———. *Politics and the Arts: Letter to M. D'Alembert on the Theatre* 1758. Translated and edited by Allan Bloom. Glencoe, IL: Free Press of Glencoe, 1960.

Saint Laurent, Cecil. *History of Ladies Underwear.* London: Michael Joseph, 1966.

Sandoz, Marc. *Jean Simon Berthélemy.* Paris: Editart, 1979.

Saraf, Manisha. "Holy Anorexia and Anorexia Nervosa: Society and Concept of Disease." *The Pharos,* Fall 1998, 2–4.

Schama, Simon. "Modes of Seduction: The Theatrical Eloquence of Haute Couture at the Costume Institute." *The New Yorker,* December 8, 1995, 100–105.

———. *Citizens: A Chronicle of the French Revolution.* New York: A. Knopf, 1989.

Second, Alberic. *Petits Mystères de l'Opéra.* Paris, 1844.

Sennett, Richard. *Flesh and Stone: The Body and the City in Western Civilization.* New York: Norton, 1994.

Solomon-Godeau, Abigail. "The Legs of the Countess." In *Fetishism as Cultural Discourse.* Emily Apter and William Pietz, eds. Ithaca NY: Cornell University Press, 1993.

Sorel, Albert. *L'Europe et la Révolution Française.* Vol. 8. Paris: Librairie Plon, 1892.

Sorell, Walter. *The Dance in Its Time.* Garden City, NY: Anchor Press/Doubleday, 1981.

Spencer, Samia, ed. *French Women and the Age of Enlightenment.* Bloomington: Indiana University Press, 1984.

Squire, Geoffrey. *Dress, Art and Society.* London: Studio Vista, 1974.

Starobinski, Jean. *1789: Emblems of Reason.* Translated by Barbara Bray. Cambridge, MA: MIT Press, 1988.

Steele, Valerie. *Fashion and Eroticism: Ideals of Feminine Beauty from the Victorian Era to the Jazz Age.* New York: Oxford University Press, 1985.

———. *Fetishism: Fashion, Sex and Power.* New York: Oxford University Press, 1996.

Steward, Mary Lynn and Nancy Janovicek. "Slimming the Female Body?: Dress, Corsets, and Physical Culture in France, 1890s–1930s." *Fashion Theory: The Journal of Dress, Body and Culture,* vol. 5, No. 2, June 2001.

Strong, Roy, Ivor Guest, Richard Buckle, Barry Kay, and Liz Da Costa. *Designing for the Dancer.* London: Elron Press, 1981.

Swann, June. *Shoes.* London: Batsford, 1982.

Swift, Mary Grace. *A Loftier Flight: The Life and Accomplishments of Charles-Louis Didelot, Balletmaster.* Middletown, CT: Wesleyan University Press, 1974.

Théleur, E. A. *Letters on Dancing: Reducing this Elegant and Healthful Exercise to Easy Scientific Principles.* London: Hicks and Read, 1831.

———. "Letters On Dancing." Sandra Hammond, ed. In *Studies in Dance History,* Fall/Winter 1990.

Toepfer, Karl. *Theatre, Aristocracy and Pornocracy.* New York: PAJ, 1991.

Treves, Frederick. "The Dress of the Period in its Relations to Health." A lecture delivered on behalf of the National Health Society, Fellow of the Royal College of Surgeons, London: Allman, 1884.

Trouille, Mary Seidman. *Sexual Politics in the Enlightenment: Women Writers Read Rousseau.* Albany, NY: State University of New York Press, 1997.

Vaillat, Léandre. *Histoire de la Danse.* Paris: Librairie Plon, 1947.

Vernet, Horace. *Incroyables et Merveilleuses: Costumes et Modes D'autrefois Paris 1810–1818.* Texte par Roger-Armand Weigert, Conservateur au Cabinet des Estampes de la Bibliothèque Nationale. Paris: Rombaldi, 1955.

Véron, Louis. "Mémoires d'un Bourgeois de Paris." Translated by Victoria Huckenpahler. *Dance Chronicle,* vol. 7, 1984.

Vigée-Lebrun, Elizabeth. *Memoirs of Madame Vigée Lebrun.* Translated by Lionel Strachey, NY: George Braziller, 1903.

Voltaire, François Arouet. *Correspondance.* T. Besterman, ed. Genève: Institut et Musée Voltaire, 107 vols. 1953–1965.

Vuillier, Gaston. *History of Dancing.* London: William Heineman, 1898.

Wallace, Carol McD., Don McDonagh, Jean L. Druesedow, Laurence Libin, and Constance Old. *Dance, A Very Social History.* New York: Metropolitan Museum of Art and Rizzoli, 1986.

Waugh, Nora. *Corsets and Crinolines.* London: B. T. Batsford Ltd., 1954.

Whitfeld, Henry. *The Absurdities of Stays; and The Evil Effects of Tight Lacing.* London: Ashfort Kint, 1845.

Wild, Nicole. *Catalogue de l'Opéra, Décors et Costumes,* 2 vols. Paris: Bibliothèque Nationale, 1987.

Wilton, Mary Margaret. *The Book of Costume or Annals of Fashion, From the Earliest Period to the Present Time. By a Lady of Rank.* London: Henry Colburn, 1847.

Winter, Marian Hannah. *Pre-Romantic Ballet.* New York: Dance Horizons, 1974.

Le Théâtre du Merveilleux. Paris: Olivier Perrin, 1962.

Winterson, Jeanette. *Art Objects: Essays on Ecstasy and Effrontery.* New York: Vintage Books, 1995.

Wollen, Peter. *Raiding the Icebox: Reflections on Twentieth-Century Culture.* Bloomington: University of Indiana Press, 1993.

Wrigley, Richard. *The Politics of Appearances: Representations of Dress in Revolutionary France.* Oxford, NY: Berg, 2002.

Wynne, Shirley. "Complaisance, An Eighteenth-Century Cool." *Dance Scope,* vol. 5, 1970, 22–35.

Index

A

Academy of Dance, 32
Achille à Scyros, 139–140
Actors
  English, 39
  immorality, 55
Aladin, 160, *161*
Allard, Mademoiselle, *45*
American Revolution, 24
Ancient Greek festivals, 77
Anglomanie, 16
Anorexia, ballet dancers, 233–234
Antique myths in ballet, 103, 111–116, 165
Antique style, Paris Opéra, 109
Antony and Cleopatra, 143–144
Arabesques, 183
Archaeological revelations, 95
Aristocracy
  in amateur theatrics, 19–21
  Baroque period, 9–14
Art criticism, 58–59

B

Back to nature philosophy, 51–57
Ballet costume
  accuracy, 41
  genres, 41–42
  London audiences, *115,* 116
  neoclassicism, *115,* 116
  noble, 41–42
  Romantic movement, 183–184
  semiotic meaning, 241, 243–244
  visions of fairylands, 47
Ballet d'action, 61, 63, 64, 113, 245
Ballet dancers
  anorexia, 233–234
  ballerinas' fantasy roles, 179
  dehumanized objects without agency,
    228–229

  education, 234
  health, 237
  intelligence, 234
  mothers, 234
  protectors, 234
  religious vocation, 234
  reputation, 235
Ballet masters, 41
Ballet of the Nuns, *see Robert le Diable*
Ballet pantomime, 41, 245
Ballets
  antique myths, 111–116
  Cahusac, Louis de, 60–61
  commercialization, 218–219
  fantasy role, 179
  fascination with foreign, 203
  French Revolution, 4
  increasing popularity, 203
  with plot, 58
  Rousseau's, 56–57
  scenarios, 63, 64
  stability, 222
  women in male roles, 86–88, *87*
Ballet slippers, 194, *see also* Toe shoes
Ballroom dances, 163
Baroque period, 9
  aristocracy, 9–14
  cleanliness, 10
  manners, 10
  women's role at court, 12–14
Batterie, 42–44
Battle of the Nile, influence on fashion, 120
La Belle au Bois Dormant, 198–202, *199,*
  200
Berthélémy, Jean-Simon, *108, 109,* 109–111
Bertin, Rose, 19
Black characters, *141,* 143
Black suits, Bourbon restoration, 148
Blasis, Carlo, 181–186

Body, *see also* Female body
   attitudes toward, 239–240
   increasing exposure of, 42–44
   as machine, 6
Bonaparte, Napoléon, *see* Napoléon
Le Bon Genre, *123, 124,* 124–126, *125*
Boquet, Louis, 46–47
Bourbon restoration, 118
   colors, 148
   fashion magazines, 148–150
   middle classes, 148
   theater, 151–164
   uniforms, 148
   women's clothes, 148
Bourgeoisie, 66
   Napoléon, 122
Bows, 129
Breastfeeding, 98
Breasts
   corsets, 25, 27
   neoclassicism, 101
Breeches, 154
British Blockade, 95
Brugnoli, Amalia, 189–191
Brummel, Bryan (Beau), 177–178
Byron, Lord, 90–91

C
Cahusac, Louis de, 60–61
Calvinism, 51
Camargo, Marie-Anne de Cupis de, 42–44,
   43
Carmagnole, 82
Le Carnaval de Venise ou la Constance à
   l'Epreuve, 152, 153
Cendrillon, 160–163, *162*
Censorship, Napoléon, 142
Ce pays-ci, 10
Change, 22
Chaotic aesthetic, 91–92
Character dances, 136–137
Charles X, 165, 178
Chateaubriand, René de, 130–134, 150
Chemise dress, 23
Chemise à la reine, 23
Cholera, 237
Choreographers, 41
Choreography
   dance costume, relationship, 3
   Romantic movement, 183–184
Ciceri, Pierre-Luc-Charles, 145, 160
   Italian scene painting, 208
Citizens, special dress, 70–71
La Clairon, 36–39, *38*
Clari ou la promesse du mariage, 155, 156
Classical dress, 5, 95
   philosophical ideas, 96

Cleanliness, Baroque period, 10
Clergy, 66
Cloaks, 88
Clothing, *see also* specific type
   expressive of personal self, 56
   as screen, 2
The Code of Terpsichore, 181–186
Colors, 174, 244
   black, 73
   Bourbon restoration, 148
   French Revolution, 70, 72, 73
   skin, 173–174
Comic ballet, 151
Comic dancers, 42
Commercialization
   ballet, 218–219
   Paris Opéra, 204
Conservatism, 147, 165, 180, 202–203
Conservative style, 16–17
Contra dance, *124*
Contredanses allemandes, 90
Copyright, 111
Corday, Charlotte, 74
Corinne or Italy, 134
Corps de ballet, 103, 227
   daily life, 222
Corsets, 3, 25, 93, 101, 125–126, 171–173,
   172, 230–233, 241–242
   breasts, 25, 27
   dance principle development, 25
   dancing, 27
   health issues, 126–128, 172–173, 230–
      233
   physical constraint, 25, 27
   posture, 27, *28*
   problems for movement, 29
   Romantic movement, 168
   shapes, 25–26
Costume, *see also* specific type
   meaning, 4
Cotton industry, 123–124
Counter-revolutionary clothing, 71–73
Coup d'état of 18 Brumaire, 94
Court dances
   development, 32
   grace, 32–33
Court dress, 11, *11,* 82–92
   England's effect, 15–17
   influences from other countries, 24–25
   Marie Antoinette, 19
   Napoléon, *119,* 120–122
   presentation, 13
Covent Garden Opera Ballet, 223
Covent Garden Opera House, Fop's Alley,
   230
Crinolines, 231
Cult of the antique, 109

D

Daguerre, Louis-Jacques, 160
Dance costume reform
  accuracy, 41
  defined, 35
  before French Revolution, 41–50
  Noverre, 63
Dance costumes, *see also* Specific type
  Bourbon restoration, 151–164
  choreography, relationship, 3
  fashion, relationship, 1
  fetishes, 224
  meaning, 3
Dancers, *see also* Specific type
  as courtesans or prostitutes, 15, 227–228
  low status, 222
  marriage, 204
  morality, 204
  pay, 221–222
  pension, 221–222
  propriety, 204
  role as sexually available object, 225
Dancing masters, 13, 31–34
  functions, 31–32
  Louis XIV's reign, 32
  manners, 32
Dandyism, 177, 229, 230
Danses populaires, 203
La Dansomanie, 136–137
Dauberval, Jean, 82–86
David, Jacques-Louis, 67–68, 78, 80, 121, 129
Décolleté, 168
Decorative clothing, purpose, 9
Degas, Edgar, 229–230
De l'Allemagne, 135
Demi-caractère ballets, 151
Demi-caractère dancers, 42
Diderot, Denis, 57–59
  painting, 58–59
  theater as agency of social reform, 57–58
Directorate, 88, 109
  social dance, 88
Display, 91
Doctrine of ideal aesthetics, 96
Drawers, 101, 242
Dressed à *la sauvage,* 100–101
Dress shoes, *104*
Le Déserteur, 83, 86
  costumes, 86

E

Education, 77–78
  ballet dancers, 234
  women, 53, 56
Egalitarian styles, England, 16–17
Elgin Marbles, *94,* 96
Ellsler, Fanny, 237–238

Émile, 53
Emotion, 62
Empire style, 101
Encyclopedists, see Philosophes
England
  dancer's discreet costume, 206
  egalitarian styles, 16–17
  English Dandy, 177
  female body, 128
  influence on French style, 15–17
  Marie Antoinette's fashions, 23
  Napoléon, 117–118
  Rousseau's praise, 53
  sea power, 117
  understatement, 178
  waltz, 90
  war with, 95
English actors, 39
Equality
  under law, 5
  for women, 240
Espagnolisme, 203
Estates, 66
  sumptuary laws, 66–67
Expression
  grace, 33
  technique, contrasted, 6

F

Fabric, 214–215
  industrialism, 171
  Napoléon, 122–124
  Romantic movement, 168
Fantasy, 207
  new technologies, 207–208
Fashion
  change, 22
  day-night dress distinctions, 148, 168
  despotic influence, 2–3
  functions, 2
  German literature, 150
  industrialization effects, 6
  influences, 2, 150
  suffering, 232–233
  unhealthy emotionally or physically, 2–3
  value of study of, 2
  as weapon of power for women, 12
Fashion magazines
  Bourbon restoration, 148–150
  French Revolution, 70
  Germany, 170
  Romantic movement, 169
Favart, Madame (M.J.B. Duroncay), 36, *37*
Feet, 105, 221
  ballet shoe development, 105
  Romantic ballerinas, 182, 187–188
  Romantic ballet, 34

Female body
  Romantic movement, 175, 176, 181
  warrior figures, 175
Feminism, 240
  defeat of revolutionary radical feminism,
    74
Fetishes, 224, 228
La Fille mal gardée ou il n'est qu'un pas de
    mal au bien, 82–86, 198
  costumes, 84
First Estate, 66
Fort-l'Évêque prison, 49
Le fourreau, 15–16
Foyer de la danse, Paris Opéra, 204–205
Fragonard, Alexandre-Evariste, 195–196
Freeing of slaves, 85, 86
French court, 4–5, 119, 120–122
  Napoléon, 119, 120–122
  presentation, 13
French Revolution, 5, 239–240
  ballet, 4
  colors, 70, 72, 73
  defeat of revolutionary radical feminism,
    74
  economics of textiles and clothing, 70
  fashion journals, 70
  gender boundary disintegration, 73–74
  hair styles, 71
  Marie Antoinette, 73, 77
  Paris Opéra, 82–86
  politics of style, 66–73
  rationalism, 68
  simplicity, 68
  women in, 69, 73–77
  women's revolutionary clubs, 74
Fête de la Fédération, 79
Fête de l'Etre Suprême, 80

G
Gardel, Pierre, 78, 79–80, 138, 139, 140–146,
    198
  Paris Opéra, 110, 111–116
Gautier, Théophile, 243–244
Gender swapping, 86–88, 87
Germany, 150, 245
  fashion magazines, 170
Le Geste, 61
Gigot sleeves, 168
Gonorrhea, 237
Gosselin, Mademoiselle, 189
Goëthe, Johann Wolfgang von, 150
Gouges, Olympe de, 76
Grace
  court dance, 32–33
  expression, 33
Greek mythology, 111–116
Greek sculptures, 95–96
Greek tragedies, 96

Greek tunics, 80
Greek vases, 95–96
Greuze, Jean-Baptiste, 58–59
Grotesque tradition, 207–208, 218
Guimard, Marie-Madeleine, 46–50, 48, 50
  aristocracy, 49
  as clothes designer, 47
  in England, 49
  entertaining, 49
  Marie Antoinette, 49
  political force of, 46
  street clothes, 47

H
Hair styles, 30–31, 98
  French Revolution, 71
  perukes, 30–31
  Romantic movement, 168–169
Hamilton, Emma, 107–108
Hats, 24, 82
  English influences, 14, 16
  Romantic movement, 169
Headgear, 10
High heeled shoes, 12, 225–226
Hips, 221
Hoops, 231
Hugo, Victor, 175–176

I
Incroyables, 71–73, 72
Industrialization, 5–6, 241, 244
  conceptualization of ballerina's body, 6
  fashion effects, 6
  Romantic backlash, 6
Ingres, Jean-Auguste-Dominique, 129
Intelligence, ballet dancers, 234
Isabey, Jean-Baptiste, 121
Italy, 117
  dance influences, 218
  Italian choreographers, 218
  Italian dancers, 218

J
Jacobin Party, 135
Jewelry, 91
Joséphine, Empress of France, 121
  fashion style, 109
Le Jugement de Paris, 115–116
Julie ou la Nouvelle Héloïse, 51, 53, 54, 56
July Revolution of 1830, 165
Jumps, 182, 243

L
La Liberté, 76
Legal prostitution, 235
Legs, 221, 228, 229–230, 243
Leitmotif, 202
Leroy, Louis-Hippolyte, 121

Lettres sur la Danse (Noverre), 61–63, 186
Lifts, Romantic ballet, 225
Lighting, 231, 243
    Romantic ballet, 208
Literature
    German, 150
    Romanticism, 150
    18th century writers, 51
Livrets, 63, 64
Louis XIV, 9–10
Louis XVI, death, *68*
Louis XVIII
    after Napoléon's defeats, 147
    early life, 147
La Lévite, 24

M
Madonna/prostitute complex, 223–224
Magri, Gennaro, 33–34
Maillots, 103, 105–107
Makeup, 173–174
Male dancers, 41, 235
Mallarmé, Stéphane, 244
Manners, 227
    Baroque period, 10
    dancing masters, 32
    as social barrier, 13–14
Manon Lescaut, 201, 202
Marianne, 76–77
Marie Antoinette, Queen of France, 17–23,
    18
    clothing cost, 19
    court costume, 19
    dislike for, 17
    education, 17
    English fashions, 23
    fashion influence of, 18–19
    French Revolution, 73, 77
    last days, 23
    performing in plays and operas, 19–20, 21
    theater, 19–20, 21
Marie-Louise of Austria, *127,* 128–129
Marriage, dancers, 204
Masks, 30, 151
Mass consumption, 6
Mechanical corsets, *172,* 173
Men's dress
    English tailoring, 171
    18th century dancers, 41
    understatement, 178
Merveilleuses, 106, 107
Middle class
    artistic tastes, 96
    Bourbon restoration, 148
    increasingly opulent lifestyle, 13–14
    values, 5–6
Military uniforms, *see* Uniforms
Milon, Louis J., 144–145

The Mirror of Graces, 126
La mode, meaning, 4
Morality, dancers, 204
La Mort de Tasse, 159, 160
Motherhood, 53
Méricourt, Théroigne de, 74–76, *75*
La Muette de Portici, 197, 198
Muscadins, 71
Music, Napoléon, 129
Muslin, 214–215
Mystery, 207
    new technologies, 207–208
Mythological ballets, 103, 111–116
    Romantic movement, 195
Mythological garb, 42

N
Napoléon, Emperor of France
    arts encouragement, 98
    assassination attempt, 135
    ballets, 136–146
    bourgeoisie, 122
    celebrated artists, 136–146
    censorship, 142
    court dress, *119,* 120–122
    culture of war, 120
    dances, 136–146
    dancing lessons, 128–129
    England, 117–118
    European relations, 117
    fabrics, 122–124
    military campaigns, 117–118
    music, 129
    neoclassicism, 94–95
    painting, 129–130
    regressive attitudes toward women, 128
    reign, 5, 118–136
    return from Elba, 118
    sumptuary laws, 120–121
    theater, 98, 135–136
    uniform, 120
National Assembly, democratization of
    fashion, 67
National costumes, 176–177
National dances, 136–137
Nationalism, 136–137
Natural aesthetics, 96–97
Natural man, 57
Nature, 51–57
Neoclassicism, 94–116
    ballet costume shocks London audiences,
        115, 116
    bosoms, 101
    dance improvisations, 107–108
    middle-class moral illustration, 96
    Napoléon, 94–95
    newly discovered female body, 98
    shift in aesthetics of clothing, 98–101, *99*

Neoclassicism (*continued*)
  shoes, 101–103
  tableaux vivants, 108
  underwear, 101
Nineteenth century heroine, 223
Nobility, 66
Noble ballet, 151
Noverre, Jean-Georges, 34, 61–64, *62*
  emotion, 62
  Voltaire, 60

O
Oriental style, 24
Ornamentation, 91
Ostentation, 10
Ottoman Empire, 24

P
Les Pages du duc de Vendôme, 156, *157, 158*
Painting, 58–59
  Napoléon, 129–130
Panniers, 12, 29–30
  elimination, 35–39
Pantomime, Noverre, 63
Paris Opéra
  antique style, 109
  commercialism, 204
  dancers, 42, 46–50
  embourgeoisement, 204, 222
  foyer de la danse, 204–205, 222–223
  French Revolution, 82–86
  Gardel, Pierre, *110,* 111–116
  scene design, 146, 160
Partnering, Romantic ballet, 225
Paul et Virginie, 141, 142–143
Peasants, 66
Personal imagery, 2
Perukes, 30–31
Petit Trianon, 21, 22–23
Philippe l'Egalité, Duc d'Orléans, 17
Philosophes, 51
  relationships, 60
Philosophisme, 16
Philosophy of natural rights, 76
Phrygian bonnets, 82
Physical culture movement, 241
Pirouettes, 34
Pointe dancing, 187, 242–243
  advent, 189–206
  early dancers, 189
  pictorial representations, 195
  Taglioni, Marie, 217
Polish styles, 24
Polonaise tunic, 24
Pompadour, Madame de, 20
  theater, 20
Posture, corsets, 27, *28*
Poverty, 6–7

Practice clothing, 185–186, 205–206, 228, 242
Presentation at court, 13
  rehearsal, 13
La Préface de Cromwell, 175
The Prodigal Son, 145, 146
Propriety, dancers, 204
Prostitutes, 235–237
  legalized prostitution, 223–224
  madonna/prostitute complex, 223–224
Psyché, 113–115, *114*
Public balls, 91
Public education, 77–78

R
Racial prejudices, 143
La Raison, 81
Le Rat, 203–204
Récamier, Madame, *106,* 107
Redingote, 16
Reign of Terror, 66, 71
Religions, 165
  new, 80
Revolution, French, *see* French Revolution
Revolutionary fans, 71
Revolutionary festivals, 77–82, *79*
  ancient Greek festivals, 77
  costume, 80
Revolution of 1830, 165–166
Revolution of 1848, 165–166
Robe de cour, 119
Robe de cérémonie, 19
Robe à la Psyché, 113–115, *114*
Robert le Diable
  tutu, *208, 209,* 209–214
  White Ballet, 210–214, *211*
Robes à l'anglaise, 19
Rochefoucauld, Vicomte Sosthène de la, 202–203
Rococo fashion, 20
Roman mythology, 111–116
Romantic ballerinas, 195
  ballet landscapes, 180
  complex range, 180
  feet, 182, 187–188
  image *vs.* reality, 223
  innovations, 179
  madonna/prostitute complex, 223–224
  penury, 222
  as Platonic ideal, 223
  roles, 180
Romantic ballet, 243
  erotic meanings, 225
  ethos, 218–219
  images of woman, 223
  lifts, 225
  lighting, 208
  partnering, 225

pictorial representation, 218–219
  Romantic movement, 218–219
  settings, 208
Romantic movement, 6, 118–120, 165
  ballet costumes, 183–184
  ballet technique, 181–189
  choreography, 183–184
  corsets, 168
  dress profile, 169
  fabric, 168
  fashion magazines, 169
  female body, 176, 181
  female warrior figures, 175
  hair styles, 168–169
  hats, 169
  literature, 150
  mythological ballets, 195
  Romantic ballet, 218–219
  street dress, 176
  waistlines, 168
Roman tunics, 80
Rousseau, Jean-Jacques, 51–57, *52*
  ballet contributions, 56–57
  intellectual womens' opinions of, 55–56
  motherhood and family, 53
  opinion of women, 53–55
  theater, 55
  views on clothing, 54–55
La Révolte des femmes, 240–241

S
Saint Sauveur, Grasset de, 88
Sallé, Marie, 44–45
Salons, 13
Salon theaters, 21
Sans-culottes, 71
Les Sauvages de la Mer du Sud, 154–156
Scarlet vests, 175–176
Scene design, Paris Opéra, 146, 160
S-curve, *26*
Second Estate, 66
Sensualist school, 120
Sestini, Vincenzio, 116
Shoe buckles, 70
Shoes, *see also* Specific type
  ballet shoe development, 103–105, *104*
  neoclassicism, 101–103
  sexual meaning, 103
  18th century, 29
Silk industries, 122
Skin, colors, 173–174
Skirts, 54–55
  shapes, 29–30
Slavery, *85,* 86
  freeing of slaves, *85,* 86
Sleeves, 29
Slim figure, 3
Slippers, 104–105

The Social Contract, 55
Social dance, 31, 88–89, *89*
  dancer development, 33
  Directorate, 88
  postrevolutionary dance craze, *136*
La Somnambule, 196
Spanish dancers, 203, 224, 245
Spartan society, 77–78
Stage costume
  reform, 35–41
  before 18th century, 25
Stage dancers, tricks, 34
Staël, Madame de, *133,* 134–135
Stays, 93
Storming of Bastille, 66
Street dances, 82
Street dress, Romantic movement, 176
Street-theater demonstrations, 78
Style à *l'Anglaise,* 15
Suffering, fashion, 232–233
Sumptuary laws, 9
  estates, 66–67
  Napoléon, 120–121
Sun King, *see* Louis XIV
La Sylphide, 139, 179, *213,* 214, 215
  Taglioni, Marie, 215, *216*
  tutu, *213,* 214
Syncretism, 245
Syphilis, 237

T
Tableaux vivants, neoclassicism, 108
Taglioni, Filippi, 210
Taglioni, Marie, *192,* 194, *200,* 210
  fashion influence, 217–218
  pointe dancing, 217
  La Sylphide, 215, *216*
  tutu, *213,* 214
  White Ballet, 210–214, *211*
Tallien, Madame de, 107, 108
Talma, François, 39, *40*
Taste, 178
Technique, 221
  expression, contrasted, 6
Theater
  Bourbon restoration, 151–164
  development of amateur, 20
  late 18th century, 20–21
  Madame de Pompadour, 20
  Marie Antoinette, 19–20, 21
  Napoléon, 98, 135–136
  reforms, 35–41
  social reform, 57
  Versailles, 20
Third Estate, 66
Théleur, E. A., 186–188
Théâtre des Petits Cabinets, 20
Théâtres de sociéte, 21

Tights, 103, 105–107
Télémaque dans l'Isle de Calypso, 112, 113
Toe dancing, *see* Pointe dancing
Toe shoes, *190, 192,* 192–194, *193,* 225–226
   blocking of top, 194
   darning, *190,* 194
   as extended phallus, 226
   significance, 224
Training, 226–227
Transparent dresses, 105–107
Travesty, 86–88, *87*
Troubadour style, 151
Trousers, 154
Tunique blanche, 103
Turkish fashion, 24
Turn out, 221
Tutu, 6, 221, 242–243
   characteristics, 214
   development, 47
   materials, 214–215
   Robert le Diable, 208, 209, 209–214
   significance, 224
   La Sylphide, 213, 214
   Taglioni, Marie, *213,* 214

U

Underwear, 44, 171–173, *172,* 240, 242
   neoclassicism, 101
Uniforms, 70, 80–82, *83,* 86
   Bourbon restoration, 148
   Napoléon, 120

V

Vaque-Moulin, Elisa, 191
Vernet, Horace, 129–130
Versailles, 10
   theater, 20

Vestris, Auguste, 138
Vestris, Gaëtan, 138
Vigée-Lebrun, Elizabeth, *18, 22,* 23, 107
Voltaire (François Marie Arouet), 59–60
   English influences, 59–60
   Jean-Georges Noverre, 60
   reforming costuming, 60
   writer of theater and ballet, 60
Véron, Louis, 204

W

Waistlines, 231–233
   Romantic movement, 168
   wasp, 231–233
Waltz, 90–91, *123,* 129, 150, 163
   criticism, 90
   England, 90
   sensuality, 90–91
Werther, 150
White Ballet, 180
   Robert le Diable, 210–214, *211*
   Taglioni, Marie, 210–214, *211*
Wigs, 30–31, 91
Women
   Bourbon restoration clothes, 148
   dancing to revolutionary songs, *69*
   defeat of revolutionary radical feminism, 74
   education, 53, 56
   equality, 240
   fashion as weapon of power, 12
   French Revolution, 73–77
   revolutionary clubs of, 74
   warrior figures, 175
   women's rights, 5, 76
Wooden shoes, 82
Writers, 18th century, 51